MACCA IN
THE LONG NOUGHTIES
Paul McCartney
tracks, life and tours
1998-2009

Ian D Derbyshire

IDD Publishing

www.iddpublishing.com

Email info@iddpublishing.com

First published in the United Kingdom 2024

British Library Cataloguing in Publications Data
A Catalogue record for this book is available from the British Library

Copyright Ian Derbyshire 2024

ISBN 978-1-0686238-0-6

Contents

Preface

Paul McCartney's solo and Wings career in the 1970s has been well chronicled by Kozinn & Sinclair (2022 and 2024), Chrisp (2023), Doyle (2013), McCartney (2002), McGee (2003), Miles (1997), Jones (2023) and Perasi (2023). But beyond chapters and sections in the Macca biographies by Carlin (2009), Norman (2016), Sandford (2007), Sounes (2010) and Driver (2023), his later career has not been covered in depth. This is despite Paul producing some of his strongest work since the 1970s during the 2000s.

Bob Dylan (1941-) told *Rolling Stone* in 2007: "I'm in awe of McCartney. He's about the only one I'm in awe of. He can do it all. And he's never let up ... He's just so damn effortless."

Vincent Benitez (2010) has commented that Paul felt a sense of "liberation" as he approached and entered his sixties. In his live sets in particular and on his albums, at times, Paul embraced his Beatles' past. But he also enthusiastically explored different and new musical styles and genres.

This book examines McCartney's music during the 2000s, but its start point is 1998: a pivotal and traumatic year. On 17 April 1998, Linda McCartney (née Eastman: 1941-98), Paul's wife for 29 years, died of cancer. This loss hit Paul hard and was followed by intense mourning and depression.

During the next two years, Paul paid tribute to Linda's with the releases of the *Wide Prairie* (1998) anthology of Linda's recordings, *Rushes* (1998), *Run Devil Run* (1999), *Working Classical* (1999) and *A Garland for Linda* (2000).

By mid-1999, Paul had begun to come to terms with the loss of Linda and he tentatively embarked on a new relationship with Heather Mills (1968-), a former model and charity campaigner. In June 2002, Paul and Heather married and in October 2003 daughter Beatrice (Bea) was born. Incompatibility drove the couple apart, culminating in separation in April 2006 and divorce in May 2008.

In August 2007, Paul found new love with Nancy Shevell (1959-), an American business executive. They married in October 2011.

Not known as a confessional songwriter, the rollercoaster of emotions Paul experienced between 1998-2009 did influence his albums *Driving Rain* (2001), *Chaos and Creation in the Backyard* (2005) and *Memory Almost Full* (2007), which are unusually introspective.

In April 2002, Paul resumed touring after an 8-year break, backed by a new band which included three younger American musicians. Between 2002-09, Paul and the band played 190 concerts before 3.7 million people, grossing $350 million. These included prestigious shows at Rome's Colosseum and Moscow's Red Square (in May 2003), Glastonbury (June 2004), *Live 8* (June 2005), Kyiv's Independence Square (June 2008), Quebec's Plains of Abraham (July 2008), Tel Aviv's HaYarkon Park (September 2008) and Coachella (April 2009).

Between 1998-2009, in addition to three main pop-rock albums, Paul released:

- *Run Devil Run* (1999): a rock 'n' roll covers album.
- Three classical albums: *Working Classical* (1999); *A Garland for Linda* (2000); and *Ecce Cor Meum* (2006).
- Four avant-garde, mash-up and electronica albums: *Rushes* (1998); *Liverpool Sound Collage* (2000); *Twin Freaks* (2005); and *Electric Arguments* (2008).

Paul also displayed his talents as an artist and poet, holding art exhibitions and publishing *Paul McCartney: The Paintings* (2000) and *Blackbird Singing: Poems and Lyrics* (2001).

Throughout these years, Paul was highly active supporting humanitarian causes: animal welfare; vegetarianism; transcendental meditation; landmine removal; and the victims of the 9/11 terrorist atrocity.

The 1998-2009 'long decade' is a full and fascinating period in Paul's life and music: one overdue a closer review.

Sources and Picture Credits

This work has been sourced from newspaper and music magazine articles and interviews from the period 1998-2009, the 2008 court judgement from Paul's divorce settlement and the secondary sources listed in **Secondary Sources: Books.**

Data on Paul's worldwide album sales is drawn from
https://chartmasters.org/paul-mccartney-albums-and-songs-sales/

The excerpts from song lyrics are included under the copyright critical review 'fair use' provision.

Descriptions of people and events are sourced from press articles and biographies. The author has sought to present these fairly and impartially.

Picture Credits

Thanks go out to David Borman, of The Netherlands-based *Maccazine*, who has given permission for me to reproduce (on the front cover and in the Photograph Section) pictures he shot in 2009 at concerts in Arnhem, in the Netherlands, Köln (Cologne), in Germany, and the O2 Arena in London. The copyright to these photographs resides with David.

The remaining photograph in the Photograph Section are reproduced under image licences from Alamy.

1970-97: Solo McCartney and Wings

In the 1960s (James) Paul McCartney (1942-) was a pivotal member of the Beatles: the world's most influential musical group. The Beatles propelled key changes in pop-rock music, helped turn the album an art-form, made pioneering use of film and video and had a deep influence on the fashion, lifestyles and hairstyles of the baby boomer generation.

Dowlding (1989) has identified Paul as the principal composer of over seventy of the 158 released Beatles songs credited as Lennon-McCartney co-writes. These included the Number 1 hits *Love Me Do, Can't Buy Me Love, Eight Days A Week, Yesterday, Paperback Writer, Penny Lane, Hello Goodbye, Lady Madonna, Hey Jude, Get Back, Let It Be* and *The Long and Winding Road.*

On 20 September 1969, John Lennon (1940-80), the Beatles' unofficial leader, privately told Paul and the band's management he wanted a "divorce" from the group. It remained uncertain whether Lennon's departure was permanent, but from December 1969 Paul began recording material on his own, at his homes and in studios in London.

In April 1970, Paul released, *McCartney,* a DIY album on which he played all instruments. In the album's press release, Paul acknowledged his "break with the Beatles" and stated that he did not know whether it would be temporary or permanent.

Music critics savaged the *McCartney* album. They considered its songs, with the notable exception of *Maybe I'm Amazed*, to be banal, second-rate and under-produced. Nevertheless, *McCartney* topped the US Billboard 200, reached number 2 in the UK and went on to sell 4.3 million units worldwide. The album marked the start of a long, hugely successful and musically diverse solo career.

Between 1970-97 Paul released:

- 17 mainstream pop-rock albums, selling 55 million units worldwide, with seven topping the UK chart and six the US Billboard 200.
- 60 singles, of which nine reached number 1 in the US and three topped the UK chart.
- Two albums of classical music, selling 300,000 units.

- Two albums of remixes (*Thrillington* and *Strawberries Oceans Ships Forest),* selling 130,000 units.
- Four live albums, selling 8 million units.
- One album of rock 'n' roll covers, *Choba B CCCP,* selling 1 million units.
- Two compilation albums, *Wings Greatest* (1978) and *All the Best!* (1987), selling over 10 million units.

Paul's popularity and critical acclaim reached peaks in 1973-78, 1980-82, 1989 and 1997.

1971-79: Wings ascendant

Paul's second album, *Ram,* released in May 1971, was credited to Paul and Linda McCartney. It featured his American photographer wife Linda, whom he had married on 12 March 1969, on backing vocals and three US New York-based session musicians: David Spinozza (1949-) on guitar; Hugh McCracken (1942-2013), on guitar; and Denny Seiwell (1943-), on drums.

Ram topped the UK album chart, reached number 2 in the US and sold 4 million units worldwide. It received negative reviews from pro-Lennon music critics in *Rolling Stone* and the *New Musical Express* (NME). But today *Ram* is widely considered to be an indie pop classic and one of Paul's strongest works.

In 1971, Paul was keen to play live again and so formed the group Wings. It took its name from an image of angels' wings that entered Paul's head whilst praying during complications in Linda's pregnancy with daughter Stella (1971-).

Paul recruited to Wings the guitarist and singer Denny Laine (1944-2023), who, as a 1964-66 member of the Birmingham-based Moody Blues, had sung lead on their 1964 hit single *Go Now.* Paul and Denny developed a mutual respect during the Beatles' last British tour in December 1965, when the Moody Blues were the support band.

Wings' other two initial members were Denny Seiwell on drums and, despite very limited musical training, Linda on keyboards and backing vocals.

Wings' debut album, *Wild Life*, was recorded in a week and released in December 1971. Raw, rushed and lacking commercially standout songs, music critics panned it. It reached 11 in the UK and 10 in the US and sold 1.7 million units worldwide: For an ex-Beatle, this was a setback.

In January 1972, Wings became a five-member group, with Henry McCullough (1943-2016), a Northern Irish blues guitarist, joining on lead guitar.

In February 1972, Wings gained experience through playing a series of unannounced gigs at UK universities. This was followed in 1972-73 by a 26-show tour of small venues in Europe and 21-show UK tour. The band travelled across Europe in a colourfully painted bus, with Paul's young children on board.

Battle-hardened through these tours, Wings released in April 1973 the album *Red Rose Speedway*. Initially envisaged as a 21-track double album to highlight the band members' individual and collective talents, Paul was persuaded by the record company that it would have more commercial impact if slimmed down to a 9-track single album. The decision that did not please all the band's members, particularly as some of the tracks left off highlighted the hard-rocking side of 1972-73 Wings.

Red Rose Speedway was sonically more polished and "poppy" than *Wild Life* and the record company was proved right. It topped the US album chart, reached number 6 in the UK and sold 2.1 million units worldwide. Its lead single, *My Love*, a love ballad to Linda, topped the US chart.

Paul decided to record the next Wings' album in Lagos, Nigeria: a city at the forefront of world music with the Afrobeat sound of Fela Kuti (1938-97). But, during rehearsals in August 1973 at Paul's farm near Campbeltown in western Scotland, tensions in the band, arising from artistic differences and financial issues, boiled over.

Delays in the resolution of the ongoing financial dispute over the dissolution of the Beatles and its troubled Apple Corps, a multi-media corporation, had left Paul short of ready funds. As a result, Wings' members were on a salary of only £70 a week in 1972: a paltry sum for a band on the rise. Feeling additionally constrained by Paul's tight control over his guitar solos, McCullough abruptly unstrapped his Les Paul and quit the band during the final stages of rehearsals. Several days later, on 29 August, Seiwell, decided against joining the 30 August flight to Lagos as he believed the band needed to recruit a new lead guitarist.

Paul, Linda and Denny Laine flew out to Lagos, with Wings continuing with three members: Paul playing drums, bass, electric guitar and piano. Assisted in the EMI studio in Lagos by Geoff Emerick (1945-2018), engineer of Beatles albums 1966-69, this slimmed-down Wings recorded *Band on the Run.*

Released in December 1973, *Band on the Run* was critically lauded, winning two Grammy Awards. Commercially, it became Paul and Wings' most successful album. It topped the US and UK charts, spent 125 weeks in the UK album chart and sold 8.6 million units worldwide.

Band on the Run kickstarted an ascendant period between 1974-76 when Wings became the world's most successful pop-rock group.

In 1974, Wings returned to five members. Paul recruited, as lead guitarist, Jimmy McCulloch (1953-79), a Scotsman formerly of Thunderclap Newman, and on drums, the London-born Geoff Britton (1943-). In January 1975, Joe English (1949-), an American, replaced Britton.

In May 1975, this five-member Wings released *Venus and Mars,* a pop-rock album which topped both the UK and US charts, selling 3.5 million units.

This was followed, in March 1976, with *Wings at the Speed of Sound,* a true band effort in which every member had a lead vocal. Propelled by the US chart-topping singles *Silly Love Songs* and *Let 'Em In, Wings at the Speed of Sound* reached number 1 in the US album chart and 2 in the UK and sold 3.9 million units worldwide.

Commercially, Wings reached their peak between September 1975 and October 1976 with a hugely successful 66-arena world tour. This tour is captured on *Wings Over America* (1976), a triple live album, released in December 1976, which sold 3.6 million units. The 31 shows in the US and Canada in May-June 1976 were attended by over 600,000 fans.

In September 1977, Linda's pregnancy with son James (1977-) led to the shelving of a planned Wings' US tour. This contributed to the departure from the band of McCulloch and English.

Reverting to its three-member core (Paul, Linda and Denny Laine), Wings recorded a UK chart-topping single, *Mull of Kintyre* – the first UK single to sell over 2 million units - and a folk-pop album *London Town*. Released in March 1978, *London Town* reached number 2 in the US and 4 in the UK, selling 3.9 million units worldwide.

In April 1978, ahead of a new 1979 Wings tour, Denny Laine persuaded his London friends, the guitarist Laurence Juber (1952-) and drummer Steve Holley (1954-), to join the group. This new five-member Wings recorded *Back to the Egg*, produced by Chris Thomas (1947-), who had worked in 1968-69 with Beatles' producer George Martin (1926-2016) and had recently produced the Sex Pistols' punk album *Never Mind the Boll**ks* (1977).

Released in June 1979, *Back to the Egg* had a harder sound, in response to the challenge of new wave music. It reached number 6 in the UK and 8 in the US but received negative critical reviews. Its worldwide sales of 2 million units were half the level of each of the three preceding albums. Wings had passed their peak.

The 1980s: remaining relevant

On 16 January 1980, Paul was arrested at Tokyo airport for carrying 229 grams of cannabis, worth £1,000, in his luggage. He was detained in custody, fined and deported on 25 January. Wings' 11-date tour of Japan was cancelled. In November 1980, Wings dissolved.

With children at school, Paul did not tour again until 1989.

The synth-pop, new wave and glam metal dominated 1980s was a difficult decade for classic rock artists from the 1960s and 1970s. Paul sought to remain musically and commercially relevant by working with a variety of producers and songwriters. He released seven albums:

- *McCartney II* (1980), a DIY album which experimented with electro-pop. It reached number 1 in the UK and 3 in the US and sold 2.3 million units worldwide.

- *Tug of War* (1982), a pop album produced by George Martin, the 'fifth Beatle.' It was recorded in the aftermath of the 8 December 1980 assassination of John Lennon in New York. Outstanding musicians appeared on the album: Eric Stewart (1945-), of 10cc; US rockabilly guitarist Carl Perkins (1932-98); US jazz-fusion bassist Stanley Clarke (1951-); Beatles' drummer Ringo Starr (1940-) on one track; and US soul-funk icon Stevie Wonder (1950-) on two tracks. Hailed in *Rolling Stone* as "the masterpiece everyone has always known Paul McCartney could make," *Tug of War* topped the UK and US charts. It sold 4.2 million units worldwide.

- *Pipes of Peace* (1983), another pop album produced by George Martin. Its highlights were *Say, Say, Say,* a duet with the 'King of Pop' Michael Jackson (1958-2009), which was Paul's last US number 1 single, and *Pipes of Peace,* which was Paul's last UK number 1 single. The album reached number 4 in the UK and 15 in the US. It sold 3.1 million units worldwide.

- *Give My Regards to Broad Street* (1984), a soundtrack to a critically and commercially unsuccessful McCartney film. Featuring reworkings of six Beatles and four McCartney solo songs, it topped the UK chart and reached 21 in the US. It sold 2.2 million units worldwide.

- *Press to Play* (1986), an album with a contemporary 1980s' sound. Produced by Hugh Padgham (1955-), who had collaborated successfully with The Police and Phil Collins (1951-), it included eight tracks co-written with Eric Stewart. It reached number 8 in the UK and 30 in the US and sold 1 million units worldwide.

- *Choba B CCCP* (1988), a rock 'n' roll covers album released in October 1988 initially only in the Soviet Union. It received worldwide release in 1991, reaching 63 in the UK and 109 in the US and sold 1 million units.

- *Flowers in the Dirt* (1989), a critically well-received album, featuring four tracks co-written with the Liverpudlian new wave artist Elvis Costello (1954-). It topped the UK album chart but reached only 21 in the US. Its lead single *My Brave Face* was Paul's last single to reach the US top 40. The album sold 3.5 million units worldwide.

1989-97: return to touring, new genres and Beatles revival

Paul's waning popularity in the US during the 1980s arose, in part, from reduced visibility: his last US concert had been on 23 June 1976.

For *Flowers in the Dirt,* Paul recruited a new touring band of experienced British musicians: Robbie McIntosh (1957-), formerly of the British-American new wave group The Pretenders, on guitar; Hamish Stuart (1949-), formerly of the Scottish funk and R&B Average White Band, on bass; Paul 'Wix' Wickens (1956-), classically trained who had played with Bob Dylan and Joni Mitchell (1943-), on keyboards; and Chris Whitten (1959-), formerly of the British-Irish folk-rock group The Waterboys, on drums.

Between September 1989 and July 1990, Paul and this band toured the world, playing 103 shows in the US, Europe, Japan and South America. The 21 April 1990 concert at Rio de Janeiro's Maracanã Stadium attracted 184,000. On this tour, Paul played an increasing number of Beatles songs. The performances are captured on *Tripping the Live Fantastic* (1990), a triple LP/double CD, and the abridged *Tripping the Live Fantastic: Highlights!*, which, together, sold 2.5 million units worldwide.

In 1991, the American Blair Cunningham (1957-) replaced Chris Whitten on drums. The new band recorded *Unplugged (The Official Bootleg)*, a 25 January 1991 acoustic-only live performance of rock 'n' roll standards, Beatles and McCartney tracks for MTV. Released as an album in May 1991, *Unplugged* reached 7 in the UK and 14 in the US. It was accompanied by a six-show Unplugged Tour between May and July 1991.

Between September 1991 and June 1992, Paul and the band took a break from touring to record the album *Off the Ground,*. Released in February 1993, it reached number 5 in the UK and 17 in the US and sold 2.5 million units. The album was promoted by a 77-show February to December 1993 New World Tour, captured on the CD/DVD *Paul is Live* (1993).

Experimenting with new genres

From the mid-1980s, commercial radio excluded Paul's new releases from playlists, deeming it no longer 'contemporary.' This prompted Paul to begin to explore new musical genres: classical music and electronica.

In the 1960s, Paul had admired the avant-garde 'new classical' electronic music of Karlheinz Stockhausen (1923-2007) and Luciano Berio (1925-2003). As he entered middle age, he began to listen also to more mainstream classical music. In 1989, the American composer Carl Davis (1936-2023) persuaded Paul to collaborate on writing a Liverpool-themed classical oratorio (a piece of music based on a story and sung by soloists and a chorus) for the 150th anniversary of the Royal Liverpool Philharmonic.

Davis was acquainted with Paul and Linda through a mutual friend Carla Lane (1928-2016), an animal welfare activist and TV comedy scriptwriter who wrote the popular British sitcom *Bread* in which Davis's wife Jean Boht (1932-2023) starred.

Unable to write a musical score, Paul hummed the melodies for Davis to transcribe. The resulting melodic and pastoral work, *Paul McCartney's Liverpool Oratorio,* was premiered in June 1991 at Liverpool Cathedral, which in 1953 had rejected the 12-year-old Paul when he had auditioned for its choir. The *Liverpool Oratorio* topped the UK classical music charts for many weeks.

Encouraged, Paul then composed *Standing Stone*, a 74-minute, four movement New Age orchestral work released in September 1997. It was commissioned in 1993 by Richard Lyttelton (1950-), president of EMI Classics, to celebrate the label's centenary.

This time, Paul used a computer software programme to generate the score from notes he played on a keyboard. The English classical and film composer Richard Rodney Bennett (1936-2012) and English composer David Matthews (1943-) assisted. *Standing Stone* also topped the UK classical music charts.

In the 1990s, Paul explored his interest in electronic music which he had previewed on *McCartney II*. Since 1985, Paul had his own recording studio at Hog Hill Mill, a former post mill, at Icklesham East Sussex near his 1,500-acre Peasmarsh Estate. This became his 'music laboratory.'

Intrigued by trance and techno music, Paul formed a secret partnership with Martin Glover (1962-), a.k.a. Youth, a former bass player with the British post-punk group Killing Joke who had forged a reputation as an accomplished techno dance-music producer. Youth produced *U.F.Orb* (1992) for The Orb and the pop-rock classic *Together Alone* (1993) for Crowded House.

Paul invited Youth to Hog Hill Mill studio to remix some tracks from *Off the Ground*. The pair bonded over shared interests in painting and poetry. Youth stayed several days, working into the early hours of each morning to create esoteric ambient mixes using Sound Tools, the precursor to Pro Tools. For the collaboration, they adopted the alias The Fireman: Paul's trumpet-playing father Jim (1902-76) had, served in Liverpool's fire service during World War II.

In November 1993, The Fireman released, *Strawberry Oceans Ships Forest,* an electronic album of *Off the Ground* techno-dance and trance remixes, using samples, loops and droning drumbeats.

Lacking promotion, *Strawberry Oceans Ships Forest* passed unnoticed. But, in a four-star review in *Rolling Stone*, Gillian Gaar (1959-) commented: "The droning wail of guitars and keyboards gives the music an exotic tinge, conjuring up images of a late-night stroll through the casbah."

Riding the Beatles' revival

In the mid-1990s, Paul's career was boosted by new interest in the Beatles among a younger generation who followed new Britpop groups and watched the *Beatles Anthology* TV documentary.

The UK's leading Britpop group, Oasis, cited the Beatles as a key influence and regularly played John Lennon's *I Am The Walrus* and Paul's *Helter Skelter* during concerts. In September 1995, Paul made a charity recording of John Lennon's Beatles' classic, *Come Together*, with the Smokin' Mojo Filters, featuring Oasis guitarist Noel Gallagher (1967-), new wave singer-songwriter Paul Weller (1958-) and actor-guitarist Johnny Depp (1963-).

Between 1991-95, the *Anthology* project combed through the Beatles' musical and video archives and the three remaining Beatles, Paul, George Harrison (1943-2001) and Ringo Starr sat for interviews for a November-December 1995 TV documentary. Comprising behind-the-scenes video clips and studio and concert footage, the *Anthology* series was watched by

420 million. In 1995-96 three *Anthology* double CDs of unreleased Beatles demos, live recordings and two 'new songs' (*Free As a Bird* and *Real Love* – fleshing out John Lennon home demos from 1977) were released. The *Anthology* albums topped the US Billboard 200 and charted high in the UK, reigniting mass interest in the Beatles.

On 11 March 1997, Paul became Sir Paul, receiving a knighthood from Queen Elizabeth II (1926-2022) for services to music.

The period spent looking back at the Beatles' output for the *Anthology* project spurred Paul to raise his game on his next solo album. He chose as producer Jeff Lynne (1947-), the Birmingham-born leader of the Beatles-influenced Electric Light Orchestra. In 1994-95, Paul had worked with Lynne at Hog Hill Mill studio on the Beatles' *Free As a Bird* and *Real Love* songs.

Released in May 1997, the resulting album, *Flaming Pie,* was a folk-rock classic and one of Paul's strongest works since *Band on the Run.* It reached number 2 in both the UK and US and sold 1.9 million units worldwide.

Devastating news

Despite Paul's career being on an upward curve, tragedy was just around the corner.

On 8 December 1995, Paul received the devastating news. A routine scan uncovered a cancerous tumour in Linda's left breast. Linda underwent a lumpectomy, followed by intensive chemotherapy, leaving her low on energy during 1996-97. Homeopathic and alternative treatments followed, including a bone marrow transplant, with regular visits to doctors.

Aware that Linda may have less than 18 months to live, Paul spent increasing time at the couple's 159-acre Blossom Wood Farm, home since 1978. Situated on the Peasmarsh Estate, the modest five-bedroom house lay in an Area of Outstanding Natural Beauty (AONB) three miles from the literary coastal town of Rye.

However, it appears that the cancer may have been detected too late. By 1998, it had spread to Linda's left breast and liver and was now incurable.

1998: Lonesome Road

Key events

February: Paul holds a week-long session at Hog Hill Mill studio with Youth to record The Fireman album *Rushes*.

18 March: Linda records her final song at Hog Hill Mill.

Late March: Paul and Linda fly to Arizona so that Linda can spend the final weeks of her life at their Tanque Verde ranch.

13 April: *Twentieth Century Blues: The Songs of Noel Coward* is released in the UK and includes *A Room With A View* recorded by Paul at Hog Hill Mill on 12 December 1997. It features a sparse arrangement, with clipped vocals, guitar and mellotron.

17 April: Linda dies at the age of 56 from cancer.

4 June to 2 July: A *Wide Open* exhibition is held at the Bonni Benrubi Gallery in New York, displaying photographs from across Linda's career.

16 June: Ringo Starr's album *Vertical Man* is released. Paul provides bass and backing vocals on *La De La* and *What In The ... World* and bass on *I Was Walkin':* tracks recorded during a 29 September 1997 visit by Ringo to Hog Hill Mill.

July: Paul and engineer Geoff Emerick hold final mixing sessions for *Wide Prairie*.

21 September: The Fireman album *Rushes* is released.

26 October: Linda McCartney's album *Wide Prairie* is released.

10-11 October: Recording session for *Working Classical*.

December: The Peter Kirtley band releases *Little Children*, a samba-rhythm charity single, with Paul on spoken vocals, in aid of Brazilian street children.

On 11 March 1998, Linda made a final public appearance, with Paul and their son James, at a Paris show in which daughter Stella's latest designs for the Chloé fashion house were unveiled. With cropped brown hair and appearing gaunt, Linda bravely told reporters that she was "feeling great."

Just over a fortnight later, Linda said goodbye to her closest friends in England and the McCartney family flew from the UK to the US. It was reported that they were headed for Santa Barbara, California, but this was a code for Linda's inner circle of friends. Instead, the McCartneys flew to Tucson and drove to their Tanque Verde ranch in the Arizona desert. Here, in one of her favourite places, Linda spent the final days of her life.

When energy permitted, Linda went on short horse rides with Paul, imbibing the sights, sounds and breezes of nature in the warmth of Arizona's early spring. Linda's final horse ride was on 15 April, after which her strength waned, and she became bed bound.

Linda passes on

At 5 a.m. on 17 April, Linda slipped into a coma. Lying at her side on the bed, Paul clasped Linda's hands and whispered: "You're up on your beautiful Appaloosa stallion Blankit. It's a fine spring day, we're riding through the woods. The bluebells are all out and the sky is clear blue."

As Paul reached the end of the sentence, Linda's eyes closed, and she gently slipped away. Aged 56, Linda was nine years older than Paul's mother Mary (1909-56) when she died of breast cancer in 1956.

Speaking several days after Linda's death, Paul released an emotional statement: "This is a total heartbreak for my family and I. Linda was, and still is, the love of my life and the past two years we spent battling her disease has been a nightmare. Her passing has left a huge hole in our lives. We will never get over it, but I think we will come to accept it."

With Linda's passing, Paul had lost his soulmate and the person he termed "my greatest supporter." The McCartney marriage had been exceptionally close. Since March 1969, Paul and Linda had never spent a night apart except for the nine days between 16-25 January 1980 when Paul was held in custody in Tokyo on cannabis charges.

Following Linda's death, Paul fell into a deep depression and was seen little in public for a year. The psychological challenges he faced were even greater than those after September 1969 when he was left "broken-hearted, shocked and dispirited" after John Lennon told Paul and Ringo he was leaving the Beatles.

In the autumn of 1969, Paul withdrew to his High Park Farm on the remote Kintyre peninsula, near Campbeltown in Scotland. There he laid low with Linda, Heather Louise (1962-), Linda's daughter from her 1962-65 marriage to University of Arizona anthropologist Joseph Melville See Jr. (1938-2000), and Paul and Linda's newborn Mary (born on 28 August 1969). This prompted 'Paul is dead' rumours. Paul stayed in bed late, drank heavily, gave up shaving and vented the anger he felt towards his former bandmates.

Later, Paul reflected that this was the one time in his career when he might have become a rock casualty, but that Linda's support and belief in his songwriting talent: "gave me the strength and courage to work again."

In 1998, without Linda at his side, the situation was hugely different.

Paul stepped back from public view. Linda's ashes were flown to the UK and scattered at Blossom Wood Farm and High Park Farm.

Carla Lane, who visited Paul at Blossom Wood Farm in late April 1998, noted: "Paul was just haggard ... he sat there like an old man, lost. He was shattered ... totally bewildered."

Another friend, Geoff Dunbar (1944-), an English animator, said: "He was racked with grief ... He sobbed like a baby."

On Monday 8 June 1998, the memorial service for Linda was held at St. Martin-in-the-Fields, London. Seven hundred mourners attended. They included Linda's distraught four children, Ringo Starr, George Harrison, George Martin, Carla Lane, rock world friends David Gilmour (1946-), Chrissie Hynde (1951-) of The Pretenders, Elton John (1947-), Billy Joel (1949-), Eric Stewart, Peter Gabriel (1950-), Pete Townshend (1945-) and two of Linda's Shetland ponies.

The Brodsky Quartet played Paul's 1970 song *The Lovely Linda* and students from the Liverpool Institute for Performing Arts (LIPA) sang

Blackbird. LIPA was the music college Paul had helped establish, in 1996, as patron and benefactor, on the site of his old school.

In an emotional address, Paul told the mourners: "I have lost my girlfriend, and it is very sad. I still can't believe it, but I have to because it is true … She said one day, 'If I could save just one animal, that is all I would like to do' …Linda McCartney Foods have told me they have sold 400 million meals, so that is a couple of animals she has saved."

At the service's end, the full congregation sang an emotional *Let It Be*.

A further memorial service was held on 22 June in New York's Riverside Church. It was attended by Linda's brother John, her two younger sisters Laura (1947-) and Louise (1950-) and her favourite Appaloosa. Chrissie Hynde and Neil Young (1945-) read emotional eulogies.

Reflecting 18 months later after Linda's death, Paul stated: "I had a year of doing nothing. Everybody told me, 'You must keep busy.' I said, 'No that's like denial.' I refused to get busy. I had a whole year of letting any emotion come sweeping over me. And it did. For about a year, I found myself crying – in all situations around anyone I met … the minute we talked about Linda, I'd say, I'm sorry about this. I've got to cry."

When his mother died, Paul was 14. At that time, there was no such thing as a grief psychiatrist. Paul reflected in 2002: "I certainly didn't grieve enough for my mother."

But in 1998, Paul underwent grief therapy with a psychologist. Paul spent hours painting in his studio, producing works which he described as "a bit disturbing." And he followed his psychologist's advice: "'A good way to grieve is to cry one day and not cry the next, alternate days so as you don't go down one tunnel.' I took his advice."

On Saturday 26 September, Paul had a brief break for a joyous occasion: to walk his 27-year-old daughter Mary down the aisle at St. Peter and St. Paul's Church in Peasmarsh for her marriage to Alistair Donald, a 32-year-old television producer she had met in school in Rye.

During 1998-99, Paul worked through the stages of grief by completing projects inspired by Linda's multifaceted life as photographer, musician, animal rights activist and advocate of vegetarianism.

Rushes: The Fireman returns

Personnel: Paul McCartney (all instruments and vocals)

Producer: The Fireman (Paul McCartney and Youth)

Recording session: February 1998 (Hog Hill Mill studio)

Release date: 21 September 1998

Highest chart placings: UK: -; US: - [did not chart].

Length: 61:20 minutes

Tracks: 1. *Watercolour Guitars* 5:48; 2. *Palo Verde* 11:56; 3. *Auraveda* 12:51; 4. *Fluid* 11:19; 5. *Appletree Cinnabar Amber* 7:12; 6. *Bison* 2:40; 7. *7 a.m.* 7:49; and 8. *Watercolour Rush* 1:45.

In February 1998, Paul invited his The Fireman partner, Martin Glover (Youth), to Hog Hill Mill studio to record what Youth declared later to be a "very beautiful ... requiem for Linda."

Since their first outing in 1993, Youth's reputation had soared: he co-produced eight tracks on the Verve's UK chart-topping and award-winning album *Urban Hymns* (1997), including *Bitter Sweet Symphony*.

During an intensive week working with Youth, Paul experimented on synthesizer, keyboards, bass, guitars, drums, tabla and harpsichord to create ten ambient electronica tracks. Eight of these appear on *Rushes*.

The songs

At a 2 October promotional webcast held at Abbey Road Studio 2, Paul's team described *Rushes* as: "an occasionally erotic CD of ambient chill-out music." Its compositions have engaging melodies and rhythms, making *Rushes* a relaxing, if overlong, chillout album.

1. **Watercolour Gardens** opens the album with a hypnotic guitar arpeggio in the acoustic style of Pink Floyd's David Gilmour. Paul would repeat this style in 2020 on *McCartney III*'s *Long Tailed Winter Bird*.

2. **Palo Verde** draws its title from a tree native to Arizona. Layering acoustic guitar and synthesizer, Paul and Youth create an aural dream landscape above which Linda's voice floats, reciting self-composed haikus (a Japanese poetry form comprising three lines): "The adrenaline rushes through you ... So amazing that you think you're on drugs ... The flowers turn into fruit." The euphoric numbed out-of-body sensation conjured up by this track is morphine-like: hence the album's title *Rushes*.

3. **Auraveda,** whose title references alternative holistic medicine, has an Indian vibe, with Paul on tabla, sitar and harmonium.

4. **Fluid** is the album's centrepiece and its theme is repeated on track five. It begins with repetitive piano notes in the style of *Tubular Bells* (1973) by Mike Oldfield (1953-). Layers of synthesizer and acoustic guitar melodies are then added. The mellow guitar tone is reminiscent of Oldfield's *Hergest Ridge* (1974). The ambience is akin to The Orb's 1991 track *Back Side of the Moon,* providing the sensation of relaxing on a tropical beach while waves lap on the shore.

After the six-minute mark, a woman can be heard erotically moaning "Oh Yeah" (taped from a 1-2-1 sex chat line), followed by discussions about UFOs and "when you least expect it, things are going to start changing" (taped from an astrology phone line).

5. **Appletree Cinnabar Amber** opens with the floating guitar-driven melody of *Fluid*. Trance-like drums and hip-hop grooves reminiscent of Massive Attack add urgency. Background voices can be heard saying: "Have you ever had an out of body experience?" and "What does the concept of time mean to you?"

6. **Bison** opens with rippling cymbals, followed by distorted bass by Youth, with Paul playing drums and a swirling mellotron.

7. **7am** is a meandering synthesizer and mellotron-driven track. It includes verses taken from Paul's October 1995 unreleased demo of *Hey Now (What Are You Looking at Me For?)*.

8. **Watercolour Rush** closes the album with a brief reprise of track 1.

Release, promotion and reception

By 1998, Paul's *Club Sandwich* magazine had revealed that The Fireman was a McCartney and Youth project. Nevertheless, Paul sought to maintain a sense of mystery.

A cryptic promotional press release stated: "The Fireman brings bison for trancing in the streets. The Fireman gives a watercolour rush, fluid. The Fireman understands darsh walls and emerdeen sky. Do You? The Fireman knows a lemon's peal. And the power of the equinox. The Fireman heard a girl's snatch-talk of a saucer flying. The Fireman likes the sound of mud. The Fireman plays it all: bass, watercolour guitar, keyboards, cymbals and the fool. The Fireman looped a shadow's clipclop. And made auraveda. The Fireman taped the talk of sex. The Moon is right. So The Fireman comes."

Hydra, an EMI label, released *Rushes* on 21 September. Inside the CD tray was the reproduction of a photograph of a naked model.

At the 2 October 72-minute webcast, Paul appeared in public for the first time since Linda's death, but in heavy disguise. He wore a black ski mask, yellow rain hat, sunglasses and headphones and did not speak. A woman from Paul's team asked questions and read the answers handed to her on pieces of paper by Paul.

The event ended with Paul playing guitar for 30 minutes, mixed by Youth, before a screen message appeared: "The Fireman Loves You."

The *Rushes* album did not chart. Nor did its 12-inch single: comprising *Fluid*, *Appletree Cinnabar Amber* and an extended version of *Bison* (7:55).

On 6 September 1999, a second 12-inch single was released: *Fluid (Nitin Sawhney Remixes)*, limited to 3,000 copies. This comprised remixed versions of *Fluid*, with propulsive electronic beats, drums and sitar: the *Out of Body and Mind Mix* (3:41), the *Out of Body Mix* (4:23) and the *Out of Body with Sitar Mix* (4:23). This did not chart.

These remixes were carried out by Nitin Sawhney (1964-), a British Indian flamenco guitarist, DJ, arranger/producer and songwriter whose 1996 album *Displacing the Priest* (1996) had won the 1998 British Ethnic Multicultural Media Academy (EMMA) award.

In July 1999, Paul visited Sawhney's South London flat to record a new guitar part for the remixes. Paul and Nitin discussed the Bengali philosopher, writer and composer Rabindranath Tagore (1861-1941), whose aphorism "in love all of life's contradictions dissolve and disappear" had been quoted by Paul in the *Pipes of Peace* album notes.

Paul and Nitin bonded and were to become lasting friends, with Nitin attending Paul's 2002 wedding and being invited on occasions as a dinner guest at Peasmarsh.

Wide Prairie: Linda's legacy album

Personnel: Paul McCartney. Linda McCartney, Wings

Producers: Paul McCartney, Linda McCartney, Lee "Scratch" Perry (tracks 7 and 14), Jennifer Maidman (tracks 10 and 11)

Recording: 1972-80*, 1987-89**, 1998***

Release date: 26 October 1998

Highest chart placings: UK: 127; US: -

Length: 52:09 minutes

Tracks (written by Linda unless stated otherwise): 1. *Wide Prairie* 4:33*; 2. *New Orleans* 3:13*; 3. *The White Coated Man* (Linda, Paul and Carla Lane) 2:13**; 4. *Love's Full Glory* 3:46*; 5. *I Got Up* (Linda and Paul) 3:19*; 6. *The Light Comes from Within* (Linda and Paul) 2:57***; 7. *Mister Sandman* (Pat Ballard) 2:50*; 8. *Seaside Woman* 3:54*; 9. *Oriental Nightfish* 2:49*; 10. *Endless Days* (Linda and Mick Bolton) 3:11**; 11. *Poison Ivy* (Jerry Lieber and Mike Stoller) 2:54 **; 12: *Cow* (Linda, Paul and Carla Lane) 4:24**; 13. *B-side to Seaside* (Linda and Paul) 2:38*; 14. *Sugartime* (Charlie Phillips and Odis Echols) 2:06*; 15. *Cook of the House* (Linda and Paul) 2:37*; and 16. *Appaloosa* (Linda and Paul) 4:44***.

In the months before Linda's death, Paul gathered the songs Linda had written over her life for a posthumous album. After Linda's death, Paul finalised the project, adding instrumental overdubs and mixed the album with Geoff Emerick, who had recently also lost his wife to cancer.

The songs

The album's sixteen tracks included three covers (*Mister Sandman*, *Poison Ivy* and *Sugartime*), five Linda and Paul co-writes, two Linda, Paul and Carla Lane co-writes, one Linda and Mick Bolton co-write and five songs written solely by Linda.

Ten of the songs were recorded in the 1972-80 Wings era, four in 1987-88 and two in 1998.

1. **Wide Prairie**, written by Linda, is a country and western song recorded by Wings in Paris (on 20 November 1973) and Nashville, Tennessee (in July 1974). Adopting an exaggerated country twang, Linda sings about growing up in Arizona and riding horses across the wide prairie. Trumpets, saxophone and trombone enliven the song.

2. **New Orleans**, written by Linda, was recorded in New Orleans in February 1975 during Wings' *Venus and Mars* sessions. It is imbued with the easy-going spirit of the Big Easy, referencing places Paul and Linda visited. Additional recording took place on 24 May 1979.

3. **The White Coated Man**, recorded on 21 March 1988 and 18 July 1989, is an anti-vivisection song with lyrical input from Carla Lane. The track opens by taking the perspective of an animal looking through bars of a cage in the morning, with Carla asking, "why can't I move?" This powerful song features electric guitar by Paul and Robbie McIntosh. An accompanying video shows a vivisection laboratory.

4. **Love's Full Glory**, written by Linda and recorded on 16 July and October 1980, is well constructed and features dreamy vocals. Lloyd Green (1937-), a Nashville session player, plays country pedal steel guitar, and Laurence Juber, acoustic guitar.

5. **I Got Up** is a punk-country song with doo wop backing vocals by Denny Laine. Co-written with Paul, it was originally recorded in Paris on 11 November 1973, with Jimmy McCulloch on guitar. Further touches were added at Hog Hill Mill studio on 20 March and 9 July 1998. The album's liner notes describe "its gutsy feel" as being typical of Linda's

refusal to put up with "bullshit" and words like "should" and "compromise" that restricted her freedom.

6. **The Light Comes from Within**, written by Linda and Paul, was Linda's final song. Recorded at Hog Hill Mill studio on 18 March 1998, it features 20-year-old James on guitar. The track has interesting chord changes and instrumental touches by Paul on bass and electronic piano. Written during one of Linda's many trips from Peasmarsh to London for cancer treatment, it is a "rage against the dying of the light" and against male chauvinist critics and greedy and power-hungry property developers. In a country and western style, Linda sings about feeling sick at being called simple and "a hick" and that she needs "a sense of cause" and to "smell the flowers." Proclaiming "oppression won't win," she declares "the light comes from within."

7. **Mister Sandman** is a song written by the American Pat Ballard (1899-1960) which reached number 1 in the US for the Chordettes. The song implores the mythical Mr. Sandman to "bring me a dream." Paul and Linda liked the song so much that McCartney Publications Ltd. (MPL) bought its rights. This version was recorded at Black Ark Studios in Jamaica on 20 June 1977. It is produced by Lee "Scratch" Perry (1936-2021), a legendary Jamaican dub and remix pioneer. Further touches were added in Scotland in August 1977. Linda adapts the song to a reggae dub rhythm.

8. **Seaside Woman** was the first song Linda ever wrote. It was composed during a family visit to Jamaica in 1971 at a time when Northern Songs claimed that her 50% writing credit for Paul and Linda's February 1971 single *Another Day* had been fraudulent. Wings recorded *Seaside Woman* on 27 November 1972 and played the song on early tours. On 31 May 1977, Linda released *Seaside Woman* as a single under the pseudonym Suzie and the Red Stripes, taking the second part of the name from the famous Caribbean beer. The cartoon video for *Seaside Woman* won a Short Film Palme d'Or at the 1980 Cannes Film Festival. With its infectious reggae rhythm, *Seaside Woman* reached number 59 in the US charts and number 90 in the UK when re-released in 1986.

9. **Oriental Nightfish** was written by Linda and recorded by Wings on 4 October 1973 during the *Band on the Run* sessions. It is Linda's most

experimental and proggy track, featuring dramatic guitar and mellotron by Paul, flute by Denny Laine and moog by Linda. Its animated promotional film, directed by Linda and Ian Eames (1949-2023), Pink Floyd's original animator, competed in the 1978 Cannes Film Festival.

10. **Endless Days**, is a melancholy child-like ballad. It was recorded on 21 October 1987 in the studio of Jennifer Maidman (1958-), a British bass guitarist and producer. Mick Bolton (1948-2021), formerly of the English glam-rock band Mott the Hoople, plays keyboards and Geoffrey Richardson (1950-), from the Canterbury-scene progressive rock band Caravan and the avant-pop Penguin Cafe Orchestra, mandolin and slide guitar. Bolton, who co-wrote the song, had given early keyboard lessons to Linda.

11. **Poison Ivy** was recorded on the same day as *Endless Days* at Jennifer Maidman's studio. It is a cover of a 1959 doo-wop hit for The Coasters and was written by Jerry Lieber (1933-2011) and Mike Stoller (1933-). One of Linda's favourite songs, her version has punkish vocals.

12: **Cow,** recorded on 24 July 1988, is an animal welfare song co-written with Carla Lane with haunting lines about a "placid creature" grazing for a final day in a summer field before being taken by truck to slaughter. The song declares "he will eat you because he didn't look." Linda plays a tinkling Casio keyboard, Carla provides spoken verse, while Paul embellishes with prominent Höfner bass, harmony vocals and impressive lead guitar solos.

13. **B-side to Seaside** is a light-hearted Linda and Paul co-write recorded on 16 March 1977 as a B-side to *Seaside Woman*. Paul plays all instruments, while Linda leads on vocals.

14. **Sugartime** is the album's second Lee "Scratch" Perry produced track and was recorded at the same session as *Mister Sandman*. Written by Charlie Phillips (1937-), an American country music singer-songwriter, and Odis Echols (1930-2013), *Sugartime* was a US hit in 1958 for The McGuire Sisters. A Linda favourite, Paul and Linda sometimes sang *Sugartime* as a party piece. This version has a full dub reggae makeover, with Paul adding calypso-style vocals.

15. **Cook of the House**, co-written by Linda and Paul, was included on *Wings at the Speed of Sound* (1976) and was the B-side to *Silly Love Songs*. A 1950s style rocker, *Cook of the House* begins and ends with the sound of food frying. In between, Linda, lists cooking ingredients and affirms that wherever she serves her guests, they like the kitchen best. This phrase was taken from a sign in the kitchen of a house Paul and Linda rented in Australia during the Wings Over the World tour.

Rolling Stone described *Cook of the House* as a non-feminist "celebration of scatterbrained wife-in-the-kitchen coziness." The song features barrelling piano runs by Paul and the horns of the British R&B saxophonist Howie Casey (1937-) and the New Orleans alto saxophonist Thaddeus Richard (1950-). Paul plays a stand-up bass that once belonged to Bill Black (1926-65), from the famous backing band to Elvis Presley (1935-77).

16. **Appaloosa**, another Linda and Paul co-write, was recorded at Hog Hill Mill studio on 7 March 1998. The song's inspiration came from the Indigenous Nez Perce tribe and their Appaloosa horses, named after the Palouse river in the north-west US. Linda rode an Appaloosa horse Blankit bred on Paul and Linda's Arizona farm. The song drew its melody from a practice piece Linda frequently used. Paul plays all instruments and there are interesting tempo changes.

Release and reception

Wide Prairie was released on 26 October 1988 and reached number 127 in the UK album charts. It received little publicity beyond a 17 December *Wide Prairie Show* webcast when Paul answered fans' questions.

The single *Wide Prairie* reached number 74 in the UK. The second single, *The Light Comes from Within,* despite being banned by UK's BBC radio on account of its strong language, reached number 56.

In a review for the UK music magazine *NME,* Mark Beaumont (1972-) gave *Wide Prairie* a 2 out of 10 rating, stating: "No matter how hard you search for the faintest trace of merit in it, *Wide Prairie* merely serves to confirm that humane burger visionary and top mother she may have been, but musician she wasn't."

In 2019, *Wide Prairie* was re-released on vinyl and garnered more favourable reviews.

In *Pitchfork*, Jayson Greene (1981-) gave the album a 6.8 out of 10 rating, finding it "silly and exuberant, almost relentlessly so, but also deeply strange."

Spill Magazine gave it a five-star review, finding it "utterly charming," with musical styles "all over the genre map," from punkish country & western doo-wop (on *I Got Up*), more conventional country and western (*Wide Prairie*), reggae (*Seaside Woman* and *Mister Sandman*), electronica (*Oriental Nightfish*) to the sparse and vulnerable *Endless Days*.

1999: Try Not to Cry

Key events

1-5 March: Paul records tracks for *Run Devil Run* at London's Abbey Road Studio 2.

15 March: Paul is inducted into the Rock and Roll Hall of Fame.

10 April: Paul performs at the *Concert for Linda*.

1 May to 25 July: Paul's paintings are exhibited at the Lÿz Art Forum, in Siegen, Germany, supported by an audio-visual presentation, *Feedback*.

20 May: Paul attends the Pride of Britain awards ceremony at the Dorchester Hotel, London. He is impressed by anti-landmines campaigner Heather Mills.

28 May: Paul records the electronic dance song *Clean Machine* at Abbey Road.

18 July: *A Garland for Linda* is premiered at Charterhouse Chapel, Surrey. It is subsequently recorded at All Saints Church, Tooting, London, on 8 September.

16 September: At Capitol Hill Studios, Los Angeles, Paul records, with producer Jeff Lynne, a cover of Buddy Holly's *Maybe Baby* for a comedy film.

13 September: The Beatles *Yellow Submarine Songtrack* is released.

18 September: Paul performs at the *PETA Party of the Century* at Paramount Studios, Hollywood. A DVD was later released on 4 September 2001.

4 October: The *Run Devil Run* album is released. *No Other Baby* is the single.

1 November: Paul's *Working Classical* album is released.

November: Paul contributes vocals to Heather Mills' charity single *VO!CE*.

14 December: Paul plays a livestreamed *Run Devil Run* concert at Liverpool's Cavern Club. A DVD was later released on 19 June 2001.

One of Linda's dying wishes was for Paul to be inducted individually into the Rock and Roll Hall of Fame (RRHoF): the Beatles had been inducted in 1988 and John Lennon in 1994. This Paul achieved at the Waldorf-Astoria Hotel, New York, on 15 March 1999.

Making one of his first public appearances since Linda's death, Stella accompanied Paul to the stage to receive the award from his friend, the Canadian folk/grunge-rocker Neil Young. Stella wore a self-designed T-shirt which bore the words: "About F***ing Time!"

In the year after Linda's death, Paul was so inactive musically that MPL, which owned the rights to more than 3,000 songs, including the entire catalogue of Buddy Holly (1936-59), registered a £369,000 annual loss.

In February-March, Paul returned to the recording studio to work on *Working Classical*, a classical memorial of songs Paul had written about Linda, and *Run Devil Run*, an album of rock 'n' roll songs Linda and Paul loved. These albums were released in October-November.

Paul also played live again, performing on 10 April at the *Concert for Linda*, on 18 September at the *PETA Party of the Century* and on 14 December at Liverpool's Cavern Club.

There were also impromptu jams at the RRHoF on 15 March, with Robbie Robertson (1943-2023), performing Carl Perkins' *Blue Suede Shoes*, and with Billy Joel, playing *Let It Be*, and on 7 September at the Roseland Ballroom, New York City, during the 24th Buddy Holly Week.

Supporting Linda's causes

During 1999 Paul tirelessly supported the animal rights and vegetarian causes Linda had championed. These included People for the Ethical Treatment of Animals (PETA), which campaigned against the fur trade, factory farming and the use of animals to evaluate products intended for human use.

Concert for Linda: 10 April

Carla Lane and Chrissie Hynde, who had been two of Linda's closest friends, organised the *Concert for Linda,* as a homage to her life and achievements. Held on 10 April at London's Royal Albert Hall, the event was attended by 5,000 and its proceeds were donated to PETA and other animal rights charities.

More than a dozen artists performed, including Elvis Costello, George Michael (1963-2016), Irish singer Sinéad O'Connor (1966-2023), Tom Jones (1940-) and Chrissie Hynde's The Pretenders. The artists sang their own songs, Beatles songs and Hynde joined guitarist Johnny Marr (1963-) to perform The Smiths' *Meat is Murder*.

Paul attended and wasn't expected to play. But, caught up in the moment, he came on stage and performed the 1958 Ricky Nelson (1940-85) hit *Lonesome Town:* one of Linda's favourite songs. The Pretenders and Elvis Costello provided instrumental backing.

At the concert's end, Paul led emotional ensemble performances of the Beatles' *All My Loving* and *Let It Be*.

PETA Party of the Century: 18 September

At the 18 September *PETA Party of the Century* and humanitarian awards at Paramount Studios, Hollywood, Paul performed six-songs from *Run Devil Run,* backed by the upcoming album's all-star band.

At this event, Paul presented the first Linda McCartney Memorial award to the Canadian American actor Pamela Anderson (1967-), for her work in saving animals. Paul's daughter Stella received a Humanitarian Award.

In a tribute to Linda, the Canadian singer-songwriter Sarah McLachlan (1968-) sang her moving 1998 hit *Angel* against the backdrop of previously unseen McCartney family videos.

Linda's vegetarian food legacy

Paul made sure that the Linda McCartney vegetarian food empire continued and invested £3 million to keep the products free of genetic modifications.

In 1989, in *Linda McCartney's Home Cooking,* Linda set out over 200 recipes for healthy and simple-to-cook vegetarian meals. The book was an enormous success, selling over 200,000 copies. It was followed, in 1991, by the launch of *Linda McCartney Foods* (LMF), a range of ready-made vegetarian meals. In December 1999, LMF became part of H.J. Heinz & Co., and in May 2007, was relaunched by the US natural foods group, Hain Celestial Group.

In 1998, LMF became sponsor of the Linda McCartney Racing Team (LMRT): a professional road bicycle team of vegetarians who competed in the UK and internationally.

To promote LMRT, on 28 May 1999 Paul recorded, at Abbey Road, a 5:14 minute electronic dance song *Clean Machine,* as the team's anthem. It was made available exclusively on the LMRT website.

With its relentless four-to-the-floor techno-house drumbeat and pre-set bassline, *Clean Machine* was described by Ian Peel, in *The Unknown Paul McCartney and the Avant-Garde* (2002), as Paul's "first full-on electronic dance track."

The LMRT was short-lived. Increasing debts and insufficient broader sponsorship led to its disbandment in 2001. A detailed account of the LMRT's difficulties is set out in John Deering's *Team on the Run: The Inside Story of the Linda McCartney Pro Cycling Team* (2002).

Working Classical: a requiem for Linda

Personnel: The London Symphony Orchestra, conducted by Lawrence Foster and Andrea Quinn, and the Loma Mar Quartet.

Producer: John Fraser

Recording: 10-11 October 1998 track 12; and 21-25 February 1999 tracks 1-11 and 13-14 (all at EMI Studios, Abbey Road, London).

Release date: 1 November 1999

Highest chart placings: UK Classical Charts: 1.

Length: 61:35 minutes

Tracks: 1. *Junk* 2:49; 2. *A Leaf* 11:08; 3. *Haymakers* 3:33; 4. *Midwife* 3:33; 5. *Spiral* 10.02; 6. *Warm and Beautiful* 2:31; 7. *My Love* 3:48; 8. *Maybe I'm Amazed* 2:04; 9. *Calico Skies* 1:52; 10. *Golden Earth Girl* 1:57; 11. *Somedays*

3:05; 12. *Tuesday* 12:26; 13. *She's My Baby* 1:47; and 14. *The Lovely Linda* 0:54.

With memorial services planned for Linda in the UK and US, Paul decided to include instrumental versions of songs he had written specifically about Linda. From his solo catalogue, Paul selected eight songs for reinvention by string quartet: *Warm and Beautiful; My Love; Maybe I'm Amazed; Calico Skies; Golden Earth Girl; Somedays; She's My Baby;* and *The Lovely Linda.* He also added *Junk,* which had not been written about Linda, but whose waltz rhythm suited a string quartet. In addition, Paul wrote two short new compositions: *Haymakers* and *Midwife.*

These 11 songs provided 28 minutes of recorded material.

To complete *Working Classical,* Paul added three longer orchestral compositions: *A Leaf; Spiral;* and *Tuesday.*

Paul worked with EMI Classics' recording producer John Fraser (1945-) to arrange the 11 songs for string quartet. The Brodsky Quartet premiered these arrangements in London. The recently formed Loma Mar Quartet then recorded the songs in February 1999.

For the three longer compositions, Paul developed orchestrations with Richard Rodney Bennett and Jonathan Tunick (1938-), a US composer who had orchestrated musicals for Stephen Sondheim (1930-2021). The pieces were then performed by the London Symphony Orchestra (LSO), conducted by Lawrence Foster (*A Leaf* and *Spiral*) and Andrea Quinn (*Tuesday*).

The songs

1. **Junk** is a song written by Paul in 1968 when in Rishikesh, India, studying transcendental meditation. It was not included on the Beatles' *White Album* or *Abbey Road* but was included on *McCartney* (1970).

2. **A Leaf** began as a piano composition soon after the *Liverpool Oratorio.* With the assistance of Fraser, Paul developed it into an orchestral piece divided into seven parts. It has the American classical style of Aaron Copland (1900-90) and George Gershwin (1898-1937), with gentle,

wistful sections building to a series of crescendos and its use of muted trumpets. On 23 March 1995, *A Leaf* was performed live in front of then Prince Charles (1948-) at the Royal College of Music. In April 1995, it was released as a CD single and reached number 156 in the UK charts. The LSO performed the *Working Classical* version.

3. **Haymakers** is a short new piece for string quartet with a joyful, pastoral and regal tone. The violins, played by Krista Bennion Feeney (1961-) and Anca Nicolau, and viola, played by Joanna Hood, are supported by a cello, played by Myron Lutzke, as a bass line.

4. **Midwife** features the same instrumentalists as *Haymakers* and proceeds at a stately pace. The title relates to Paul's mother Mary, who was a midwife.

5. **Spiral** is an impressionistic, pastoral piece, influenced by the English composers Edward Elgar (1857-1934) and Ralph Vaughan Williams (1872-1958). Strings and flute are prominent. Performed by the LSO, it begins with a slow, swirling section comprising a solo flute underpinned by strings. At the five-minute mark, there is a brief troubled and discordant section, before a return to a gentle, soothing, meditative theme played on flute and violin. The song's inspiration came from a visit by Paul to Newgrange, a Neolithic monument in the Boyne Valley, County Meath, Ireland. According to Irish mythology, Newgrange is the dwelling place for deities. Paul Du Noyer (2015) considers *Spiral* to be Paul's finest work in the classical field.

6. **Warm and Beautiful** is a 1976 love ballad for Linda that appeared on *Wings at the Speed of Sound*. The string quartet version emphasises the song's melody.

7. **My Love** is Paul's most famous love song to Linda. Released in 1973, it topped the US singles chart. This 1999 instrumental version veers dangerously towards elevator music.

8. **Maybe I'm Amazed** is Paul's first great solo song and remains a live staple. The string quartet version is well arranged, with the cello prominent.

9. **Calico Skies** is an acoustic folk love song from *Flaming Pie* (1997), Paul's last album with Linda. It works well in string quartet format.

10. **Golden Earth Girl** is an *Off The Ground* (1993) song written about Linda's love of nature. This version includes delightful flute and oboe.

11. **Somedays** is a song from *Flaming Pie* written by Paul in two hours on 18 March 1994 while Linda was conducting a photo session. The string quartet brings out the song's delicate melody.

12. **Tuesday** originated as the theme for an animated film based on *Tuesday* (1991), a wordless picture book for children by the American illustrator David Wiesner (1956-). The song's orchestration has similarities to *A Leaf,* with an American classical and cinematic style.

13. **She's My Baby** appeared on *Wings at the Speed of Sound.* The 1976 version's prominent bass made it a dance song. The 1999 string quartet version is quite different.

14. **The Lovely Linda** opened Paul's debut solo album *McCartney* and, at 42 seconds, is the shortest song in his catalogue. It was written at High Park Farm, Campbeltown, in 1969. The 1999 version closes the album to retain thoughts of Linda in the listener's mind.

Release and reception

The album's title *Working Classical* is a pun by Paul on the words "working class." He explained: "I'm a lucky ordinary guy … I'm very proud of my working-class roots. A lot of people like to turn their backs on their past … I'm always working class, I'm always from Liverpool and my roots are always in rock 'n' roll – but I like the odd cello!"

On 16 October 1999, *Working Classical* was premiered at the Liverpool Philharmonic Hall. The album was released on EMI Classics on 1 November 1999.

Like *Standing Stone* (1997), *Working Classical* topped the UK classical music charts.

As with Paul's earlier orchestral works, many classical music critics were critical: *Classics Today* slated it as "yet another crossover disaster."

But in *Gramophone*, Adrian Edwards was more positive, stating: "All of us who recall the imaginative instrumental touches that graced those early Lennon-McCartney airs, *She's Leaving Home* and *Eleanor Rigby*, will be drawn to this collection."

Run Devil Run: a rock 'n' roll album for Linda

Personnel: Paul McCartney (vocals, bass guitar, electric and acoustic guitars, percussion); David Gilmour (electric guitar, lap steel guitar, backing vocals); Mick Green (electric guitar); Dave Mattacks* (drums, percussion); Ian Paice (drums, percussion); Pete Wingfield (keyboards, piano, Hammond organ); Geraint Watkins* (piano); and Chris Hall (accordion).

* May sessions only

Producers: Chris Thomas, Paul McCartney, with engineering by Geoff Emerick and Paul Hicks

Recording session: March and May 1999 (Abbey Road Studio 2)

Release date: 4 October 1999

Highest chart placings: UK: 12; US: 27.

Length: 40:46 minutes

Tracks: 1. *Blue Jean Bop* 1:57; 2. *She Said Yeah* 2:07; 3. *All Shook Up* 2:06; 4. *Run Devil Run* 2:36; 5. *No Other Baby* 4:18; 6. *Lonesome Town* 3:30; 7. *Try Not to Cry* 2:41; 8. *Movie Magg* 2:12; 9. *Brown Eyed Handsome Man* 2:27; 10. *What It Is* 2:23; 11. *Coquette* 2:43; 12. *I Got Stung* 2:40; 13. *Honey Hush* 2:36; 14. *Shake a Hand* 3:52; and 15. *Party* 2:38.

In March 1999, Paul emerged from ten months of near seclusion from the public to record, in Abbey Road Studio 2, London, the rock 'n' roll covers album *Run Devil Run*: a project Linda had wanted Paul to do.

Paul's British rock musician friends rallied around to assist this return to music making.

David Gilmour, who first met Paul at Abbey Road in 1967 when Pink Floyd were recording *Piper at the Gates of Dawn* and the Beatles *Sgt. Pepper's Lonely Hearts Club Band,* agreed to play guitar.

Also in the band was Mick Green (1944-2010), a guitarist formerly with Johnny Kidd & the Pirates and Billy J. Kramer & the Dakotas who Paul knew from the early 1960s.

In addition, there were two musicians Paul admired but had never met before: Iain Paice (1948-), a powerhouse drummer with the British heavy metal group Deep Purple, and, on keyboards, the Englishman Pete Wingfield (1948-).

And, for the May session, Dave Mattacks (1948-), of folk-rock pioneers Fairport Convention, played drums, while the Welshman Geraint Watkins (1951-) featured on keyboards.

Paul booked Abbey Road Studio 2 for five days to record the album at breakneck speed. Paul sought to rekindle the adrenalin rush of the Beatles' 1,200 gigs in Hamburg in 1960-62 and the Liverpool Cavern Club in 1961-63 when the band swiftly learned covers of songs requested by the audience. And, in an interview with Laura Gross (included in *Run Devil Run*'s limited edition set), Paul said he wanted to re-experience the disciplined way of working used by George Martin on the Beatles' pre-1966 albums. This involved three-hour morning and afternoon sessions during each of which the band would be expected to record two songs.

For *Run Devil Run,* Paul allowed the studio band fifteen minutes to rehearse each song. They then launched into an instinctive live take: the catchphrase for the week was "no thinking.." Where band members were unfamiliar with the song, Paul gave a quick demo. This approach gave *Run Devil Run* its high-energy feel.

Chris Thomas co-produced the album with Paul. Engineering, in May, was by Geoff Emerick and Paul Hicks. They created a punchy, crisp and uncluttered sound that was modern despite the songs being retro in style.

Recording *Run Devil Run* proved to be cathartic and therapeutic. It reset Paul's mind to his early teenage years in 1956-57 when the propulsive sounds of the new US rock 'n' roll on the radio helped ease the pain felt from his mother's early death.

Chris Thomas commented that recording the tracks brought a smile back on Paul's face and that the album was a parting gift to Linda.

The songs

The album contains twelve covers of rock 'n' roll and rockabilly songs from the 1950s that Paul had fond memories of but which had not been performed by the Beatles. Some are well-known songs, but three are obscure Paul and Linda favourites: *Coquette; She Said Yeah;* and *Movie Magg*.

In addition, the album contains three new McCartney songs written in that era's 'three-chords-and-a-howl' style. Paul stated he found it challenging writing to genre, but all three songs he created would not have been out of place on the Beatles' first two albums.

Throughout the album Paul's vocals are equally strong on rockers and ballads and he plays surging lines on his Höfner violin bass, bought in the early-1960s for £30. Paul and the band successfully recreate an updated early 1960s' Cavern Club sound.

1. **Blue Jean Bop** is a song written and recorded by Gene Vincent (1935-71) on his debut album in 1956, the year Paul's mother Mary died. It starts with Paul singing, with atmospheric echo, "blue jean baby, with your big blue eyes." Paul's version stays close to the cherished original. Vincent's *Be-Bop-A-Lula* was the first song Paul bought and, during their residency in Hamburg, the Beatles met Vincent. They mimicked Vincent's leather clad style before the Beatles' manager Brian Epstein (1934-67) insisted they switch to suits in order to have mass-market appeal.

2. **She Said Yeah** is a song recorded in 1959 by the US R&B singer Larry Williams (1935-80). While it did not chart, it was popular among early-1960s British invasion groups, including the Beatles, who covered three Williams' songs: *Bad Boy; Dizzy Miss Lizzy;* and *Slow Down*.

3. **All Shook Up**, written by Otis Blackwell (1931-2202), was Elvis Presley's first UK number 1, in June 1957, when Paul was 15. Paul covers

it enthusiastically, adopting his Elvis voice. For good measure, Paul adds whelps of "Yeah!" This track was recorded in May 1999, with Mattacks on drums and Watkins on keyboards. David Gilmour is on backing harmonies. It is a heavier version than the Elvis original.

4. **Run Devil Run** is a new song written by Paul. Its title comes from a bottle of bath salts called Run Devil Run, with reputed properties to expunge demons. Paul saw these in Miller's Rexall Drugs, a voodoo and herbal medicine store on 87 Broad Street, Atlanta, Georgia, when visiting with his son James. Paul wrote the verses later when sailing on holiday. The song has the narrative style of Chuck Berry (1926-2017) but uses an aggressive, accelerated 176 bpm tempo. The verses end with a Wings-style harmony and there is a rip-roaring keyboard break.

5. **No Other Baby** is a slow anthemic song, with a simple bass and guitar riff. It had been a 1958 George Martin-produced single for the British skiffle group The Vipers. Paul had never owned a copy of the record but had performed the song periodically during pre-concert soundchecks. Delivered by Paul with heartfelt passion, it is a standout track. Its lyrics express Paul's grief and state of mind in 1998-99, declaring "no other baby can thrill me like you do."

6. **Lonesome Town** is a mournful country-rock song which was a US number 7 hit for Ricky Nelson in 1958. A Linda favourite, the song summed up Paul's situation in 1998-99 following her death. Paul's vocals are an octave higher than the original and are supported by harmony vocals by David Gilmour.

7. **Try Not to Cry**, the second track written by Paul, is a bluesy R&B song with fine guitar. Its biographical lyrics find Paul declaring that he wants to enjoy being alive and to sing but finds it difficult "not to cry, cry, cry, cry over you."

8. **Movie Magg** is a 1955 rockabilly song written by Carl Perkins, a sharecropper's son. It is a story about riding on a mule called Becky with his girlfriend Maggie to a movie show. Perkins collaborated with Paul on the song *Get It* in 1981, for the *Tug of War* album. During that session, Perkins explained why he wrote *Movie Magg*. Paul recorded it in 1999 as a tribute to his late friend. Paul plays acoustic guitar, backed by drums. Keyboards and electric guitars were not used on this recording.

9. ***Brown Eyed Handsome Man***, is a 1956 Chuck Berry B-side to *Too Much Monkey Business*, which reached number 4 in the US and was also recorded by Buddy Holly. Paul performs it in a Cajun zydeco-style, with Chris Hall on accordion.

10. ***What It Is***, Paul's third new song on the album, is a piano-driven boogie-woogie. Paul wrote and played it to Linda during her closing months. It declares that Linda "makes the world go around for me."

11. ***Coquette*** is a piano vamping jazz standard written by Johnny Green (1908-89) and Carmen Lombardo (1903-71). Fats Domino (1928-2017) recorded it in 1958 as a B-side to his number 6 US hit *Whole Lotta Lovin'*.

12. ***I Got Stung*** is a fast-paced rocker which was a 1959 UK number 1 for Elvis Presley. Green plays lead guitar, having previously recorded the song with the Pirates in 1981.

13. ***Honey Hush*** is a rockabilly blues song written and recorded in 1953 by Kansas City 'blues shouter' Big Joe Turner (1911-85) and covered in 1956 by the US rockabilly singer Johnny Burnette (1934-64). It was a song Paul first heard on a Dansette record player as a teenager during a sleepover at John Lennon's art school flat in Liverpool. Paul's hard-rocking version became a favourite in his live shows.

14. ***Shake a Hand*** is a song written by the US R&B trumpeter Joe Morris (1922-58) which was recorded in 1959 by Little Richard (1932-2020). It was a song Paul frequently played on the jukebox of a favourite bar in Hamburg where the Beatles played pool. Paul sings with impassioned vocals in a style that is a cross between Little Richard and Lennon. Gilmour and Green trade guitar solos.

15. ***(Let's Have a) Party*** is a feelgood rock 'n' roll song written by Jessie Mae Robinson (1918-66) and recorded by Elvis Presley for his 1957 film *Loving You*. It reached number 2 in the UK singles chart. Paul's version is more intense and ferocious than the Presley original.

Release, promotion and reception

Run Devil Run was released on 4 October 1999 and was promoted on UK television by Paul and members of his *Run Devil Run* band. There were appearances on *Later with Jules Holland* (recorded on 2 November and broadcast on 6 November), *Red Alert – National Lottery* (on 13 November), *The Tube* (on 20 November) and the *Parkinson* talk show (recorded on 2 December and broadcast on 3 December).

On 14 December, Paul and his all-star band performed twelve songs from the album, plus *I Saw Her Standing There,* at Mathew Street's new Liverpool Cavern Club (opened in 1984): the original Cavern Club, situated on the other side of the street, had been demolished in 1973.

There was an audience of 300 selected guests, while 15,000 watched on large screens outside. The concert was livestreamed over the internet to a reported 50-150 million worldwide. In June 2001, a *Live at the Cavern Club* concert film was released on VHS and DVD.

Music critics gave *Run Devil Run* positive reviews of four stars out of five. They considered it far superior, in its passion and recording quality, to Paul's earlier rock 'n' roll covers album, 1988's *Choba B CCCP* (the 'Russian album'), which had been recorded in two days (also with Mick Green).

For Peter Ames Carlin (2009), the selection of songs made *Run Devil Run* the most "deeply autobiographical" album of Paul's career. For Paul du Noyer (2015), the album's hard-rocking displayed McCartney's "indestructible musical spirit" in the face of his recent life challenges. While for Chris Wheatley, writing in *Record Collector* (2023), *Run Devil Run* "celebrated the spirit of the 1950s with authenticity and verve."

Run Devil Run reached number 12 in the UK, selling 135,000 units, and 27 on the US Billboard 200, selling 275,000 units. Its worldwide sales-to-date have been 800,000 units.

On 24 October, Paul released the single *No Other Baby,* which reached 42 in the UK. On its B-side were *Brown Eyed Handsome Man* and *Fabulous*, a song which, performed by Charlie Gracie (1936-2022), had reached number 6 in the UK chart in 1957. *Fabulous* had been the first song recorded during the *Run Devil Run* sessions.

Paul meets Heather

In April, Paul became a grandfather, with the birth of daughter Mary's son, Arthur.

By spring 1999, Paul was gradually coming to terms with the loss of Linda and was ready to consider starting a new relationship.

On 20 May 1999, Paul attended the *Daily Mirror* Pride of Britain Awards at London's Dorchester Hotel. He had been invited to present the Linda McCartney Award to Juliet Gellatley, founder and president of the animal rights charity *Viva!* (estd. 1994) and the Vegetarian and Vegan Foundation. He was seated beside UK Prime Minister Tony Blair (1953-) and the British business magnate Richard Branson (1950-), head of the Virgin Group .

It was at this ceremony that Paul first saw Heather Mills. A tall and striking 31-year-old former model, with long blonde hair and blue eyes, Mills was an amputee. On 8 August 1993, she lost her left leg below the knee after being hit, when crossing Kensington Road in central London, by a police motorcycle travelling rapidly behind a bus. She also suffered a crushed pelvis, broken ribs and a punctured lung. The Police Authority awarded her £200,0000 in compensation.

Since 1991, Heather had immersed herself in charity work, helping those affected by the Yugoslav Civil War. She had set up a refugee crisis centre in London and drove deliveries of food and clothes to Croatia.

In 1994, using the £180,000 she received from selling her story to the *News of the World* and from other interviews, she established the Heather Mills Health Trust (HMHT). The Trust raised funds to aid child amputee war victims, redistributed unused prosthetic limbs and advocated the removal of landmines: an issue Princess Diana (1961-97) had campaigned for in 1997.

At Pride of Britain in May 1999, Heather introduced the winner of the bravery award: Helen Smith, a wheelchair-bound PhD student who had lost both legs and an arm to meningitis. Noticing that that Helen's microphone had been attached to the lectern at standing height, making it difficult for her to be heard, Heather grasped it from its stand and handed it to Helen. The ballroom's 500 guests responded with spontaneous applause.

Later, Heather delivered an impassioned speech. It impacted Paul powerfully. Piers Morgan (1965-), editor of the *Daily Mirror* and the brainchild behind the awards, said later that Paul told him: "I like the way she talks, she's a gutsy girl." Piers suggested Paul contact Heather to support her charities.

In a November 2004 interview, Paul admitted: "I just liked the look of her, same as had happened when I saw Linda. I was just physically attracted. Then we got together and found we had so much in common. And I was thinking, what if I hadn't seen her?"

The day after the awards, Heather flew to Cambodia with the Duchess of Kent (1933-) to shoot a piece for the *That's Esther* UK BBC TV programme on the Voluntary Service Overseas (VSO) charity's work helping children. During this 12-day trip, Heather became engaged to the documentary's director, the 47-year-old Chris Terrill, whom she had developed a friendship with before flying out.

On Heather's return to the UK, she found an answerphone message from Paul. Thinking it was likely to be a spoof, she deleted it. But, after receiving a further message, they talked.

Paul told Heather he was interested in the landmines issue and had seen a *Tomorrow's World* programme on UK BBC TV about bionic arms that took nerve impulses from the residual limb. He believed these would help landmine survivors and offered to help in funding this. Heather welcomed this offer of support but advised Paul that what amputees in less affluent countries really needed were much cheaper artificial limbs.

A week later, Paul and Heather met in Paul's London office to explore the issue further. Following the meeting, Paul asked Heather to assemble a business plan for relief to the maimed children affected by a contemporary crisis in Sierra Leone.

In June 1999, Heather worked on this plan and set about converting the HMHT into a registered charity. This was achieved in February 2000.

Heather's wedding to Chris Terrill was set for 8 August 1999, but a week before she called it off. It was Heather's third broken engagement since 1993.

In July-August 1999, Paul and Heather discussed the Sierra Leone project further by phone and in person,. Impressed with the business plan, Paul wrote out a £150,000 cheque to the HMHT.

In her book, *A Single Step* (2002), Heather stated that, in August, she told Paul that she had split up with her boyfriend and "Paul's face lit up." He invited Heather to dinner at his favourite vegetarian restaurant in Knightsbridge, London, to "talk about this more."

A private courtship

This began six-months of private courtship. Paul and Heather met several times a week for meals, walks and drives in the country. They spent time together at Paul's small historic 3-bedroom cottage 'Lizzie' (named after its Elizabethan timber) in the Forecastle, near Rye, in East Sussex. There they each cooked meals and Paul presented Heather with wildflowers from his estate. They also spent time in August 1999 in the northeast US, at Paul's holiday home in the Hamptons, where he relaxed on his Sunfish sailing dinghy, *Linda*.

At times, Paul felt guilt that he might be 'betraying' Linda. But, from 'strange, metaphysical occurrences,' such as animal and bird noises on his estate, Paul came to believe that Linda was sending messages that it was OK for him to seek a new love.

Heather had little familiarity with Paul's music. When young, she had listened to her father's classical music and had liked the heavy rock of AC/DC and Led Zeppelin. She declared later: "I wasn't even a Beatles fan. I barely even knew any of the songs. I liked one song by Wings but that was it. He loved that."

What attracted Heather was Paul's energy and romantic nature. She described him as "a cross between Peter Pan and Captain Hook" and her "knight in shining armour."

Recording VO!CE

In November 1999, Heather and her sister Fiona, who lived in Greece, stayed overnight at Peasmarsh. During this stay, Paul contributed background vocals to *VO!CE,* a charity single for Heather's disability charity.

VO!CE was a co-write, with Heather, who supplied the lyrics, and Paul and Nikko Patrelakis, an electronic dance music (EDM) arranger in Greece. The song involves a monologue by Heather about the need to listen to people with disabilities. This is set against a musical backdrop of electronic dance rhythms and drums. In the background, Paul sings "someone you love" and "why don't you ask her she has a voice?"

In Hog Hill Mill studio, Heather was a tough taskmaster, insisting Paul make repeated takes until he achieved the gospel vocal tone she had in mind.

The single was released in November 1999 and included the *Paul McCartney's Mello Extension,* a 7:17 minute chilled instrumental. Marketed as "Heather Mills feat. Paul McCartney," *VO!CE* reached number 87 in the UK singles charts. Promotion was low-key to ward off press questions whether Heather was Paul's new girlfriend.

Heather met Paul's children in November but the couple spent Christmas apart, with their families. On 23 December 1999, Paul felled a Christmas tree on his Sussex estate and drove three hours to deliver it to Heather's house. Arriving late, he stayed. The next morning Paul planted the tree in the garden. Heather and Paul decorated the tree together before Paul left to join his family for Christmas Eve.

2000: In Transition

Key events

Early February: Paul and Heather's relationship becomes public.

1 February: The Beatles receive the Best Band Ever award from the NME.

14 February: *A Garland for Linda* charity album is released.

9 March: At Sear Sound, New York, Paul records the Elvis Presley hit *That's All Right Mama,* with Presley backing band members Scotty Moore on guitar and D.J. Fontana on drums. It is released on the 2001 tribute album, *Good Rockin' Tonight: The Legacy of Sun Records.*

March to May: *Standing Stone* concerts in England, Germany and the US.

May: Paul records a cover of *I'm Partial to Your Abracadabra* for the 2001 *Brand New Boots and Panties* Ian Dury tribute album.

5 June: The soundtrack for the film comedy *Maybe Baby* is released and includes McCartney performing the title track.

21 August: The *Liverpool Sound Collage* avant-garde album is released.

14 September: The *Paul McCartney Paintings* book is published.

5 October: *The Beatles Anthology* book is published.

13 November: *1 (The Beatles),* a compilation album of the Beatles' chart-topping singles is released. It reaches number 1 in over 35 countries, including the UK and US, and goes on to be the best-selling album of the 2000s worldwide.

2 December: The Linda McCartney Centre for cancer treatment is opened at Royal Liverpool University Hospital, following the raising of £4 million by the Forget-Me-Not Cancer Appeal.

On 31 December 1999, Paul introduced Heather to his large multi-generational extended family at the McCartney's traditional New Year's Eve party. As usual, the event was held at Rembrandt, a mock Tudor house in Heswall, an affluent part of the Wirral, Merseyside, bought by Paul for his father in 1965. Adhering to a well-honed routine of drinks, games and singalongs, the McCartneys welcomed in the new millennium.

With Paul focusing on his developing relationship with Heather, 2000 was musically a year of relative inactivity. In February, Paul released *A Garland for Linda,* a remembrance album with one new composition, and, in August, *Liverpool Sound Collage,* an avant-garde album. He also recorded tribute songs to Elvis Presley and Ian Dury (1942-2000).

Financially for Paul the most important release of the year was *1 (The Beatles),* a 27-track compilation of the Beatles' chart-topping singles. Released on 13 November, it held number 1 position in the UK's album chart for nine consecutive weeks and debuted at number 1 in the US. It went on to become the best-selling album worldwide of the 2000s, selling over 31 million copies.

A growing friendship with Heather

In January 2000, Paul invited Heather to join him in the Caribbean, on the Turks and Caicos Islands, where Paul had been holidaying with his children. Heather joined Paul on 10 January, as his children flew home. They spent a week together at the exclusive Parrot Cay island resort: sailing, swimming and enjoying beachside candle-lit dinners.

When Paul returned to the UK, Heather invited him to a late thirty-second birthday celebration on 29 January 2000 at her Sussex barn: she had turned 32 on 12 January. Around a hundred attended: Heather's friends and those connected to her charities. Paul and Heather danced together, but their privacy was respected.

In February, the couple's cover was blown when Paul and Heather were spotted leaving a London restaurant with Ringo Starr and his US actor wife Barbara Bach (1947-).

Several days later, the couple's relationship became public when a photographer spotted Paul and Heather in a park in London with Paul's daughter Mary and her young son. Paul agreed that the lensman could take a shot of Paul and Heather together if he then left them alone. Paul told the photographer: "We've grown close. We're very good friends. She is a very impressive woman. We are an item …. If this is to develop, then give us a chance."

The next day, the posed photograph and accompanying story appeared in the UK's *News of the World* Sunday newspaper. It also made UK TV news and on Monday was across the UK press.

A media storm ensued, with reporters and paparazzi photographers tracking Heather and Paul's daily movements. This continued for months and tabloid newspaper articles appeared recounting the remarkable life story of Heather Mills.

A remarkable life story

At the time Heather met Paul, she was already a well-known figure in the UK from her campaigning and media work and her frank 1995 autobiography, *Out on a Limb*.

Heather updated this autobiography in 2002's *A Single Step,* while the celebrity biographer Neil Simpson (1966-) later published, in 2007, an unauthorised biography, *The Unsinkable Heather Mills*.

Heather's father, her first husband and her mother's partner contested some of the stories in her autobiography. But the overall picture remained clear: Heather's upbringing and early adult life had presented a series of challenges which she had surmounted to become by the 1990s a respected charity campaigner and media star.

Heather was born on 12 January 1968 in the army town of Aldershot in southern England, into a family with military roots. Her grandfather (on her mother's side) had been a colonel in the British Army in India and her father Mark had been a paratrooper.

During her early years, the family moved regularly as Mark changed jobs: living at one time in Libanus village in the Brecon Beacons (in Wales), then in Rothbury, near Alnwick in north-east England, followed by Washington, Tyne and Wear.

At the age of six, Heather's mother Beatrice suffered a serious car accident and was hospitalised for several months. It led to Heather and her younger sister Fiona being briefly taken into care. Three years later, Beatrice left the family to live with Charles Stapley (1925-2011), an actor in the popular UK television soap opera *Crossroads*.

Mark was left in charge of three children and relied on them to do cooking and cleaning. At times, the family was so short of money that, as admitted in her autobiography, Heather shoplifted groceries from the age of ten.

When Heather was only 13, Mark was jailed for 18 months for debt and fraud. Heather moved with her sister Fiona to Clapham, London, where she lived with Beatrice and Stapley. On Saturdays, Heather assisted at a jewellery shop in Clapham, but was caught stealing jewellery. She received a probationary sentence as she was only 15.

From the age of 16, Heather worked in London in a succession of jobs, including in the bar of a Soho hostess club and as a clothes and swimwear model. Aged 18, she began a relationship with Alfie Karmal, seven years her senior who was in the process of a divorce. They began living together in 1987.

In 1988, despite Alfie's remonstrations, Heather left to start a lucrative £1,500 a day 12-month contract as the face of a cosmetics firm in Paris. Midway through and feeling homesick, she asked to be released from the contract. But this was refused by a director who had fallen secretly and obsessively in love with Heather. Heather swiftly took a taxi to Calais and fled France by a ferry to Dover.

Soon after her December 1988 return to England, Heather proposed to Alfie. They married on 6 May 1989 and set up home in the London commuter belt. Their modern four-bedroom house in Hoddesdon, Hertfordshire, 20 miles north of London, had a swimming pool.

Two months after the wedding, Heather set up a modelling agency ExSell, with a mission of looking after models properly. After an ectopic pregnancy in late 1990, she sold this modelling agency.

In March 1991, while carrying a second ectopic pregnancy, Heather left Alfie: they formally divorced in late 1991. She flew to Slovenia (then part of Yugoslavia) and set up home, in a bedsit, with Milos Pogacar (1962-), a skiing instructor. Heather had met and fallen in love with Milos during a skiing holiday with Alfie's first wife.

The timing for this new romance proved to be inopportune.

On 25 June 1991 Slovenia declared independence from Yugoslavia, triggering a June-July 1991 war. Ahead of the fighting, Heather fled Slovenia by car, with Milos. However. Milos struggled to adapt to life in London and in August 1991 returned to Slovenia.

During 1991-92, Heather made periodic trips to Ljubljana, Slovenia, but the relationship foundered. But Heather became committed to assist victims of the Yugoslav Civil War. From 1992, she regularly drove convoys of food and clothing from the UK to Croatia.

A Garland for Linda

Personnel: Paul McCartney (composer); Richard Rodney Bennett (composer); Michael Berkeley (composer); John Rutter (composer); John Tavener (composer); Ralph Vaughan Williams (Composer); Rozanna Panufnik (composer); Giles Swayne (composer); Judith Bingham (composer); David Matthews (composer and concertmaster); Philippa Davies (flute); Robert Cohen (cello); and the Joyful Company of Singers (conducted by Peter Broadbent).

Producer: John Fraser

Recording: November 1999

Release date: 25 April 2000

Highest chart placings: UK Classical Charts: 9

Length: 55:11 minutes

Tracks: 1. *Silence and Music* (Ralph Vaughan Williams) 4:50; 2. *Prayer for the Healing of the Sick* (John Tavener) 8:53; 3. *Water Lilies* (Judith Bingham)

7:35; 4. *Musica Dei Donum* (John Rutter) 5:36; 5. *The Doorway of the Dawn* (David Matthews) 4:53; 6. *Nova* (Paul McCartney) 6:28; 7. *I Dream'd* (Roxanna Panufnik) 3:30: 8. *Farewell* (Michael Berkeley) 3:30; 9. *The Flight of the Swan* (Giles Swayne) 6:16; and 10. *A Good-Night* (Richard Rodney Bennett) 2:51.

While Paul and Heather's romance was starting to blossom, Paul continued to bring to completion projects commemorating Linda, notably *A Garland for Linda*.

This choral tribute album to Linda was modelled on *A Garland for the Queen*, in which ten British classical composers, including Ralph Vaughan Williams, composed new works to celebrate the 1953 coronation of Queen Elizabeth II.

Nine British classical composers contributed pieces to *A Garland for Linda*. They included Richard Rodney Bennett, John Rutter (1945-) and John Tavener (1944-2013). There is also a new McCartney song *Nova*, written between November 1998 and May 1999.

Produced by John Fraser, the album was recorded in November 1999 at All Saints Church, Tooting, London with The Joyful Company of Singers chamber choir, under the baton of Peter Broadbent.

The songs

Each musical piece includes a text pertinent to the themes of passing, memories and the power of music to "uplift sad minds." As he explained on 27 January 2000, Paul's composition **Nova**, was inspired by "what I was feeling about Linda at the time, and I just wanted to somehow include her spirit of goodness."

Set to an alternately calm and anxious choral melody, *Nova* has haunting lyrics of loss and love. The piece begins with questioning where God is "hiding" and whether there was "something in our past imperfect?" This progresses to the affirmatory "I am here in every song you sing" and in "the wings of a rising lark" and every "flake of snow" and that "I'll be that arm that guides … 'til the end of time." It concludes with a simple "Amen."

Nova unveils Paul's almost pantheistic spiritualist beliefs.

Release and reception

EMI Classics released *A Garland for Linda* in the UK on 14 February 2000. Funds raised by the album and supporting events, including a 110-page songbook and fundraising dinner, went to the Garland Appeal charity. The aim was to raise £2 million for non-animal-related research to help eradicate breast and liver cancer, promote early cancer detection awareness and support music which has the power "to move people and to provide a source of hope."

The album reached number 9 in the UK's classical album chart.

Gramophone's Rob Cowan (1948-) found the work an "edifying memorial, superbly sung, beautifully recorded ... (with *Nova* being) one of (Paul's) best solo works since the Beatles and Wings."

Music Web International's Rob Barnett considered the album "not simply a *memento mori* but one to which you will want to return again ... (*Nova* is) touching and strong ... the choral voices circle ascending and descending like some great stratosphere-dwelling bird."

A Garland for Linda was performed in spring 2000 at small venues and churches in England and the US east coast.

Liverpool Sound Collage

Personnel: Paul McCartney, The Beatles (1963-65 and 1967-68), Youth, and Super Furry Animals

Producer: Paul McCartney; with Paul Hicks as engineer

Recording: 1999-2000

Release date: 21 August 2000

Highest chart placings: UK: -; US: - [did not chart].

Length: 58:21 minutes

Tracks: 1. *Plastic Beetle* 8:23; 2. *Peter Blake 2000* 16:54; 3. *Real Gone Dub Made in Manifest in the Vortex of the Eternal Now* 16:37; 4. *Made Up* 12:58; and 5. *Free Now* 3:29.

Commissioned by British pop artist Peter Blake (1932-), elements of the *Liverpool Sound Collage* formed a soundscape for visitors to *About Collage*: a multi-media pop-art exhibition in 2000 at the Tate Liverpool art gallery.

Blake had known Paul since the early 1960s when he created *The Beatles 1962,* a Warholesque pop-art poster-picture. With his then wife Jann Haworth (1942-), Blake designed the iconic, collage-based front cover art for *Sgt. Pepper's Lonely Hearts Club Band* (1967).

The *Liverpool Sound Collage* is an avant-garde work which employs the musique concrète ('concrete music') Stockhausen approach of sampling sounds from the natural environment, musical instruments, synthesisers and other electronic devices.

This approach had been used in 1968 by John Lennon, with the help of Yoko Ono (1933-) and George Harrison, for *Revolution 9,* an 8:22 minute track on the Beatles' *White Album.* Abroad at the time when *Revolution 9* was assembled, Paul was unimpressed when he heard the piece. But he appreciated Stockhausen and the non-standard music of John Cage (1912-92) and, between 1966-68, had immersed himself in London's avant-garde music scene.

Indeed, it was Paul who had created the Beatles first slice of avant-garde electronica: the 13:48 minute *Carnival of Light.* It had been commissioned for the London Roundhouse's 28 January 1967 *Million Volt Light and Sound Rave.* During a break in the recording of *Penny Lane,* Paul asked his bandmates: "Would you mind giving me 10 minutes? I've been asked to do this thing. All I want you to do is just wander round all of the stuff and bang it, shout, play it." The result was a cacophony of distorted guitar, organ and drums. It was heard at the Rave but then locked securely away in the Beatles' vaults.

The *Liverpool Sound Collage* is an advance on *Revolution 9* and the *Carnival of Light.* It mashes together snippets of conversations between the Beatles during 1963-68 recording sessions, samples of Beatles music and Paul's

Liverpool Oratorio, drum machine loops and comments by passers-by recorded on a Dictaphone in Liverpool by Paul on 14 December 1999, ahead of the Cavern Club gig.

Youth and Cian Ciarán (1976-), the keyboard player with the Welsh psychedelic rock band Super Furry Animals (SFA), provided Paul assistance.

Cian and Paul had met at the 1 February 2000 *NME* awards ceremony. "A bit worse for wear," Cian introduced himself to Paul and declared: "I'll do the best remix (of unreleased Beatles recordings) you'll ever hear." Three weeks later, Paul left a message on Cian's answer machine, stating: "Alright Cian, it's Paul here. I'm going to take you up on your remix offer."

In return, Paul agreed to guest on the SFA's 2001 album, *Rings Around the World.* Reprising his 1967 performance on the Beach Boys' *Vegetables,* Paul rhythmically chewed celery and carrot on the *Rings Around the World* track *Receptacle for the Respectable.*

The songs

The *Liverpool Sound Collage* stands out as Paul's most unconventional and inaccessible solo work. It includes washes of electronic sonic distortion and is bereft of melodies and rhythmic structures.

1. ***Plastic Beetle*** comprises drum machine loops, synthesisers, backward pianos and traffic noise on which are layered snippets of studio dialogue and singing from the following Beatles' sessions: *I Call Your Name,* on 1 March 1964; *Think for Yourself,* 8 November 1965; *Good Night,* 28 June 1968; *This Boy,* 17 October 1963; and *Mr. Moonlight,* 18 October 1964. The track is credited to Paul McCartney and the Beatles.

2. ***Peter Blake 2000*** was used as the soundtrack to Blake's *On Collage* exhibition and was produced by Cian Ciarán and SFA, who add synthesisers, bass and keyboards. This track samples Beatles dialogue and vocals from the *Think for Yourself* session and from the 1 February 1967 take 9 of *Sgt. Pepper's Lonely Hearts Club Band.* It also includes extracts from the end of *Magical Mystery Tour* and string section samples from Paul's *Liverpool Oratorio.*

3. ***Real Gone Dub Made in Manifest in the Vortex of the Eternal Now*** is an electronic track assembled by Youth. It includes Beatles' dialogue from the *Think for Yourself* session, extracts from the *Liverpool Oratorio* and samples of people in the streets of Liverpool interviewed by Paul.

4. ***Made Up*** is shorter and different mix by Youth of track three.

5. ***Free Now*** is a cut-down version of track two. It is the album's most accessible track.

Release and reception

Released on 21 August 2000, the *Liverpool Sound Collage* did not chart in the UK or US and sold just 40,000 units. A challenging listen, Paul described it as: "an outbreak from my normal stuff … a little side dish that is not to be confused with my other work." But as part of Tate Liverpool's *About Collage* multi-media experience, it was more effective.

Surprisingly, the *Liverpool Sound Collage* was nominated for a 2001 Grammy Award for Best Alternative Music Album. Less surprisingly, it lost to Radiohead's *Kid A*.

Painter Paul

Paul had a lifelong interest in art. At the age of 11, he chose as his school prize a book on the art of the Spanish surrealist painter Salvador Dali (1904-89) and the Cubist Pablo Picasso (1881-1973). Later, aged 14, Paul won a further prize for his drawing of St. Aidan's Church on the Speke housing estate where his family had lived.

Unlike John Lennon, Stu Sutcliffe (1940-62), the Beatles' first bassist, and Klaus Voormann (1938-), a Hamburg days' friend, Paul had gone to a grammar school and not an art college. Paul said later: "I felt that only people who'd gone to art college were allowed to paint."

In mid-1960s London, bachelor Paul spent hours at London's Fraser and Indica galleries, befriending art critic John Dunbar (1943-), gallery owner 'Groovy Bob' (Robert) Fraser (1937-86) and contemporary artists including Peter Blake and Richard Hamilton (1922-2011). He became an art collector, buying paintings by Picasso, French impressionist Pierre-

Auguste Renoir (1841-1919) and Belgian surrealist René Magritte (1898-1967), including *The Listening Room* (1952), which inspired the Apple logo.

But it was not until 1982 that Paul began painting his first canvases. The trigger was the encouragement of Willem de Kooning (1904-97), a Dutch-born abstract expressionist artist who lived near Paul and Linda's US home in East Hampton. Like de Kooning, Paul's painting style is abstract and surrealist. He makes use of vibrant positive colours, often yellow, inspired by Linda's blonde hair.

Seventy of Paul's abstract paintings were first shown at the Kunstforum Lÿz gallery in Siegen, Germany, between 1 May to 25 July 1999, attracting 45,000 visitors. The exhibition was curated by Wolfgang Suttner, an art teacher and McCartney fan, who, from hearing an interview at the time of Paul's 19 September 1993 concert in Dortmund, became aware that Paul had many unseen paintings.

Following five years of correspondence, Paul agreed that Suttner could exhibit his works. After the exhibition's success, the art book *Paul McCartney: The Paintings* was published in September 2000. It contained reproductions of 117 colour and 17 duotone illustrations of Paul's works.

The British art critic Brian Sewell (1931-2015) dismissed Paul's paintings as "self-indulgent impertinence." But Paul's biographer Howard Sounes (2010) found his paintings to have a "dream-like quality." Comparing Paul to other rock and singer-songwriter painters, Sounes ranked Paul as below Joni Mitchell but "fractionally above" Bob Dylan.

Tribute songs to Elvis Presley and Ian Dury

Across his solo career, Paul has recorded tribute and charity album songs for artists he admired. In 2000, he recorded *That's All Right Mama*, for the compilation album, *Good Rockin' Tonight: The Legacy of Sun Records* (2001), and *I'm Partial to Your Abracadabra*, for the *Brand New Boots and Panties* (2001) cancer charity tribute album to Ian Dury.

That's All Right Mama

Good Rockin' Tonight commemorated the 50th anniversary of Sun Records, the label at the forefront of early rock 'n' roll. Artists including Bob Dylan, Elton John, Sheryl Crow (1962-), Tom Petty (1950-2017), Eric

Clapton (1945-), Van Morrison (1945-), Carl Perkins, Robert Plant (1948-), Jimmy Page (1944-), Jeff Beck (1944-2023) and Chrissie Hynde contributed cover tracks.

Paul covered *That's All Right Mama*, Elvis Presley's 1954 debut single, accompanied by two members of Presley's backing band: guitarist Scotty Moore (1931-2016) and drummer D.J. Fontana (1931-2018).

That's All Right was originally written and recorded in 1946 by the Chicago blues singer Arthur 'Big Boy' Crudup (1905-74). Elvis Presley accelerated its tempo, transforming it into one of the earliest rock 'n' roll songs. The Beatles covered it on 2 July 1963 for the UK *Pop Go the Beatles* radio show and Paul recorded a version in 1987 on *Choba B CCCP*.

I'm Partial to Your Abracadabra

In late 1999, Paul became aware that Ian Dury, a larger-than life new wave pub rock singer, was terminally ill with colorectal cancer.

Paul admired Dury's songs, with their colourful lyrics and debts to vaudeville.

Although Paul had never met Ian before 1999, they shared mutual friends: the British painters Peter Blake and Humphrey Ocean (1951-). Dury had studied art in 1964-67 at the Royal College of Art under Blake and went on to teach art at the Canterbury College of Art (CCA), with Ocean as one of his students. In 1971, when Dury set up the pub rock band Kilburn and the High Road, he persuaded Ocean to play bass.

In 1974, Ocean left to concentrate on art. His early work included the inner-sleeve art for *Wings at the Speed of Sound* (1976) and he was tour artist for the May-June 1976 Wings Over America tour. Ocean's drawings and sketches, which display Paul and the band in relaxed mood, can be seen in *The Ocean View*, a hardbound volume included in the 2013 *Wings Over America* deluxe edition archive box set. Ocean's 1983 painting of a seated Paul forms part of London's National Portrait Gallery collection. Paul also later used Ocean's 2004 etching *Black Love Chair* for the *Memory Almost Full* (2007) album cover.

In late 1999, Paul visited the ailing Dury at his home in Hampstead, north London. Paul provided Dury with a list of consultants and therapists who had helped Linda with palliative care and supplied vouchers to cover the cost. Dury died at home on 27 March 2000.

In May 2000, Paul recorded a cover version of *I'm Partial to Your Abracadabra*, a track from Dury's 1977 standout album *New Boots and Panties*. Paul was backed by Dury's band The Blockheads. Jools Holland (1958-), formerly of Squeeze, played keyboards.

Rather than seeking to replicate Dury's languid Cockney vocal style, Paul decided to go for a raucous, hard rocking delivery. The song appeared on the 2001 cancer charity album *Brand New Boots and Panties*.

2001: Back in the Sunshine Again

Key events

January: Heather and Paul spend a romantic holiday in India.

16 February to 2 March: *Driving Rain* sessions in Los Angeles.

19 March: Paul's *Blackbird Singing: Poems and Lyrics* book is published.

7 May: *Wingspan: Hits and History* is released and a TV documentary. The compilation sells 1.2 million copies, reaching 2 in the US and 5 in the UK.

14 June: Paul and Paul Simon perform at the AAM benefit concert in Beverly Hills.

19 June: Paul records *Your Loving Flame* and *Vanilla Sky* at Henson Studios. The *Vanilla Sky* film soundtrack album is released on 4 December.

22 July: Heather Mills accepts Paul's proposal of marriage.

11 September: From the runway at New York's JFK airport, Paul sees smoke over the Twin Towers, caused by the al-Qaeda terrorist attack.

20 October: Paul performs at *The Concert for New York City*. A CD is released on 27 November 2001 and a DVD on 29 January 2002.

29 October: *From a Lover to a Friend* is released as a single.

5 November: *Freedom* is released as a single. Proceeds are donated to the Robin Hood Foundation for 9/11 victims and emergency workers.

12 November: *Driving Rain* album is released.

29 November: George Harrison dies of cancer in Los Angeles.

11 December: Paul performs three songs (*Your Loving Flame*, *Freedom* and *Let It Be*) at the Nobel Peace Prize 100th Anniversary Concert in Oslo's Spektrum Arena.

Paul and Heather grew emotionally closer during 2001: a year which saw profound change and activity in Paul's personal and professional life.

The couple began the year with a month-long romantic holiday in India. It included stays at former Maharaja palaces functioning now as luxury hotels. This was Paul's first visit to India since the Beatles' stay at the ashram (spiritual retreat) of Maharishi Mahesh Yogi (1918-2008) in Rishikesh, north India, in early 1968. On 12 January, Heather's thirty-third birthday, the couple travelled overnight on the *Palace on Wheels* train from Delhi to Jaipur: a city in Rajasthan famed for its romantic pink sandstone palaces.

In February, Paul and Heather flew to New York for Valentine's Day shopping. At the top of the Empire State Building, Paul wrote the couple's names on the stonework.

They then travelled west to Los Angeles. Between 16 February and 2 March, Paul spent two weeks recording, at Henson Studios for his next album, *Driving Rain*.

For this West coast stay, Paul and Heather decided to rent a French-style mansion on 9536 Heather Road, Beverly Hills, owned by Courtney Love (1964-), the widow of Nirvana's Kurt Cobain (1967-94). They nicknamed it 'Heather's house' – after the road's name rather than Heather - and liked it so much that Paul later bought it for $4 million.

On 22 July, when back in Britain, Heather accepted Paul's proposal of marriage. The wedding was set for 2002.

On 20 October, Paul headlined a New York City charity concert to support victims of the 9/11 terrorist atrocity.

On 12 November, the album *Driving Rain* was released.

Paul proposes to Heather

On 18 May, after the couple returned to the UK, MPL provided a loan of £800,000 to enable Heather to buy Angel's Rest, a whitewashed seafront house on a private shingle beach near Hove, in Sussex. Heather agreed to repay the loan at £1,000 a month over a 25-year term, but in 2002 the loan was written off as a gift by Paul.

On 20 July 2001, Paul and Heather attended the annual graduation ceremony at LIPA. Paul presented awards to the singer-songwriters Joan Armatrading (1950-) and Benny Gallagher (1945-) and to the one-time Sex Pistols' Svengali Malcolm McLaren (1946-2010).

After the ceremony, Paul and Heather enjoyed a short break at the exclusive lakeside Sharrow Bay Hotel on Ullswater, in the picturesque Lake District, in northwest England. They had stayed at the hotel a year before.

On 22 July 2001, Heather recounted in *A Single Step*, that as the couple were walking to dinner, Paul asked Heather to "wait a minute" while he collected a present for her from their room. He returned with the gift behind his back, dropped to his knees and presented Heather with a box containing a ring. It was a £15,000 diamond and sapphire engagement ring he had bought secretly in Jaipur, India, when holidaying together in January 2001.

Paul declared: "I love you Heather. Will you marry me?" Lost briefly for words, Heather gathered herself and responded "Yes," leaving Paul with "tears running down his face."

The wedding was set for "sometime in 2002."

Energised by these changes in his personal life, in 2001 Paul played live again on 14 June and 20 October and wrote and recorded a new album, *Driving Rain*.

Driving Rain

Personnel: Paul McCartney (vocals, bass guitar, guitars and piano); Abe Laboriel Jr. (drums, percussion and backing vocals); Rusty Anderson (guitars and backing vocals); Gabe Dixon (keyboards and backing vocals); David Kahne (programming, orchestral samples, synths and guitar); James McCartney (co-write, percussion and guitar on tracks 9 and 12); Ralph Morrison (violin on track 11); string quartet featuring David Campbell on viola (on track 13); and Eric Clapton (guitar on track 16).

Producer: David Kahne, who recorded on 16-track analogue tape, transferring to Logic Audio digital equipment to engineer the tracks.

Recording sessions: 16 February to 2 March and 19 June 2001, at Henson Studios, Los Angeles; and 20 and 23 October, at Madison Square Garden and Quad Studios, New York.

Release date: 12 November 2001

Highest chart placings: UK: 46; US: 26.

Length: 67:21 minutes

Tracks: 1. *Lonely Road* 3:16; 2. *From a Lover to a Friend* 3:48; 3. *She's Given Up Talking* 4:57; 4. *Driving Rain* 3:26; 5. *I Do* 2:56; 6. *Tiny Bubble* 4:21; 7. *Magic* 3:59; 8. *Your Way* 2:55; 9. *Spinning on an Axis* 5:16; 10. *About You* 2:54; 11. *Heather* 3:26; 12. *Back in the Sunshine Again* 4:21; 13. *Your Loving Flame* 3:43; 14. *Riding into Jaipur* 4:08; 15. *Rinse the Raindrops* 10.08; and 16. *Freedom* 3:34.

By early 2001, Paul had enough ideas for a new album of new songs: his first in four years. On the album's launch, Paul said: "I feel as though it's a good time in my life, having had a bad time. It's also an album made in the USA, like bits of *Ram* ... it seems quite positive."

Driving Rain included songs written during the mid- and later-1990s in the Maldives, Caribbean and Arizona, two co-writes with son James, three songs written in January 2001 while holidaying with Heather in Goa, India, several built up from assorted fragments and one arising from a studio jam.

The album has an organic rawness harking back to *McCartney* (1970) and *Wild Life* (1971). One reason was that Paul arrived at the recording sessions with a strained voice, caused by a heated telephone conversation with a carpet salesperson in India whom Paul claimed had "ripped me off." But the main reason was that Paul followed the approach he had used when recording *Run Devil Run*: bringing each day the bare bones of a song which was then rehearsed briefly by the studio musicians before being recorded "live, quick and simple." Subsequently, David Kahne added layers of synthesiser and strings from his "trusty bank of sounds" to some tracks.

Fourteen of the album's tracks were recorded between 16 February to 2 March. Daily sessions ran from 11:30 a.m. to 6:30 p.m. *Your Loving Flame* was recorded on 19 June and *Freedom* on 20 and 23 October.

Seven other songs were worked on but did not make the album. These included the Beatlesque *(I Will) Always Be There,* the ballads *If This is Wrong* and *You Are Still Here,* and a 'train song,' *Washington.*

The producer and musicians

Ahead of recording, Paul asked his MPL's New York office to suggest potential producers. One of the names proposed by Bill Porricelli was David Kahne (1958-), an American who had worked with The Bangles and Tony Bennett (1926-2023). Intrigued that Kahne was also a musician and composer, Paul agreed to a two-week session in February 2001 at Kahne's favoured Henson Studios (formerly A&M studios) in Los Angeles.

The pair gelled with Paul saying: "I liked his approach, he's very musical, but modern … he's very quiet and very on the ball and … what he wanted to do and what I wanted to do was very similar."

Kahne went on produce further McCartney projects: *Back in the U.S.* (2002); *Back in the World Live* (2003); *The Space Within US* (2006); and *Memory Almost Full* (2007). He also produced Eps, singles and albums by Paul's son James: *Available Light* (2010); *Close at Hand* (2011); *Me* (2013); and *Beautiful* (2024).

Ten days before the recording sessions, Kahne asked Paul if he wished to do the album with a band or to multi-track it himself. Paul responded: "Probably with a band, but, if it doesn't work out, we'll multi-track it."

Kahne booked three accomplished session musicians: Abe Laboriel Jr. (1971-), on drums and percussion; Rusty Anderson (1959-), on guitars; and Gabe Dixon (1977-), on keyboards. McCartney met the backing band on the first day of recording.

Abe Laboriel Jr. was the son of Abraham Laboriel Sr. (1947-), a renowned Mexican American bass guitarist who can be heard playing on thousands of studio recordings by artists as diverse as Stevie Wonder, Elton John and Michael Jackson. Abe's mother was a classically trained singer. Growing up in Los Angeles, Abe began playing drums at the age of four and was later mentored by the renowned drummers Jeff Porcaro (1954-92) and Chester Thompson (1948-). During the 1990s, Abe toured with US guitarist Steve Vai (1960-), Canadian singer-songwriter k.d. lang (1961-) and Geordie singer-songwriter Sting (1951-).

Rusty Anderson came from Orange County in California and had been a professional guitarist from the age of 14. He had played with bands including The Police and Van Halen and on sessions for The Bangles, Elton John and Santana. Rusty had also formed his own psychedelic rock bands: The Living Daylights; and Edna Swap.

The Tennessee-born Gabe Dixon, after leaving the University of Miami, had formed a band which Kahne signed in 1998.

These musicians gave *Driving Rain* a spontaneous band feel in which guitars and drums are prominent. All three session musicians were also adept backing singers. With Paul freed to concentrate on bass and vocals, *Driving Rain* has some of Paul's strongest bass lines.

Paul asked Abe, Gabe and Rusty to play live with him on 14 June at an Adopt-A-Minefield (AAM) benefit concert in Los Angeles and the 20 October Concert for New York City, at Madison Square Garden. He then invited them to join his April-November 2002 world tour. Abe and Rusty agreed, but Gabe declined, choosing to concentrate on his own album.

The songs

Driving Rain contains some of Paul's most introspective and emotional songs, presented raw without the pop sheen sprinkled by Jeff Lynne on *Flaming Pie*.

As stated by Jamie Atkins in *Record Collector* (2023), *Driving Rain* is: "a collection songs steeped in duality, torn between grief and the optimism of new love … (with) little sense of pandering to commercial concerns … it tells us a lot about his state of mind at the time."

1. **Lonely Road** gets the album off to a rocking start. It begins with a repeated, but tentative, bass line. This gathers pace until all instruments are firing for its infectious chorus. Paul rocks out with raw, double-tracked vocals and Rusty impresses on fuzzy electric guitar. It is the first of three songs on the album that had been written in January 2001 by Paul using his Martin miniature travel guitar while on holiday in Goa. Paul described it as a "defiant song against loneliness."

The lyrics speak of struggling "to get over you" and "find something new" and conclude "don't want to walk that lonely road again."

2. **From a Lover to a Friend** is a dreamy ballad with melodic bass, prominent piano, fragile vocals, unusual time signatures and a sophisticated harmonic structure. It is an example of Paul's ability to meld together fragments from different song ideas to create a collage song. To make the edits work, Paul added odd bars to convert from 4:4 time to 5:4 and 2:4 in places.

The lyrics, while strung together instinctively, related subconsciously to Paul coming to terms with the death of Linda and his feelings for Heather. Paul sings "let me love again, now that you turned out to be someone I can trust." It was Paul's favourite song on the album. Adrian Allan (2019) has termed it "perhaps the most introspective and questioning song from (Paul's) entire post-Beatles career."

3. **She's Given Up Talking** is a strong track, featuring swirling guitar by Rusty, electronic percussion, fuzz Höfner bass, Hammond organ and distorted vocals and drums. It is a song about 'selective mutism' written by Paul when on holiday several years earlier in Jamaica. It related to a neighbour, one of whose children suddenly decided not to speak with teachers and classmates at school but talked non-stop at home. In *The Lyrics* (2021), Paul states: "Years later the family told me it was just a phase. She's grown up and she talks now."

4. **Driving Rain** is an up-tempo song let down by a banal chorus. Paul wrote it in February 2001 at the piano in the evening following a lunchtime drive with Heather on the Pacific Coast Highway from Los

Angeles to Malibu. The opening part of the phrase, "Something's open (– it's my heart)," came from a burglar alarm warning at the house Paul was renting in Los Angeles.

5. *I Do* is a melodic love ballad about Heather in the style of *Pipes of Peace* but with vocal shifts to a higher register and orchestral samples. Written in Goa, Paul described it as an "if you only knew' song."

6. ***Tiny Bubble*** is an Al Green (1946-) style soul song, driven by Paul's overdubbed Höfner bass and tasteful guitar and organ breaks by Rusty and Gabe. It began in Paul's small studio in Scotland as a stream of consciousness demo about the world being a tiny bubble. The chorus is reminiscent of the George Harrison Beatles' track *Piggies* (1968).

7. ***Magic*** tenderly recounts how Paul first met Linda at the Bag O'Nails pub/music venue in London on 15 May 1967. He reflects that it "must have been some sort of magic" that persuaded him to get up to talk to Linda as she was leaving and invite her to join him at The Speakeasy. The song has strong Höfner bass lines.

8. ***Your Way*** has a Wings-era country vibe, with Rusty on pedal steel guitar and Vox bass guitar and Abe and Rusty on backing vocals. Written in Jamaica by Paul at the same time as *She's Given up Talking,* it has simple instinctive lyrics.

9. ***Spinning on an Axis*** is a song co-written with Paul's son James when in New England, visiting American relatives. While watching the sun go down, they discussed how the earth turning away was causing the effect. James played a riff on a small keyboard over which Paul parody rapped with thoughts of spinning on an axis. They taped this on cassette and Paul developed it for the 2001 sessions. The track is loose and imaginative, with distinctive percussive and guitar effects and falsetto vocals.

10. ***About You*** is an up-tempo track written in Goa in January 2001 Its lyrics attest that Heather's love had given Paul the power to move on.

11. ***Heather*** is an uplifting keyboard-driven largely instrumental work. Its jaunty melody ends with Paul singing about flying to the moon "for a year and a day" and dancing "to a runcible tune with the queen of my

heart, Heather." The lyrics are based on *The Owl and the Pussycat* (1870): a nonsense poem by the English poet and musician Edward Lear (1812-88).

The song came about after Heather heard Paul at the piano one morning after breakfast and asked: "which Beatles track is that?" Paul responded that he was just noodling, but Heather insisted he make a Dictaphone recording so as not to lose it. She asked what's the name of the song. Paul replied: "Oh, it's called Heather."

12. ***Back in the Sunshine Again*** is a languid, bluesy track, with a memorable riff and Beatles-sounding middle section. With impressive keyboards and emotive vocals, it is another strong track. James, who played rhythm guitar on the recording, co-wrote the song with Paul in Arizona in 1997, contributing the riff and bridge. Paul said: "It's a good time, back in the sun song - about leaving behind all our troubles and moving forward into the sunshine."

13. ***Your Loving Flame*** is a restless, slow-paced (61 bpm) romantic ballad. It was written by Paul in November 1999 on the top floor of the Carlyle Hotel in New York in a room with a black Steinway baby grand piano and view of Central Park. Paul said: "I thought I was walking into a Cole Porter movie."

In her autobiography *A Single Step* (2002), Heather said that Paul called her from the hotel, telling her he had been thinking about and missing her. He put his phone on speaker mode and said: "I've written this song for you." It was his first song for Heather. Paul performed an early version in December 1999 on the UK television *Parkinson* show, with David Gilmour on lead guitar.

14. ***Riding into Jaipur*** is an Indian-themed track with Rusty on tanpura, an Indian plucked drone instrument, and Paul playing his Martin backpacker mini-guitar. It recalls elements of *Auraveda* on *Rushes*. Paul wrote the melody on his Martin guitar while holidaying with Linda in the Maldives. As Paul noted, this mini guitar had a distinctive "sound on certain frets like a sitar." Paul added the title and lyrics during an overnight luxury *Palace on Wheels* train journey with Heather to the 'Pink City' of Jaipur, India, in January 2001.

15. **_Rinse the Raindrops_** came from a studio jam on two verses of words Paul had written while sailing. Paul added a rough melody and bridge. At the end of a day's recording session, the band jammed for thirty minutes. Kahne edited overnight the pieces he liked and told Paul: "I couldn't get it down any shorter than this." This 10-minute song features discordant guitar by Rusty and raw, screaming vocals by Paul in the style of the Beatles' _Why Don't We Do It In The Road?_ (1968).

16. **_Freedom_** is a song written by Paul in response to the 9/11 al-Qaeda terrorist attack on New York. Paul first performed it at the 20 October 2001 Concert for New York City. A march-time anthemic rocker with a chorus hook, it features Eric Clapton on guitar. The lyrics, influenced by phrases used by US Republican President George W. Bush (1946-) post 9/11, declare: "I will fight for the right to live in freedom."

Paul envisioned _Freedom_ as a _We Shall Overcome_ song that would inspire healing. He wrote from the perspective of someone coming to the US from a repressive regime: "What it means to me is, 'Don't mess with my rights, buddy. Because I'm now free.'"

As with _Give Ireland Back to the Irish_, a 1972 Wings' single, Paul struggled writing political songs that were as effective as John Lennon's _Give Peace a Chance_ (1969). In 2004, Paul confided during an interview with Alan Franks: "They're not easy to write these protest songs." Howard Sounes (2010) termed _Freedom_: "a heavy-handed football chant" with lyrics that read like Republican bumper stickers.

On 3 February 2002, Paul performed _Freedom_ at Super Bowl XXXVI and played it extensively during his 2002 _Driving USA Tour_. But right-wing Christian nationalists came to misuse the song to promote human-rights curtailing aspects of President Bush's October 2001 USA Patriot Act – which strengthened US government surveillance of phone and electronic communications and expanded the range of terrorism offences - and the US-led 2003 war against an Iraqi regime accused by the Bush administration of developing weapons of mass destruction.

In July 2004, Paul told John Harris (1969-) of the UK's _The Guardian_: "Now it's all got completely ugly – the whole Iraq thing." Paul stopped playing *Freedom* live after 5 November 2002, as: "it had become identified with the war effort and I think that's a bad thing."

Release and reception

Originally planned for release in September 2001, the 9/11 outrage led Capitol Records to delay *Driving Rain*'s production so that *Freedom* could be included as a bonus track.

On 29 October, *From a Lover to a Friend,* backed with *Riding into Jaipur,* was released as a single in the UK. It reached number 45. The CD maxi-single included a stripped-down remix and a chill-out remix.

On 5 November, *Freedom* (backed with *From a Lover to a Friend*) was released as a single in the US. It reached number 20 in the adult contemporary charts and 97 in the broader US singles charts.

The album was released on 12 November. Its cover featured a grey grainy photo of Paul's face and raised right hand which had been taken using Paul's Casio camera-watch.

Many music critics gave *Driving Rain* positive reviews of 3-4 stars out of five. *Uncut's* Ian McDonald (1948-2003) wrote: "Possibly a grower, this album is certainly better than anything Macca's done for some while, if not the late masterpiece some of us have been hoping for."

But the album was not a commercial success.

In the UK, *Driving Rain* was Paul's lowest-selling mainstream album. It peaked at number 46 in its week of release - *World of Our Own* by Westlife was the number 1 - and remained only three weeks in the top 100.

In the US, *Driving Rain* sold only 66,000 copies in its first week, but recovered to peak at number 26. Paul's spring 2002 tour helped keep US sales at a steady level and by May 2002 *Driving Rain* had been certified gold, selling 500,000 units. It sold 870,000 units worldwide.

For McCartney fans, *Driving Rain* is a marmite album. It is short on catchy melodies and earworm hooks, but the songs are mature and thoughtful. Released at the height of the CD era, its most obvious weakness was a bloated length.

AAM concert: 14 June

During 2001, Paul continued to support the animal welfare and vegetarian charities Linda had championed. And he was now joined and supported in this by Heather. Since the mid-1990s, Heather had followed a wholefood and vegetarian regime to help combat infection from the many operations she endured following her 1993 accident.

Heather and Paul also became committed supporters of AAM, a US charity that helped survivors of landmine accidents and, on 4 June 2001, they launched a UK branch.

On 14 June 2001, at an AAM fundraising concert at the Beverly Wilshire Hotel in Beverly Hills, California, Paul joined US singer-songwriter Paul Simon (1941-) on stage for a rendition of the Beatles' *I've Just Seen a Face*. Paul also performed *Yesterday*, *The Long and Winding Road, Let It Be* and (for the first time with his new band) *Driving Rain*. He also read his satirical poem, *Jerk of All Jerks*.

Between 2001-05, Paul was a regular at AAM benefit concerts: performing with Brian Wilson (1942-) in 2002; James Taylor (1948-) in 2003; Neil Young in 2004; and Yusuf Islam/Cat Stevens (1948-) and Tony Bennett in 2005. During these years, Paul donated £3.4 million to AAM and its partner organisation, No More Landmines. (AAM and No More Landlines ceased to exist in 2015).

The Concert for New York City: 20 October

At 8:50 a.m. on the morning of 11 September 2001, Paul and Heather were seated in an airplane on the runway of JFK Airport in New York City awaiting take off for their flight to London. As Paul looked towards the Manhattan skyline, he saw a plume of smoke rising above the World Trade Center (WTC). The pilot, who had been informed of the tragic events that had begun at 8:46 a.m., asked passengers to remain calm while he awaited updates.

At 9:03 a.m., a second terrorist-hijacked commercial aircraft crashed into the WTC's South Tower and at 9:37 a.m. a third plane struck the west side of the Pentagon (US defence headquarters) in Arlington County, Virginia.

Commercial flights were grounded. A steward came over to Paul and Heather and said: "Something serious has happened in New York and we've got to get you out of here."

Paul and Heather went to Paul's 11 Pintail holiday home at Amagansett, an ocean-front hamlet in East Hampton, on the south shore of Long Island. It had been bought by Paul in December 1998 because too many memories of Linda remained at the East Hampton holiday home where he had previously stayed. At 11 Pintail, Paul and Heather watched television news coverage of the terrorist attacks.

When international flights resumed, Heather flew to London to fulfil charity commitments. On her return to New York, she suggested Paul hold a charity concert to help those affected by 9/11.

Paul was wary. He did not wish it to appear that he might be using the 9/11 tragedy to promote his forthcoming album. But he did want to help. A week after 9/11, Paul and Heather visited Ground Zero (the site of the New York attacks). They were affected greatly. Paul decided to hold a benefit concert and donate proceeds from his single *From a Lover to a Friend* to aid the families of New York firefighters.

The emotional concert, held at Madison Square Garden, New York, on 20 October 2001, featured performances by British and US musical artists, actors and comedians as well as short speeches by politicians. David Bowie (1947-2016) performed *America* and *Heroes*, Bon Jovi *Livin' on a Prayer, Wanted Dead or Alive* and *It's My Life*, Mick Jagger (1943-) and Keith Richards (1943-) *Salt of the Earth* and *Miss You*, Billy Joel *Miami 2017* and *New York State of Mind*, Eric Clapton and Buddy Guy (1936-) *Hoochie Coochie Man* and *Everything's Gonna Be Alright*, The Who, *Who Are You, Baba O'Riley, Behind Blue Eyes* and *Won't Get Fooled Again*, Elton John and Billy Joel *Your Song*, and rapper Jay-Z (1969-) *Izzo (H.O.V.A.)*.

Taking the stage in a New York Fire Department T-shirt, Paul and his band closed proceedings with impassioned performances of the Beatles' *I'm Down, Yesterday* and *Let It Be* and, from his new album, *Lonely Road* and *From a Lover to a Friend*. Paul also played his new song *Freedom* twice, with Eric Clapton on lead guitar.

Encouraged by the audience's positive reaction, Paul released *Freedom*, as a single on 5 November, with new vocals recorded at Quad Studios, New York.

The Concert for New York City, which was broadcast live on VH-1, raised $35 million. On 27 November 2001, a 32-track double CD, *The Concert for New York City: To Benefit the Robin Hood Relief Fund*, was released and a 245-minute DVD on 29 January 2002. The CD included four of the songs played by Paul: *I'm Down; Yesterday; Let It Be;* and *Freedom* (finale).

Ten years later, on 12 September 2011, a documentary film, *The Love We Make*, directed by Albert Maysles (1926-2015), was released, selling 75,000 units. It chronicles Paul's journey through the traumatised post 9/11 streets of Manhattan and his planning of and performance at the Concert for New York. Previously, Maysles had directed *Gimme Shelter* (1970), a documentary of the Rolling Stones' 1969 US tour.

Vanilla Sky: 4 December

In 1999, actor/producer Tom Cruise (1962-) persuaded US film director Cameron Crowe (1957-) to film *Vanilla Sky*, an English language remake of the remarkable Spanish science-fiction thriller *Abre los Ojos (Open Your Eyes)*.

Crowe (1957-), who was married (1986-2010) to Nancy Wilson (1954-), guitarist and vocalist in the US rock band Heart, was renowned for making music a central element in his films. He asked Paul to contribute the title song. Paul played several songs from the *Driving Rain* sessions, but Crowe said he was looking for something folkier.

Paul went away and, drawing inspiration from a restaurant visit, came up with an opening line: "the chef prepares a special menu." Within ten minutes, he completed *Vanilla Sky*: a simple rustic song embellished by snatches of Spanish guitar and flute.

On 4 December 2001, *Vanilla Sky* was released as a single. It was nominated for Best Original Song at the 2001 Academy Awards and Golden Globe Awards but lost out respectively to *If I Didn't Have You,* by Randy Newman (1943-), and *Until,* by Sting.

2002: Back in the U.S.

Key events

28 January: Paul receives a Lifetime Achievement Award from Amnesty International.

3 February: Paul performs *Freedom* at Super Bowl XXXVI in New Orleans.

24 March: Paul performs *Vanilla Sky* at the Kodak Theatre Hollywood for the 74th Academy Awards.

1 April to 18 May: *Driving World Tour* begins, with 27 shows in North America.

24 May to 4 August: Paul's paintings and sculptures are exhibited at the Walker Art Gallery in Liverpool. Queen Elizabeth II visits on 25 July.

3 June: Paul performs at the *Party at the Palace*, in Buckingham Palace Gardens, London, for Queen Elizabeth II's Golden (50th) Jubilee.

11 June: Paul and Heather marry at Castle Leslie in Ireland.

18 September: At the 2nd Annual AAM Gala in Los Angeles Brian Wilson and Paul duet on *God Only Knows* and Paul plays nine Beatles and solo songs.

20 September: *Wingspan*, a book of photographs and interviews, is published.

21 September to 18 November: *Driving World Tour* resumes, with 23 shows in 22 US cities, 3 shows in Mexico City and 5 shows in Tokyo and Osaka, Japan.

28 October: Paul postpones a planned November concert in Melbourne, Australia, after the 12 October terrorist bombings in Bali, Indonesia.

11 November: *Back in the U.S.* live album is released.

29 November: Paul performs at the *Concert for George* at the Royal Albert Hall.

Paul and Heather began 2002 with a romantic holiday in Kerala, south-west India. On 12 January, Paul presented a diamond and sapphire bracelet to Heather for her 34th birthday.

In 2002 Paul's career and life moved forward at an express pace with an appearance at Super Bowl XXXVI on 3 February, a return to touring in April, marriage to Heather in June and *Driving World Tour* shows in the US, Mexico and Japan between September and November.

Paul's 2002 tour was the world's highest grossing. It has been captured for posterity on *Back in the U.S.* (2002) and *Back in the World* (2003).

Paul's first tour since 1993

The 2002-03 *Driving World Tour* was Paul's first since December 1993.

Paul warmed up by playing *Freedom*, on 3 February 2002, at the Super Bowl XXXVI pre-game show in New Orleans. His backing band comprised Abe and Rusty, from the *Driving Rain* sessions, along with his long-time associate, the English keyboard player 'Wix' Wickens. The fifth member was Brian Ray (1955-), a Californian guitarist and former musical director, for 14 years, for Etta James (1938-2012). Brian had worked with David Kahne and Abe. In Paul's band, Brian played bass when Paul moved to piano.

Leg one of *Driving U.S.* began on 1 April at Oakland, California. It involved one show in Toronto, Canada, and 26 sold-out shows in 19 US cities, ending on 18 May at Fort Lauderdale, Florida. Heather accompanied Paul.

The cities visited were: Oakland and San Jose (California); Las Vegas (2 nights); Chicago (2 nights); Toronto; Philadelphia; East Rutherford (New Jersey); Boston; Uniondale (New York); Washington D.C. (2 nights); Madison Square Garden in New York City (2 nights); Cleveland (Ohio); Auburn Hills (Michigan); Los Angeles; Anaheim (California); Denver; Dallas (2 nights); Atlanta (2 nights); Tampa (Florida); and Sunrise (2 nights on 17-18 May), near Fort Lauderdale in Florida.

These 27 concerts were attended by 410,000 and grossed $53 million. Paul had thought about playing smaller 5,000-seat venues but, not wishing to deprive fans of the chance to see him perform again, opted for 12,000 to 18,000-seat arenas.

The 75,000 tickets for the first five concerts, priced between $50 and $250, sold out by telephone and the internet within 30 minutes. The early shows included two nights at the 15,000-seat MGM Grand Hotel and Casino in Los Angeles, for which Paul received a record $5.6 million fee.

Touring in the wake of 9/11, Paul enthusiastically waved the US flag during shows. Referencing back to the Beatles tour of the US in August-September 1964, nine months after the assassination of President John F. Kennedy (1917-63), Paul told the audiences: "There is a sort of healing thing going on again and I'm proud to be part of that."

At the 23 April Washington D.C. MCI Center concert, Paul provided hundreds of guest tickets to relatives of people who lost their lives in the 9/11 attack on the Pentagon.

At the 27 April New York Madison Square Garden concert, Paul received an honorary badge of a NYPD detective for his 9/11 related charitable work.

The US media coined the phrase 'Macca-mania' to describe the audiences' emotional responses. The *Las Vegas Review-Journal* review declared: "No other concert crowd I have ever seen has lavished so much affection on a performer. It was wave after wave of love, all the way up to the rafters."

Paul later said: "The tour in America ... really revitalised me ... the American audience has been so cool, so warm and informed and receptive."

The setlist was Beatles-heavy. On the 1975-76 Wings Over the World tour, Wings played five Beatles' songs. During Paul's 1989-93 tours, the Beatles quotient in the setlist rose to over a half and in 2002 (and on subsequent tours) it reached two-thirds. Five songs from the *Driving Rain* sessions were played: *Lonely Road; Driving Rain; Your Loving Flame; Vanilla Sky;* and *Freedom.*

The concerts drew fans from across the generations: from grandparents to grandchildren. When Paul and the band played the Beatles songs *All*

My Loving, We Can Work It Out, Can't Buy Me Love and *I Saw Her Standing There*, screens projected videos of the 1963-65 mop-tops on stage and being chased post-show by screaming fans.

Each concert lasted two-and-a-half hours, comprising 36 songs (including encores) and careful sequencing. The shows began with 30-minutes of high energy, up-tempo Beatles, Wings and solo classics. Paul then challenged his audience with three cuts from *Driving Rain*. This was followed by 30-minutes of Paul singing and playing ballads on guitar and piano, including tributes to George (*Something* played on a ukelele) and John (*Here Today*).

At the concert's midpoint, the band returned to join Paul for 30 minutes of Beatles, Wings and solo rockers that brought the audience to their feet. *Live and Let Die* was accompanied by spectacular pyrotechnics.

The anthemic *Let It Be* and *Hey Jude* closed the main set, with Paul orchestrating a singalong in which female and male audience members sang separately and then all together.

After several minutes of rapturous applause, Paul and the band returned to the stage to play two extended sets of encores: *The Long and Winding Road, Lady Madonna* and *I Saw Her Standing There*; followed by *Yesterday, Sgt. Pepper's Lonely Hearts Club Band* and *The End*.

For the 1 April opening show at Oakland Arena, the setlist was:

1. *Hello Goodbye*; 2. *Jet*; 3. *All My Loving*; 4. *Getting Better*; 5. *Coming Up*; 6. *Let Me Roll It*; 7. *Lonely Road*; 8. *Driving Rain*; 9. *Your Loving Flame*; 10. *Blackbird*; 11. *Every Night*; 12. *We Can Work It Out*; 13. *Mother Nature's Son*; 14. *Vanilla Sky*; 15. *You Never Give Me Your Money*; 16. *The Fool on the Hill*; 17. *Here Today*; 18. *Something*; 19. *Eleanor Rigby*; 20. *Here There and Everywhere*; 21. *Band on the Run*; 22. *Back in the U.S.S.R.*; 23. *Maybe I'm Amazed*; 24. *C Moon*; 25. *My Love*; 26. *Can't Buy Me Love*; 27. *Freedom*; 28. *Live and Let Die*; 29. *Let It Be*; 30. *Hey Jude*; 31. *The Long and Winding Road*; 32. *Lady Madonna*; 33. *I Saw Her Standing There*; 34. *Yesterday*; 35. *Sgt. Pepper's Lonely Hearts Club Band*; and 36. *The End*.

Each concert had an almost identical setlist. The only variations were *Mother Nature's Son, Vanilla Sky* and *C Moon* being replaced at some shows with *Michelle, She's Leaving Home* and *Let 'Em In*. And at the 13 April show in Toronto's, at the 15,000-seat Air Canada Centre, *Mull of Kintyre* was performed, with 14 pipers and eight drummers from the Peel Regional Police Pipe Band joining Paul and the band on stage.

During these 2002 shows, Paul played four Beatles songs live for the first time: *Hello Goodbye; Getting Better; You Never Give Me Your Money*; and *Something*.

More paintings on display

On 24 May 2002, Paul and Heather visited Liverpool for the opening of an exhibition of Paul's art at the Walker Art Gallery. It comprised 70 paintings, as well as wood sculptures and photographs. There was a 16-page souvenir programme.

Two of Paul's paintings were later used as covers for albums: *Twin Freaks* (2005) and *Egypt Station* (2018). The most recent painting and exhibition centrepiece was *Big Heart*: a large red heart surrounded by yellow green and blue. Paul dedicated this to Heather.

The exhibition continued until 4 August 2002. On 25 July, Queen Elizabeth II visited and was shown around by Paul and Heather.

Party at the Palace

On 3 June, Paul headlined the *Party at the Palace*, an all-star concert held in the garden of Buckingham Palace, the Queen's London residence. The show commemorated Queen Elizabeth II's Golden Jubilee of fifty years on the throne. There were 12,000 spectators. An estimated 1 million watched outside the Palace, in the Mall and around the Queen Victoria Memorial, and 200 million watched worldwide on television. An abridged version of the concert was released on CD and DVD in July 2002.

The performers at the Palace included many of Paul's showbiz friends, including Brian Wilson, Eric Clapton, Tony Bennett, Rod Stewart (1945-), Tom Jones, Brian May (1947-) from Queen, Phil Collins, Elton John and Shirley Bassey (1937-). The house band comprised Phil Collins on drums, 'Wix' Wickens on keyboards, Ray Cooper (1947-) on percussion, Pino Palladino (1957-) on bass and Phil Palmer (1952-) on guitar.

Paul closed the concert with seven songs. He began on acoustic guitar, cheekily playing *Abbey Road's* irreverent *Her Majesty. Blackbird* then followed. There was then a brief speech by George Martin about the Beatles' musical and cultural impact after which Eric Clapton joined Paul on stage. Taking lead vocals, Clapton launched into an impassioned performance of *While My Guitar Gently Weeps,* the George Harrison Beatles song which featured Clapton's iconic guitar solo.

The party finished with Paul playing *Sgt. Pepper's Lonely Hearts Club Band (reprise)/The End* followed by mass singalong encores of *All You Need Is Love, Hey Jude* and *I Saw Her Standing There.*

A very private 'rock 'n' roll wedding': 11 June

Paul and Heather's wedding was on 11 June and the venue chosen was St. Salvator's Church, a 17th century church on the 1,000-acre Castle Leslie Estate, in County Monaghan, Ireland. It was next to Glaslough, a tiny village (population 400) where Owen Mohan and Mary Mohan (née Danaher), Paul's grandparents on his mother's side had been born into poor farming families. They left Ireland in the 1900s, moving to Liverpool where Owen worked as a coalman (delivering coal to houses) and Paul's mother Mary was born in 1909.

On 19 May, three weeks before the big event, there were fears the wedding might be called off. Paul and Heather were staying at the Turnberry Isle Resort and Club near Miami, unwinding after the end of stage 1 of the *Driving U.S.* tour. A heated row was heard coming from Paul and Heather's room in the early hours. According to one report, Paul shouted: "I don't want to marry you. The wedding's off." Heather's engagement ring was thrown from the window of the couple's fifth floor suite. Security guards had to use metal detectors to recover the ring, which was flown back to the UK.

The couple overcame their differences and on Tuesday 11 June 2002, one week before Paul's sixtieth birthday, they tied the knot. It was a private, but extravagant, "rock 'n' roll wedding," in Paul's words, costing £2.5 million. This was hugely different from Paul and Linda's 12 March 1969 Marylebone Register Office wedding which had reputedly cost less than £100.

Paul and Heather went to significant efforts to keep the wedding private and exclude the prying media. They asked all 300 guests to keep the wedding date secret and, if bringing a mobile phone, ensure it was switched off.

But on Sunday 9 June Sir John Leslie, the estate's 84-year-old owner, inadvertently let the cat out of the bag. Speaking to reporters, he said, "It's on Tuesday. But it's all a big secret, so I can't tell anyone."

On Monday 10 June, hundreds of photographers and fans stood outside the castle's gates. News helicopters circled overhead as reporters and cameras had been banned from the castle and church. Paul and Heather had rejected an offer of £1.5 million from a celebrity magazine for exclusive coverage of the wedding. Instead, they sanctioned the release to media organisations of a single official wedding photo in return for a £1,000 donation to the AAM charity.

Geoff Baker (1956-), Paul's publicist since 1989 and who had previously been a showbiz journalist with the *Daily Star*, provided limited information on the wedding and its guests. Among the 300 attending were Paul's children, Paul's brother Mike (1944-), his former brother-in-law John Eastman and Paul's Liverpool friends and family, who were flown to Belfast on a special chartered jet.

The rock stars and celebrities attending included Ringo Starr, George Martin, Chrissie Hynde, David Gilmour, Jools Holland, Twiggy and Nitin Sawhney. Sections of the media suggested that Eric Clapton, Elton John, Sting and former US President Bill Clinton (1946-) also attended.

Heather wore an ecru lace dress, designed by London's Eavis & Brown and not by Paul's daughter Stella. She walked down the aisle holding the hand of her sister Fiona, as her elderly father did not attend. Mike McCartney was again Paul's best man.

The 30-minute wedding ceremony included three special touches: Heather entered the church to strains of Paul's 2001 song *Heather*; Ringo gave a reading based on the Beatles' song *All You Need is Love*; and, after exchanging vows and receiving a blessing, as Paul and Heather walked down the aisle, an organ played the *Wedding March* written by Paul for the 1966 film, *The Family Way*.

The wedding reception was held under three giant 170 metre marquees beside the castle's lake. The marquees were adorned with flowers and lights and joined by covered walkways to conceal the guests from media helicopters.

The banquet was Indian-themed, with vegetarian food served on gold plates and complemented by champagne and vintage wines. Indian and Irish music played in the background and there was an extensive dance floor, with sound system and seating.

At the reception, Paul gave an uproarious speech and then danced with Heather to their favourite song *The Very Thought of You*. As a wedding treat, Tony Bennett had recorded a new and very personal version of this song.

As the reception reached its close, Paul and Heather boarded *Barnaby Rudge*, a vintage 40-foot flower-garlanded converted trawler/yacht brought over from Rye. They sailed a short distance to a specially constructed pier to watch a dazzling firework display. They then retired for their wedding night to the Castle's Red Room, which, according to Sandford (2006), featured the "first fully plumbed bath in Ireland, and a bed said somehow to be 'lucky.'"

For their honeymoon, Paul and Heather flew to the Seychelles where they stayed at the eco-friendly island of Cousine, far away from the press pack.

On their return to the UK, the couple chose to live at Woodlands Farm, adjacent to the Peasmarsh Estate. This was because Blossom Wood Farm held too many memories as 'Linda's house.'

In late 2002, Paul and Heather unveiled plans to build on Peasmarsh a new two-bedroom Norwegian-style lakeside log cabin house called The Cabin. It was to have a gym annexe and a pavilion for watching wildlife.

In summer 2002, Heather, asked by the press how she found married life with Paul, she affirmed that the couple's marriage was really happy: "It's intense all the time and we love each other's company. Our favourite thing is to stay at home. I cook a meal and he dances around the room like Fred Astaire."

Back on tour in the US, Mexico and Japan

After this extended summer break, Paul and his band returned to the road on 21 September for the second leg of *Back in the U.S.* This comprised 23 shows in 22 US cities and ended on 29 October.

The US cities played (in date order) were: Milwaukee (Wisconsin); St. Paul (Minnesota); Chicago; Hartford (Connecticut); Atlantic City (New Jersey); Boston (2 shows); Cleveland; Indianapolis (Indiana); Raleigh (North Carolina); St. Louis (Missouri); Columbus (Ohio); New Orleans (Louisiana); Houston (Texas); Oklahoma City; Portland (Oregon); Tacoma (Washington); Sacramento (California); San Jose; Anaheim; Las Vegas; Los Angeles; and Phoenix (Arizona).

A *Driving Mexico* leg of the tour began on 2 November, with three concerts (on 2, 3 and 5 November) in Mexico City before a nightly audience of 17,500 at the Palacio de los Deportes. Each night's reception was warm and loud.

The tour concluded with a one-week *Driving Japan* leg. This comprised three concerts, on 11, 13 and 14 November, before 40,000 each night, at the Tokyo Dome and two shows, on 17 and 18 November, again before 40,000, at the Osaka Dome.

According to Billboard, Paul's 2002 *Driving World Tour* was the year's highest grossing tour, bringing in $126 million revenue from one million spectators: an average of $2 million per show.

The *Back in the U.S.* second leg was seen by 337,000, grossing $43.5 million. The Mexico shows, seen by 52,450, grossed $4.8 million and the Japanese shows, seen by 201,000, grossed $22.6 million.

Back in the U.S. CD and DVD

On 11 November 2002, as the tour of Japan began, Paul released a double CD and DVD, *Back in the U.S.: Live 2002,* in the US and Japan. It was Paul's first album not released on vinyl.

The CD contains 35 songs recorded at US shows between 1 April and 18 May 2002, representative of a typical setlist.

Disc one: 1. *Hello Goodbye* 3:46 (from Detroit show); 2. *Jet* 4:02 (Dallas); 3. *All My Loving* 2:08 (Cleveland); 4. *Getting Better* 2:10 (Denver); 5. *Coming Up* 3.26 (Madison Square Garden, New York); 6. *Let Me Roll It* 4:24 (Chicago); 7. *Lonely Road* 3:12 (Sunrise); 8. *Driving Rain* 3:11 (Chicago); 9. *Your Loving Flame* 3:28 (Madison Square Garden); 10. *Blackbird* 2:30 (Boston); 11. *Every Night* 2:51 (Dallas); 12. *We Can Work It Out* 2:29 (Chicago); 13. *Mother Nature's Son* 2:11 (Dallas); 14. *Vanilla Sky* 2:29 (Dallas); 15. *Carry That Weight* 3:05 (Tampa); 16. *The Fool on the Hill* 3:09 (Washington D.C.); 17. *Here Today* (Toronto); and 18. *Something* 2:33 (Tampa).

Disc two: 1. *Eleanor Rigby* 2:17 (Denver); 2. *Here, There and Everywhere* 2:26 (Chicago); 3. *Band on the Run* 5:00 (Dallas); 4. *Back in the U.S.S.R.* 2:55 (Dallas); 5. *Maybe I'm Amazed* 4:48 (East Rutherford); 6. *C Moon* 3.51 (Washington D.C.); 7. *My Love* 4:03 (Dallas); 8. *Can't Buy Me Love* 2:09 (Atlanta); 9. *Freedom* 3:18 (Dallas); 10. *Live and Let Die* 3:05 (Dallas); 11. *Let It Be* 3:57 (Atlanta); 12. *Hey Jude* 7:01 (Madison Square Garden); 13. *The Long and Winding Road* 3:30 (Denver); 14. *Lady Madonna* 2:21 (Madison Square Garden); 15. *I Saw Her Standing There* 3:08 (Sunrise); 16. *Yesterday* 2:08 (Dallas); and 17. *Sgt. Pepper's Lonely Hearts Club Band (Reprise)/The End* 4:39 (Sunrise).

The release garnered controversy as the CD's credit notes reversed, from Lennon-McCartney to Paul McCartney and John Lennon, the songwriting credits for its 19 Beatles songs. Paul had written all of these songs with limited input from John, so he thought it reasonable that the new generation of listeners should be aware of this.

In 1976, Paul had done the same in 1976 for the five Beatles songs played live on the *Wings Over America* release and John had not publicly objected. Paul had sought to do likewise in the mid-1990s for the *Beatles Anthology* CDs and book. George, Ringo and Yoko Ono vetoed this.

Ringo described Paul's 2002 decision as "underhanded", Yoko threatened legal action and the press likened it to "walking on a dead man's grave." Shaken by this reaction, Paul relented and declared in May 2003: "It's an unfairness I'm willing to live with." His subsequent live CDs and DVDs kept the original Lennon-McCartney credits.

The *Back in the U.S.* performances on CD and DVD capture Paul in good voice and exhilarated to be back on stage. The audience and his band are both having a fun time, with Abe establishing himself as an entertainer on drums and multi-instrumentalist 'Wix' Wickens forming the band's glue.

The DVD's behind-the-scenes footage reveals the tour's organisation, with a 140-person crew moving equipment, staging and special effects from show to show. The DVD also contains snatches of Cirque du Soleil's pre-show performances and Paul's soundchecks, which included blues jams of *Bring it to Jerome*, *Midnight Special* and *San Francisco Bay*.

Back in the U.S. reached number 8 in the US album charts, selling 224,000 copies in its first week and going on to sell 1 million units. It reached 4 in Japan. The DVD sold 550,000 copies.

Back in the World Live CD

On 17 March 2003, an international edition of the CD, *Back in the World Live*, was released. In its track listing, *Vanilla Sky*, *C Moon* and *Freedom* were cut out and replaced with *Calico Skies* (from Osaka Dome), *Let 'Em In* (from Tokyo Dome) and the Beatles' *Michelle* and *She's Leaving Home* (from the Mexico City shows). The performance of *Hey Jude* came from the Mexico City show.

Back in the World Live reached number 5 in the UK and spent 13 weeks in the charts. Together, *Back in the U.S.* and *Back in the World* sold 2 million units worldwide.

Tour photographer Bill Bernstein published in 2004 a tour travelogue: *Each One Believing: Paul McCartney On Stage, Off Stage, and Backstage*.

The Concert for George

On 30 December 1999, a knife-wielding schizophrenic broke into George Harrison's Friar Park home in Henley-on-Thames, England, inflicting 40 stab wounds and puncturing the lung of the former Beatle during a frenzied attack. On leaving hospital, George relayed an Indian proverb: "Life is fragile like a raindrop on a lotus leaf."

This attack came two years after George had been diagnosed with throat cancer. Radiotherapy provided temporary relief but in May 2001 cancer returned, infecting George's lungs. Battling the disease, George underwent hospital treatment in Italy and New York.

Paul and George had been the first of the Beatles to meet, sharing school bus journeys, going on hitchhiking holidays and sharing a room on tours. But, as he matured, George came to resent being treated as Paul's 'kid brother.' By the 1969 Get Back recording sessions, George and Paul began to get on each other's nerves. After the Beatles ended, George appeared to be one of the main barriers to a reunion.

Despite this, Paul and George retained great personal affection and continued to meet and talk. Alerted by George Martin in June 2001 that George Harrison was terminally ill, Paul phoned to relay his concern.

In November 2001, Paul visited George at Staten Island University Hospital, in New York. The cancer had spread to George's brain. Realising the end was near, Paul held the hand of George who stated he was at peace and told Paul: "Well, you know I'm going to be fine."

On 29 November 2001, Harrison died in Beverly Hills, Los Angeles at the age of 58: he was staying at 'Heather's house.' After hearing news from George's widow Olivia (1948-), Paul met the press outside his Sussex estate. He told them that George was a brave, beautiful and funny man whose music would live forever and stated: "I'll always love him - he's my baby brother."

In July 2002, Paul, along with Ringo and George Martin, attended a private commemoration of George's life at Friar Park.

On 29 November 2002, on the first anniversary of George Harrison's death, a *Concert for George* memorial show was held at London's Royal Albert Hall. Organised by Olivia, George's son Dhani (1978-) and George's close friend, Eric Clapton, profits from the concert were donated to the Material World Charitable Foundation.

Like the December 1971 *Concert for Bangladesh*, organised by George, the concert involved a mixture of Indian and Western musicians. It also featured four members of the Monty Python's Flying Circus comedy troupe, with whom George was close friends. Artists performing included Ringo Starr and George's friends Tom Petty, Jeff Lynne, Eric Clapton and Billy Preston (1946-2006).

Unlike 1971's *Concert for Bangladesh*, Paul participated in the *Concert for George*. He performed George's *For You Blue* (1970) on acoustic guitar and, with Ringo on drums and Eric Clapton on guitar, *Something* (playing ukelele), *All Things Must Pass* and *While My Guitar Gently Weeps*. The concert ended with Billy Preston and Eric Clapton leading versions of George's solo hits *My Sweet Lord* and *Wah-Wah*, with Paul on piano and backing vocals.

A concert DVD and CD was released on 17 November 2003.

2003: Back in Europe

Key events

23 February: Paul performs a 90-minute show to 150 guests at a 50th birthday party at Rancho Blues Club, San Diego, for a $1 million donation to AAM.

17 March: Paul's *Back in the World Live* CD is released.

25 March to 1 June: Paul undertakes the *Back in the World* tour: 33 shows in 21 cities in the UK and Europe, including Rome and Moscow.

29 April: *Hope (War Child)*, a charity album, is released to aid victims of the Iraq War. It includes Paul singing a re-recorded version of *Calico Skies*.

30 May: Paul plays a secret end-of-tour gig at Liverpool's Cavern Club.

September: Paul begins sessions for *Chaos and Creation in the Backyard*.

23 September: Paul performs 10 songs, including *Two of Us* with James Taylor, at the Beverly Hilton for the 3rd annual AAM benefit gala which raised $1.2 million.

22-23 October: Paul and his band re-record, with Dave Stewart of the Eurythmics, the 1995 song *Whole Life* for the 46664 anti-AIDS campaign. In January 2005, it is included on the Nelson Mandela Foundation's *46664 1 Year On: The EP*.

28 October: Paul and Heather's daughter Beatrice (Bea) is born.

17 November: The Beatles *Let it Be … Naked,* the *Concert for George* and a remixed 12-inch single of Paul's 1980 track *Temporary Secretary* are released.

17 December: Rusty Anderson's *Undressing Underwater* album is released, with Paul on bass and backing vocals on the track *Hurt Myself,* recorded in September 2002.

The first half of 2003 involved heavy touring by Paul and his band, with March to June shows in Europe, including prestigious concerts in Rome and Moscow.

On 29 May, it was announced that Heather was pregnant. Aware that Heather had suffered ectopic pregnancies during her 1989-91 marriage to Alfie Karmal, Paul remained at home to assist her.

On 28 October, daughter Beatrice (Bea) was born, making Paul a father again at the age of 61.

Paul did not resume touring until May 2004. Instead, he concentrated his musical energies on studio sessions for forthcoming albums. He also re-recorded, with Dave Stewart (1952-), his 1995 composition *Whole Life*.

During 2002-03 Paul also kept abreast of the remixing, at Abbey Road studios, of a stripped-down version of the Beatle's album *Let It Be* (1970). Paul had long been dissatisfied with elements of the original album's production by Phil Spector (1939-2021), particularly the overly lush strings on *The Long and Winding Road*. Paul believed the album should have been less "produced" so that it would sound more organic. The remixed *Let It be ... Naked*, released on 17 November 2003, achieved this.

Back in the World Live

The *Back in the World* tour moved to Europe, commencing before 15,000 at the Palais Omnisports de Paris-Bercy in Paris 25 March 2003. This 10-week European leg consisted of 33 mainly sold-out shows in 21 cities. Staging and equipment were transported between shows in 40 trucks by a 116-member crew.

Being spring, the shows, with a few exceptions, were held in 10,000 to 20,000-seat indoor arenas. Nearly 1.1 million people saw Paul during this leg, including 200,000 in England during 11 shows in five cities.

Heather appeared at most concerts and, each time, Paul dedicated *My Loving Flame* to "a very special person ... my lovely wife Heather."

The tour was preceded by band rehearsals on 14-15 March at the Docklands Arena in London.

The 2003 shows followed the successful formula of 2002, with a Beatles-heavy setlist and extremely limited song rotation. Throughout most of each concert, Paul donned a collarless Nehru jacket, but, for the encores, he wore a red *No More Landmines* T-shirt. As well as his usual anecdotes before songs, Paul also made a point of sprinkling in local phrases (in Spanish, French, German, Italian etc depending on venue) he had practised with a linguist ahead of the show.

Reviewing the opening Paris show, Ray Connolly (1940-), the *Daily Mail's* music critic and a Beatles expert, a little unkindly wrote: "[It was] as if we were listening to the best Beatles tribute band in the world."

In an interview at the time of his 2000s tours, Paul told Paul Du Noyer (2015) that, in deciding the setlist, he always asked himself what the audience would like to hear: "If I go to see the Stones, I really hope they're going to do *Satisfaction* and *Honky Tonk Women* and *Jumping Jack Flash* … with me that means doing some Beatles, some Wings, some recent stuff … I have this nightmare where I'm playing to the audience, and they start walking out."

Paul's live versions also strayed little from the recorded. This was the antithesis to a Bob Dylan concert where song tempos and structures were changed radically, making it sometimes difficult to identify what was being played. Paul commented that when a band member told Dylan, "*Mr. Tambourine Man* went down well tonight," Dylan would reply, "OK, take it out of the set." Paul said: "I tend to go, 'Right keep it in.'"

After Paris, Paul played at the 18,000-capacity Palau San Jordi in Barcelona (on 28 and 29 March) and 13,500-capacity Sportpaleis Antwerp (on 1 and 2 April), Belgium.

This was followed by a fortnight of concerts in England: Paul's first in his homeland in a decade. The first show was on 5 April at the 13,600-seat Hallam Arena in Sheffield. A second Sheffield show, on 6 April, had to be cancelled 90 minutes before the start as Paul had lost his voice to a cold. Under doctor's instructions, he was unable to talk for 48 hours.

The tour resumed on 9-10 April with two nights at the 16,000-capacity Manchester Evening News Arena in Manchester. Ahead of the soundcheck on 9 April, Paul spent an hour with a doctor. His band suggested dropping *Birthday* from the set to protect his voice, but Paul declined. Paul sounded hoarse and strained, but his voice was much improved at the 10 April concert, which was attended by Paul's brother Mike and several Liverpool friends.

The April stage of Paul's England tour closed with two nights (13 and 14 April) at Birmingham's 13,000-capacity National Indoor Arena and four nights (18, 19, 21 and 22 April) at the 19,000-capacity Earls Court, in London. John Lennon's eldest son, Julian Lennon (1963-), attended the 22 April show.

Three days later, on 25 April, Paul returned to mainland Europe, playing the 30,000-capacity Gelredome in Arnhem, the Netherlands. This was followed by concerts in Germany, at Cologne's 14,000-seat Köln Arena (27 and 28 April) and Hannover's 10,000-seat Preussag Arena (on 30 April). Work commitments prevented Heather from attending the German shows.

On 2 May, Paul played in Copenhagen, Denmark, before a sellout crowd of 47,000 at the Parken Stadium, with its dome closed. Ahead of the show, Paul met Denmark's Queen Margrethe II (1940-).

Paul and the band then played shows at the 14,000-seat Stockholm Globe Arena, in Sweden, on 4 and 5 May. In the audience on 5 May was ABBA's Björn Ulvaeus (1945-).

On 8 May, Paul returned to Germany, performing at the Koenig Pilsener Arena at Oberhausen. Originally scheduled for the 50,000-capacity Auf Schalke Arena in Gelsenkirchen, insufficient ticket sales led to a switch to the 14,000-capacity arena in Oberhausen.

Inside and outside the Colosseum: 10-11 May

A few days later, on Saturday and Sunday 10 and 11 May, Paul played two prestigious concerts in Rome, Italy. The first was inside the Colosseum, a 2,000-year-old Roman amphitheatre, the second was outside.

The fragile condition of the Colosseum's interior restricted the audience on 10 May to 400, on temporary seating, at £1,000 a ticket. The catacombs below were illuminated to striking effect. The audience included Boomtown Rats' singer and 1985 *Live Aid* organiser Bob Geldof (1951-), Rome's mayor, the US ambassador to Italy and Heather. Proceeds went to charities, including AAM.

Paul began the show declaring: "We understand it's the first time there's been a band in the Colosseum - since the Christians! So, we're happy to be here."

In this intimate setting, Paul rejigged his set. He played an acoustic show which featured songs previously restricted to soundchecks: George Harrison's *All Things Must Pass* and covers of *Honey Don't* and *Midnight Special*. Paul also played the Beatles' *I've Just Seen a Face*, *Things We Said Today* and *Two of Us*, as well as *Volare (Flying)*, a hit for the Italian crooner Domenico Modugno (1928-94) in the summer of 1958.

The 11 May show was a free concert in the Via del Fori Imperiali, outside the Colosseum. Attended by around 500,000 people, it was the biggest show in Paul's career to this date. It was the second-ever concert held outside the Colosseum: the first, a year earlier, had been by Ray Charles (1930-2004). For this show, Paul played his normal tour set but with the addition of *Volare*.

Paul had been scheduled to fly back to England at 2:40 a.m. soon after the show. But at 1 a.m. he changed his mind. He delayed his return to London until 6 p.m. and spent part of Monday cycling around the Eternal City.

The tour hits Central Europe and Germany

Not long after Paul and Heather returned to the UK from Rome, Heather flew to the US for eight days of work for her charity projects.

Paul's tour resumed on 14 May in Vienna, Austria, at the 16,000-capacity Stadthalle. At the show's end, Paul and the band flew by private jet to Budapest, Hungary, arriving at 3 a.m. on 15 May.

Paul spent the day ahead of the evening's Budapest concert cycling around the city's picturesque Margitsziget island, on the Danube river, between Buda and Pest. He met prime minister Péter Medgyessy (1942-), who presented Paul with a Hungarian flute. A local photographer tutored Paul on pronunciation of Hungarian phrases.

The 12,500 fans at the Budapest Sport Arena warmly appreciated Paul's efforts to speak Hungarian and it was one of the best audiences of the tour. Paul spent 16 May exploring Budapest further by bike, before leaving at 6 p.m. for Germany.

On 17 and 18 May, Paul played outdoor shows before 20,000 people at Königsplatz square in Munich. On the second night, aware that Klaus Voormann was in the audience, Paul dedicated *Here Today* to "John and Klaus."

On 21 May, Paul played an outdoor evening concert before 27,400 at the AOL Arena in Hamburg. Backstage, he met Tony Sheridan (1940-2013), a collaborator with the Beatles during the Hamburg years, Horst Fascher (1936-), who had managed Hamburg's Star-Club in the early 1960s, and Astrid Kirchherr (1938-2020), a German photographer who had been Stu Sutcliffe's girlfriend.

Paul McCartney in Red Square

The highlight of the 2003 tour was the 24 May concert in Moscow's Red Square.

Back in 1988, Paul recorded *Choba B CCCP (Back in the USSR)*, a studio album of rock 'n' roll covers for distribution only in the Soviet Union (USSR). It was released at the hopeful time of *glasnost* (openness) and *perestroika* (political and economic restructuring) initiated by the Soviet Union's reform-communist leader Mikhail Gorbachev (1931-2022).

It seemed at that time that the post-1945 Cold War between the Soviet Union and the West was ending and that the Soviet Union was liberalising politically and economically. Later, on 24 August 1991, hardline communists launched an abortive coup against Gorbachev. This precipitated a chain of events that brought the disintegration of the Communist Party and, on 26 December 1991, the dissolution of the USSR. It was succeeded by Russia and other republics.

During the communist era, the Beatles were banned in the Soviet Union. Despite this, they built up a devoted underground following among non-conformers and elements of the Soviet youth. In Western Russia and the Baltic States, Beatles music could be heard by tuning in to Western 'pirate stations,' notably Radio Luxembourg. More generally, proscribed Beatles records were exchanged in the underground economy for the price of a half or third of the average weekly wage. These underground followers drew on Beatles songs such as *Hello Goodbye* and *Let It Be* to learn English phrases.

On 25 August 1998, Ringo Starr, supported by his All-Star Band, became the first former-Beatle to play in Russia, playing at the Rossia Concert Hall in Moscow.

Some years later, Paul received an invite to deliver a masterclass at the St. Petersburg Conservatoire. It arose from Paul's connections to Brian Eno (1948-), the ex-Roxy Music electronica and ambient music composer who had presented a masterclass at LIPA. Eno and his wife Anthea, who had lived in St. Petersburg in 1997, had befriended people in the Conservatoire who were keen for Paul to visit.

Paul delivered this masterclass on 21 May 2003. During their stay in St. Petersburg, Paul and Heather received a private tour of the Hermitage Museum of art and culture and supported, with their presence, a newly founded charity for orphans. Impressed by the immense talent of the Conservatoire's young musicians, Paul focused his masterclass advice on how to remain calm and confident when performing. To Paul's delight, the Conservatoire, at which Pyotr Ilyich Tchaikovsky (1840-93) had studied, awarded him an honorary doctorate.

Paul's historic concert in Red Square, in the centre of Moscow, was held on the night of Saturday 24 May. Ahead of the event, Paul and Heather met Vladimir Putin (1952-), Russia's president since May 2000. With a fast-growing economy and active on the world stage, Putin was highly popular in Russia in 2003. But over time he became a repressive, war-mongering dictator.

Paul and Heather met a relaxed Putin in his private quarters in the Kremlin, the seat of government adjoining Red Square. They talked privately about their families and landmine clearance. Noticing a piano in the room, Paul played *Let It Be,* generating applause from Putin. Paul asked if Putin would be attending the concert. Putin said he was unsure but would do so if his schedule allowed.

Paul recounted later that Putin spoke "pretty good English" and shared a working-class background with the Beatles. Paul probed Putin's views on the Beatles and Putin told him that hearing the Beatles music as a boy "was like a gulp of freedom…. (and) a window to the world."

Paul and Heather also met Russia's defence minister Sergei Ivanov (1953-) and the retired Gorbachev. Ivanov declared himself to be a long-time Beatles fan. He told Paul that he cherished the day in 1984 when he was able: "to fulfil one of my wishes in life … when I could buy all the Beatles records." Gorbachev told Paul: "I do believe the music of the Beatles taught the young people of the Soviet Union that there is another life."

The Red Square concert was attended by 120,000: comprising 20,000 in paid seats and 100,000 lining the surrounding streets. The show began at 8:30 p.m. as the sun began to set.

The audience included Gorbachev, with his daughter and son-in-law, Moscow mayor Yuri Luzhkov (1936-2019) and the Russian rock singer and guitarist Andrey Makarevich (1953-), who, inspired by the Beatles, formed in 1969 Mashina Vremeni (Time Machine) Russia's oldest and still active rock band.

Wearing a red *No More Landmines* T-shirt, Paul called out in Russian, "Privet rebyata" ("Hello everybody"). His 38-song set included 26 Beatles' tracks, including the rarely played *She's Leaving Home* and *Two Of Us*. Paul and his band received rapturous applause when they launched into *Back in the U.S.S.R.*

Midway through the set, as Paul was performing his anti-war song *Calico Skies*, President Putin arrived. Aware of Putin's presence, Paul sang with feeling the lines: "May we never be called to handle all the weapons of war we despise."

Thunderous cheers greeted the spectacular fireworks display during *Live and Let Die* and the set closed with an extended sing-along of *Hey Jude*. As a final encore, Paul reprised, for a 'special person,' *Back in the U.S.S.R.*: Putin having missed the song when it had been played earlier.

On 14 June 2005, a DVD *Paul McCartney in Red Square* was released, selling 250,000 units. It contained 20 songs from the set:

1. *Getting Better*; 2. *Band On The Run*; 3. *Can't Buy Me Love*; 4. *Two Of Us*; 5. *I Saw Her Standing There*; 6. *We Can Work It Out*; 7. *I've Just Seen a Face*; 8. *Live and Let Die*; 9. *Let 'Em In*; 10. *Fool on the Hill*; 11. *Things We Said Today*; 12. *Birthday*; 13. *Maybe I'm Amazed*; 14. *Back in the U.S.S.R.*; 15. *Calico Skies*; 16. *Hey Jude*; 17. *She's Leaving Home*; 18. *Yesterday*; 19. *Let It Be*; and 20. *Back in the U.S.S.R.* (reprise).

The DVD intermixes live songs with documentary footage covering Paul's visits to St. Petersburg and the Kremlin, discussions of the impact of the Beatles' music in the USSR and footage of Paul cycling (illegally) around Red Square the day after the concert. While exaggerating the Beatles' contribution to the downfall of communism, the DVD provides a fascinating insight into Paul's May visit.

The tour closes in Ireland and Liverpool

After returning to the UK from Moscow, on 27 May Paul flew to Dublin for his first show in Ireland in forty years. The sold out 32,000 crowd in the RDS (Royal Dublin Society) Stadium included Irish rock band U2's guitarist The Edge (1961-). Heather attended, with the video screens showing her dancing to Paul's rockers and joining in with the *Hey Jude* encore.

During their stay, Paul and Heather cycled in Dublin and drove out to visit surrounding areas.

On 29 May, Paul played the rescheduled Sheffield show. Three weeks earlier, on 7 May, the UK's Channel 4 television had aired *Heather Mills: The Real Mrs McCartney,* a documentary which challenged Heather's account of her upbringing and life pre-Paul. Heather's distress about this documentary had led on 11 May, according to the account in Norman (2016), to an intense argument with Paul in the hotel during their stay in Rome.

At Sheffield's Hallam Arena, an audience member raised a sign saying, "Screw Channel 4, We Love Heather!" The crowd responded with a cheer. Earlier in the day, it had been announced that Paul and Heather were having a baby.

The 2003 tour ended on Sunday 1 June with an outdoor concert before 30,500 people at Liverpool's King's Dock. No longer (since 1972) a working dock, the area was used now for outdoor events.

The night before this show, Paul held an end-of-tour party for 180 friends and family at the Cavern Club. On the door, the event was described as a 'private retirement party.' Inside Paul joined the band Love Train for a set that included *Let It Be* and Chic's *We Are Family*.

The 1 June King's Dock concert was attended by Peter Blake, Liverpool's Scottish soccer legend Kenny Dalglish (1951-) and Queen's drummer Roger Taylor (1949-). The set included covers of *Honey Hush,* a song John had introduced a teenage Paul to, and *Baby Face*. Paul also played a country and western version of a Liverpool favourite, *Maggie Mae*, and his 1956 composition *I Lost My Little Girl.*

A father again at 61

On 21 June 2003, Heather's charitable work received recognition from the UK's state-funded distance-learning Open University (OU). The OU made Heather an honorary graduate and in 2004 awarded an honorary doctorate.

Heather's activities included campaigns during 2003 for Oxfam (a UK-founded charity fighting against world poverty), the National Society for the Prevention of Cruelty to Children (NSPCC) and the AAM. She also provided private counselling to amputees.

'Cannabis or me'

In July-August 2003, Paul and Heather spent an extended summer break on eastern Long Island in the Hamptons. According to later divorce papers, during this break, Paul's use of cannabis became a cause of disagreement and Heather gave Paul a 'cannabis or me' ultimatum.

Later, in a January 2006 press interview, Heather claimed that: "Paul and Linda smoked it every day for the whole of their lives together. But I would not get married to him if he was taking drugs. I hate it."

Paul and Heather returned to the UK to attend Stella's 30 August wedding at Mount Stuart House on the Scottish Isle of Bute. Stella's fiancée was Alasdhair Willis (1971-), a Middlesborough-born fashion magazine publisher and branding consultant.

In October, Heather attended a Paris fashion show wearing jeans designed by Stella.

Paul's London outburst

In September 2003, during a warm late English summer, Paul and Heather returned to Woodlands Farm. The 2007 divorce papers alleged that during this period there was an impassioned row. The next morning the cleaner allegedly encountered broken crockery, glasses and lamps and a tomato ketchup stain on the wall.

Some days later, on 17 September, Paul had dinner and drinks in Soho, London, near the MPL office, with Geoff Baker, his publicist, John Hammel (1949-), his road manager and executive personal assistant since 1975, and music industry friends.

At 1 a.m. on 18 September, impulsively, Paul decided to visit Tower Bridge where the American illusionist David Blaine (1973-) was 12 days into a 44-day stunt of fasting inside a Plexiglas box suspended nine metres high.

Baker later stated: "I was drunk and stoned and nobody seemed to be paying much attention to us. I thought, 'Hang on the real star's here – never mind that prat in the box'."

Without consulting Paul, Baker invited Kevin Wheal (1961-), a 'snapper' from London's *Evening Standard*, to photograph them. Approaching at pace with his camera, Wheal surprised Paul, who allegedly told him "f*** off - it's a private visit.."

Hammel pulled Wheal away, but the photographer claimed Paul pushed him and hurled a missive of abusive words. An irate Paul told Baker he was fired. But within hours Paul had rescinded the decision. He went on to downplay the incident as just "a group of friends on a night out."

The police did not issue any charges but the incident was reported in the *Evening Standard* and *The Guardian*.

Bea is born

Following this adverse publicity, Paul kept a low-profile during October 2003 at his 7 Cavendish Avenue home in London. He looked after Heather during the final weeks of her pregnancy, with, on occasions, the couple being spotted walking in a nearby park.

On 28 October 2003, Heather entered the Hospital of St. John and St. Elizabeth in St. John's Wood, London. She gave birth, by caesarean section, to a daughter, Beatrice Milly McCartney. The baby, who weighed 7 lbs and was born 17 days early, was named Beatrice (Bea) after Heather's mother and Milly after one of Paul's aunts, the younger sister of Paul's father Jim. Aged 61, Paul was a father again.

Paul described Bea as "a beautiful baby" and vowed to give her a private life. Speaking to *Viva!* after her birth, Paul said that, like his other children, Bea would be brought up as a vegetarian. Paul and Heather released a single approved picture of Bea to the press in return for donations to AAM.

The addition of a young baby was to bring joy but also new challenges for the couple.

Back in the recording studio

With the changes in family circumstances, Paul took a sabbatical from touring until May 2004.

In September 2003, he started recording sessions for his next album, *Chaos and Creation in the Backyard*. Paul stated: "I'm taking it really easy and am not in any hurry to get it finished, particularly with our new arrival on the way … I want to make it a great album that we'll be able to take on the road."

Paul began by recording demos for nine songs with his band and David Kahne. Many of these songs appeared later on *Memory Almost Full* (2007).

After these initial sessions, Paul felt an urge to try something new. He asked George Martin, who had retired from producing because of hearing difficulties, if he could suggest a producer. George and his record producer son Giles Martin (1969-) recommended Nigel Godrich (1971-), an English recording engineer and producer with a growing reputation.

Godrich was best known for his work with the alt-rock Radiohead: a band Paul and his son James admired. Paul was also impressed with Godrich's work with the US indie artist Beck (1970-), having produced the critically acclaimed *Mutations* (1998) and *Sea Change* (2002), and the Scottish indie-rock band Travis, producing *The Man Who* (1999) and *The Invisible Band* (2001).

Unsure whether they would get on, Paul initially committed to two weeks of recording at Godrich's favoured RAK Studio in London. They worked on three tracks: *Follow Me; This Never Happened Before;* and *Comfort of Love*.

On the track *Follow Me,* Abe, Brian and Rusty provided instrumental backing. Paul had told Godrich: "You know, I'd like to work with my live band, because they're my guys."

But after the first week, Godrich told Paul that he would like to take him out of his "safety zone" and "try something different … I want to make an album that's you."

Godrich told Paul that, while Abe was a great drummer, he liked the sound and feel of Paul's drum playing. Godrich asked Paul to play all instruments - using his old Höfner bass and Epiphone electric guitar on which he had played the *Paperback Writer* opening riff and *Taxman* solo – so that the album would have a uniform feel. Godrich would then add layers and loops of sound.

Paul later stated: "(It was) very embarrassing. I had to say to the guys, 'Look, he wants to go in this other direction and he's the producer so I can't really say, 'No, you've got to work with my band.' I said, 'How do you feel about it?;' and they were really cool."

Whole Life

On 22-23 October 2003, Paul invited his touring band and David Kahne to Abbey Road Studio 2 to record *Whole Life,* a grungy rocker Paul had written in 1995 with Dave Stewart of the Eurythmics.

Only shortly before the recording session did Paul tell his band that Dave Stewart would join. Rusty and Paul played electric guitar, Brian bass, Abe drums and Dave Stewart acoustic guitar.

Whole Life was released in January 2005 on the Nelson Mandela Foundation's *46664 1 Year On: The EP* to support the anti-AIDS campaign. Number 46664 was the prisoner number South Africa's anti-apartheid campaigner Nelson Mandela (1918-2013) was given during his 18 years of detention on Robben Island between 1964-82.

2004: A Glastonbury Triumph

Key events

Late February: Paul records material that appears later on *Memory Almost Full* (2007).

April: Further recording for *Chaos and Creation in the Backyard*.

25 May to 26 June: Paul and his band undertake a 14 show *'04 Summer Tour* across Europe. It includes a 20 June show at St. Petersburg, Russia. The tour closes on 26 June at the UK's Glastonbury Festival.

22 June: Brian Wilson releases the album *Gettin' In Over My Head*. Its track *A Friend Like You* features Paul on acoustic guitar and vocals.

September to November: Recording for *Chaos and Creation in the Backyard*.

20 September: Paul releases *Tropic Island Hum* (recorded in 1987) as a single.

27 September: Paul's *The Music and Animation Collection DVD* is released. It has three animated short films directed by Geoff Dunbar: *Rupert & The Frog Song; Tuesday;* and *Tropic Island Hum.*

15 October: Paul plays 14 songs at the Century Plaza Hotel, Los Angeles, for the 4th annual AAM benefit gala, raising $2 million. Neil Young also performs.

24 October: Paul plays 14 songs at Neil Young's 18th annual Bridge School benefit concert to assist children with severe impairments, at Mountain View, California. Paul and Neil perform together on Neil's *Only Love Can Break Your Heart.*

24-25 December: Paul and Heather appear on a celebrity edition on the UK television edition of *Who Wants to be a Millionaire* and win £32,000 for AAM.

In February 2004, Paul, Heather and baby Bea moved into the newly completed £1 million The Cabin on the Peasmarsh Estate.

In March, Heather told the press that motherhood: "is the most demanding and most rewarding job in the world - all mothers should be paid a wage. I've just started to get a babysitter to give me a bit more time."

In the spring and autumn, Paul conducted further recording for his forthcoming albums.

In May-June, Paul and his band undertook a 14 show '04 Summer Tour in Europe, including a 20 June concert in St. Petersburg and a 26 June headline appearance at Glastonbury Festival.

McCartney-related musical releases in 2004 were limited to:

- *A Friend Like You*, a track on Brian Wilson's June album release *Getting' In Over My Head*, on which Paul played acoustic guitar and provided backing vocals.
- The September release of *The Music and Animation Collection* DVD. This comprised three animated short films directed by Geoff Dunbar and based on Paul's ideas from the 1980s: *Rupert & The Frog* Song; *Tuesday;* and *Tropical Island Hum.* The DVD sold 50,000 units. *Tropic Island Hum,* recorded in 1987, was released as a single.

Recording continues: February and April 2004

In February 2004, Paul and his band returned to Abbey Road Studios and recorded, with David Kahne, seven new tracks: *Only Mama Knows*; *You Tell Me; Vintage Clothes; That Was Me; Feet in the Clouds; House of Wax;* and *The End of The End.* These would appear on *Memory Almost Full* (2007).

In April 2004, Paul recorded with Nigel Godrich again. This time it was at Ocean Way Recording Studios, on Sunset Boulevard in Los Angeles: the legendary studio where, in November 1965, the Mamas and Papas recorded *California Dreamin'*.

During this session, Paul recorded six songs: *A Certain Softness; Growing Up, Falling Down; At The Mercy; I Want You to Fly; Riding to Vanity Fair;* and *This Loving Game.*

Paul worked mainly alone. But on three tracks he was supported by musicians recruited by Godrich: Jason Falkner (1968-), a multi-instrumentalist who had been a member of the 1990s' Beatles-influenced indie-rock band Jellyfish; and James Gadson (1939-), a renowned R&B drummer who had worked with The Temptations, B.B. King (1925-2015) and Marvin Gaye (1939-84).

Heather's increasing US media profile

In 2004, Heather's charitable activities received further recognition. At the annual International Charity Gala in Düsseldorf, Germany, she received the Children in Need award, while University of California, Irvine, created the Heather Mills McCartney Fellowship in Human Security for graduate student research on human security issues.

In April 2004, Heather's US profile increased significantly when she hosted an episode of *Larry King Live.* Paul persuaded Paul Newman (1925-2008), the 79-year-old US movie legend, to be the interviewee. However, Newman's refusal to talk about his private life resulted in an awkward conversation in which Heather spoke more than the interviewee.

Despite this setback, Heather remained keen to accept further media opportunities in the US. This prompted tabloid press stories that the McCartneys might relocate to America. But, while Paul enjoyed his holiday breaks at Amagansett and in Los Angeles, he was determined that the UK would remain his family's home base. In November 2004, Paul told journalist Alan Franks: "no, we are not moving to America." But he added: "Today, I just think what an amazingly lucky person I am to have found Heather … My mum dies, and I find John. Linda dies, and I find Heather."

The '04 Summer Tour of Europe

In May-June, Paul and his band embarked on the *'04 Summer Tour* of 14 outdoor concerts in football stadiums, parks and festivals in 12 European countries before 600,000 people. This short tour climaxed, on 26 June with a headline show at the Glastonbury Festival.

The tour began on 25 May at Gijón, in north-western Spain.

On the night of 24 May, a full dress-rehearsal was held before fans with FanAsylum VIP packages. But some fans were ejected after 30 minutes for being too noisy. This was the last time Paul held a full dress-rehearsal. In future, he would play only 40-minute soundchecks, open to fans on special packages.

The 25 May Gijón show drew a crowd of 25,000 at the Estadio El Molinón. Paul played 34 songs, including eight from his solo and Wings era. Five songs received their live debut: *Flaming Pie*; *In Spite of All Danger*, composed by Paul and George in 1958 and the first song recorded by The Quarrymen (the skiffle-rock group from whom the Beatles evolved); and the Beatles' *Helter Skelter*, *You Won't See Me* and *I'll Follow the Sun*.

Paul also played *She's a Woman* for the first time since the Beatles' 29 August 1966 final concert at Candlestick Park, San Francisco; *Drive My Car* and *Penny Lane* for the first time since 1993; and *For No One,* for the first time since an intimate 23 March 1995 Royal College of Music benefit performance at St. James Church, London.

Over 30 of the songs in the Gijon set were played throughout the *'04 Summer Tour.*

The next show was in Lisbon, Portugal, on 28 May before 46,000 fans at the Parque Bela Vista, on the opening night of a six-day *Rock in Rio* festival. The festival was modelled on *Rock in Rio,* an annual music festival first held in Rio de Janeiro, Brazil, in 1985. The seventy performers included Guns N' Roses, Metallica, Britney Spears (1981-) and Sting. .

Paul arrived on 26 May and spent the day before the concert sailing from Lisbon to Sesimbra and cycling in Lisbon's Parque das Nações.

A DVD of Paul's performance in Lisbon, taken from Brazil's Globo television coverage, was released unofficially.

Shows followed in Spain, Switzerland, Germany and the Czech Republic

- On 30 May, Paul and his band played to a crowd of 30,000 at the Estadio La Peneita in Madrid. Between songs, Paul made use of the Spanish he had learned 50 years earlier at school.
- On 2 June, they then played before 30,000 at the Letzigrund Stadium in Zurich, Switzerland. The audience was drenched by constant rain.
- Next stop was Leipzig, eastern Germany. Heather and baby Bea attended Paul's first-ever concert in eastern Germany, which had been behind the Iron Curtain before 1990. The 4 June concert was the inaugural event at the Zentralstadion, built for 90 million euros. Rain did not dampen the enthusiasm of the 45,000 crowd. Appropriate to the conditions, Paul played *Yellow Submarine*.
- Next, on 6 June, Paul played his first-ever show in Prague, in the Czech Republic. A crowd of 50,000 watched in Park Kolbenova.

Paul and the band then played five concerts in Scandinavia.

- On 8 and 9 June, Paul played in a football stadium in the Danish coastal town of Horsens. A crowd of 20,000 attended each night, including Denmark's Prince Joachim (1969-) and Princess Alexandra (1964-). Paul, Heather, Bea and her nanny stayed in the Queen Suite on the top floor of the Hotel Kongebrogaarden. According to some reports, Paul spent $45,000 a night for accommodation, food and drink for himself and the crew. After the second show, Paul and Heather flew back to England to celebrate their second wedding anniversary.
- On Saturday 12 June, Paul and Heather flew to Gothenburg, Sweden, to join the band for a concert before 36,000 at the Ullevi stadium. The Swedish audience was initially quiet, but responded well to Beatles' songs and by the second half were rocking. Paul dedicated *Eleanor Rigby* to Ray Charles, who had toured with the Beatles in the early 1960s and had died on 10 June.
- Paul arrived in Oslo, Norway on 13 June ahead of the show on 14 June before 23,000 at the Valle Hovin Stadion. Unexpectedly, he flew back to London, returning to Oslo shortly before the show. When the show ended, Paul returned to London.
- The band travelled on to Helsinki, Finland, on 15 June, two days ahead of a 17 June concert at the Olympiastadion before 35,000 fans in cold and rainy conditions.

The next show, on Sunday 20 June, was a prestige concert in St. Petersburg, Russia, before a crowd of 70,000 near the Tsar's Winter Palace, where the February 1917 Russian Revolution had begun.

Paul, Heather and Bea arrived in St. Petersburg on Paul's 62nd birthday on 18 June and received a present from President Putin. They stayed as special guests in an elite secluded cottage at the Konstantin Palace in Strelna, one of the Royal Palaces of the Russian Tsars. On the Saturday, they visited the famous Peterhof fountains and met with the region's governor.

Paul received a rapturous reception. Twelve of the 35 songs from the show are included on the *Paul McCartney in Red Square* DVD:

1. *Jet*; 2. *Got To Get You Into My Life*; 3. *Flaming Pie*; 4. *Let Me Roll It*; 5. *Drive May Car*; 6. *Penny Lane*; 7. *Get Back*; 8. *Back in the U.S.S.R.*; 9. *I've Got A Feeling*; 10. *Sgt. Pepper's Lonely Hearts Club Band*; 11. *The End*; and 12. *Helter Skelter*.

The penultimate concert of the *'04 Summer Tour* was in Paris, on 24 June before 50,000 at the Stade de France. In this show, Paul performed *Michelle*.

Glastonbury 2004

The *'04 Summer Tour* closed on 26 June 2004 at the UK's leading music festival, Glastonbury, at Worthy Farm in Somerset.

Paul stated in 2007: "I'd had my eye on playing Glastonbury forever because it's an iconic festival … A couple of guys I knew (went and) they said, 'We were coming back from the main stage at midnight and all the people were sitting around their campfires singing Beatles songs.' I went – ding! A little lightbulb went off. I said, 'Well, I can do that!'"

Paul asked the festival's farmer-founder Michael Eavis (1935-) if he could play in 2003 but Paul decided to defer a year as the Saturday night slot had already been allocated to Radiohead.

Paul and his crew brought all their lighting effects and pyrotechnics to Glastonbury's main Pyramid Stage for the Saturday 26 June evening show. He delivered an enthusiastic two-hour 33-song set which included a seven-song encore. It included Paul's first ever live performance of *Follow Me*, later released on *Chaos and Creation in the Backyard* (2005).

The 120,000 crowd, packed in a muddy field after a day of torrential rain, sang along passionately to Beatles' hits, with Paul leading mass singalongs of *Hey Jude* and *Helter Skelter*. Paul came off stage to embrace Michael Eavis and was described as "weeping tears of joy."

Eleven songs from Glastonbury are included on *The McCartney Years* (2007) DVD box set: 1. *Jet*; 2. *Flaming Pie*; 3. *Let Me Roll It*; 4. *Blackbird*; 5. *Band on the Run*; 6. *Back in the U.S.S.R.*; 7. *Live and Let Die*; 8 *Hey Jude*; 9. *Yesterday*; 10. *Helter Skelter*; and 11. *Sgt. Pepper's Lonely Hearts Club Band*.

A Somerset newspaper declared that Paul: "completely stole the show ... Paul put absolutely everything into his passionate, greatest hits performance ... it felt as if he had been waiting for that show all his life."

In February 2005, NME accorded Paul's Glastonbury performance the Shockwaves award for Best Live Event of 2004, beating the Festival's Friday and Sunday headliners Oasis and Muse.

Further recording sessions

On 28 May 2004, during his tour stop in Lisbon, Portugal, Paul met Andrew Slater (1957-), president and CEO of Capitol Records since May 2001. A former record producer, Slater had worked in 1992 with The Wallflowers, an alternative rock group led by Bob Dylan's son Jakob Dylan (1969-). As CEO at Capitol, Slater oversaw a temporary revival in the label's fortunes with the signing and successful promotion of the English rock-pop band Coldplay and the American hip-hop artist Chingy (1981-).

Paul played Slater eight demos from his September 2003 and April 2004 recording sessions with Godrich and seven demos from his February 2004 sessions with Kahne.

Slater was most impressed with the Godrich sessions, declaring the songs had "all the personality of the early '70s McCartney records, while still sounding very fresh and modern." This persuaded Paul to go with the songs that Godrich had produced and shelve the material from the Kahne sessions for a later release.

Between September and November 2004, Paul and Godrich held further recording sessions: in September at George Martin's AIR Studios, at Lyndhurst Hall, in north London; and in October-November at Ocean Way in Los Angeles.

Playing virtually all the instruments, Paul worked on seven tracks: *Fine Line*; *Too Much Rain*; *Jenny Wren*; *English Tea*; *Promise to You Girl*; *Anyway*; and *She Is Beautiful*.

On *Anyway*, Paul and Godrich used two string arrangers: David Campbell (1948-), the Canadian father of Beck, and the English composer Joby Talbot (1971-).

Three of the tracks Paul worked on during these sessions were never released: *Watching My Fish Drown; A Modern Dance;* and *Perfect Lover.*

March 1998: One of the last pictures of Linda McCartney, taken by her daughter Mary at Peasmarsh, shortly before Linda made her final trip to America (PA Images/Alamy Stock Photo)

May 1999: Paul at an exhibition of his paintings at the Lÿz Art Forum in Germany (United Archives GmbH/Alamy Stock Photo)

Hog Hill Mill Studio, near Rye, East Sussex, where Paul recorded, in **November 1999**, the *VOICE* charity single with Heather (N Boyd/Alamy Stock Photo)

7 May 2001: Paul launches the *Wingspan* compilation album (Landmark Media/Alamy Stock Photo)

20 October 2001: Paul performs *Freedom* at the Concert for New York (Michael Brito/Alamy Stock Photo)

17 April 2002: Paul performing at the Continental Airlines Arena, East Rutherford, New Jersey, during the Driving USA tour (Newscom/Alamy Stock Photo)

25 July 2002: Paul and Heather with Queen Elizabeth II at an exhibition of Paul's paintings and sculptures at the Walker Art Gallery in Liverpool (Anwar Hussein/Alamy Stock Photo)

24 May 2003: Ahead of the evening concert in Moscow's Red Square, Paul and Heather meet and talk with Russian President Vladimir Putin (Associated Press/Alamy Stock Photo)

26 June 2004: Paul and his band perform the headline set on the Pyramid stage at the UK's Glastonbury Festival (Edd Westmacott/Alamy Stock Photo)

28 May 2005: Paul and Heather in Neuss, Germany, for the AAM benefit gala (DPA Picture Alliance Archive/Alamy Stock Photo)

2 July 2005: Paul and George Michael performing the Beatles' *Drive My Car* at the Live 8 charity concert in London's Hyde Park (Antonio Pagano/Alamy Stock Photo)

2 March 2006: Paul and Heather on an ice floe off Prince Edward Island, Canada, protesting the annual cull of seal pups (Rolf Hicker Photography/Alamy Stock Photo)

15 June 2006: Paul with James Brown and Brian Wilson at the Songwriters Hall of Fame ceremony at the Sheraton Hotel, New York (ZUMA Press Inc./Alamy Stock Photo)

5 June 2007: Paul's *Memory Almost Full* is released in the US on Starbuck's Hear Music record label (Associated Press/Alamy Stock Photo)

Left: **February 2008:** Paul with his solicitor Fiona Shackleton at the Royal Courts of Justice during the hearing into his divorce settlement with Heather Mills (Trinity Mirror/Mirrorpix/Alamy Stock Photo)

Right: **24 November 2008:** Paul signs copies of his new Fireman album *Electric Arguments* at the HMV records store in Oxford Street, London (PA Images/Alamy Stock Photo)

17 April 2009: Paul and his band perform an acclaimed set at the Coachella Music Festival, in Indio, California (WENN Rights Ltd/Alamy Stock Photo)

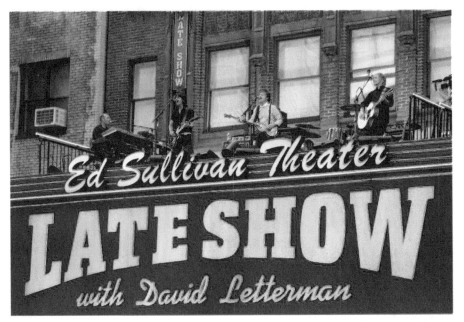

15 July 2009: Paul and his band perform a short outdoor concert on top of the marquee of the Ed Sullivan Theater for the Late Show with David Letterman (Ethan Vasquez/Alamy Stock Photo)

Left: **9 December 2009:** Paul at the Gelredome in Arnhem, the Netherlands (David Borman)

Right: **9 December 2009:** Paul, Rusty and Brian in Arnhem (David Borman)

16 December 2009: Paul and his band at the Köln Arena in Cologne, Germany (David Borman)

16 December 2009: Performing *Live and Let Die* at the Köln Arena (David Borman)

16 December 2009: Paul and band at the close of the Köln concert (David Borman)

The **22 December 2009** Good Evening London concert at the O2 Arena (David Borman)

22 December 2009: Paul and his band at the O2 Arena in London (David Borman)

22 December 2009: A backdrop of Paul and George at London's O2 Arena (David Borman)

22 December 2009: A backdrop of the 1967 Beatles at the O2 Arena (David Borman)

15 January 2010: Paul and Nancy at the 15th Annual Critics' Choice Movie Awards at the Hollywood Palladium in Los Angeles (Tsuni/USA/Alamy Stock Photo)

2005: A Late Career Classic

Key events

10 January: *46664 1 Year On: The EP* is released, including Paul's *Whole Life*.

6 February: Paul and his band perform at Super Bowl XXXIX at Alltel Stadium in Jacksonville, Florida, and he announces an autumn US tour.

April: Further recording session for *Chaos and Creation in the Backyard*.

21 April: Paul performs *Lady Madonna* and *Yesterday* at the Lincoln Center in New York City to benefit Paul Newman's Association of Hole in the War Gang Camps, a charity that brings respite and joy to cancer-affected children.

28 May: Paul performs *All You Need Is Love,* with Yusuf Islam (Cat Stevens), and *Let It Be* at the 5th annual AAM benefit gala in Neuss, Germany.

13 June: Paul releases *Twin Freaks*, a vinyl only electronic mash-up album.

14 June: The DVD *Paul McCartney in Red Square* is released.

2 July: Paul and his band perform at *Live 8*.

28 July: At Abbey Road Studio 2, Paul performs tracks from his upcoming album.

10 September: In Miami, Paul performs *Fine Line* for the *ReAct Now: Music & Relief* concert for those affected in New Orleans by Hurricane Katrina.

12 September: Paul releases the album *Chaos and Creation in the Backyard*.

16 September to 30 November: Paul and his band undertake a 37-show 'US' Tour.

3 October: Paul's children's environmental novel *High in the Clouds* is released.

17 October: Stevie Wonder releases *A Time to Love*, his first album in 20 years. It features Paul on guitar on the title track.

During 2005 Paul was highly active musically. He released two new albums, *Twin Freaks* and *Chaos and Creation in the Backyard*, and made live appearances in February at Super Bowl XXXIX and July at Live 8. He closed the year with a 37-date September to November tour of North America.

In October *High in the Clouds,* an environmental novel for children written by Paul, was published. In the same month, Stevie Wonder's album *A Time to Love* was released, featuring Paul on guitar on the title track.

Away from music, there were growing tensions in Paul's marriage.

Super Bowl XXXIX: 6 February

Paul and his band were booked to perform the prestigious half-time show on 6 February 2005 at Alltel Stadium in Jacksonville, Florida, for Super Bowl XXXIX: an American football game between the New England Patriots and Philadelphia Eagles.

The Super Bowl show was broadcast by the Fox network, owned by the Australian media mogul Rupert Murdoch (1931-) who had a newspaper empire in the US, UK and Australia.

Paul's appearance was cast in doubt after the Murdoch-owned UK's *Sunday Times* published on 28 November 2004 a seven-page magazine article investigating "the intriguing and colourful past of Heather Mills McCartney." The article included the cruel and outrageous assertion that "losing her was perhaps the best thing that ever happened to Heather as it fed her desire for self-publicity."

Heather was so incensed that she believed Paul should withdraw from the Super Bowl half-time show.

Paul was sympathetic to Heather's grievance but was reluctant to pull out from his band's Super Bowl appearance. Instead, he talked with newspaper editors about Heather's compassionate work for those affected by landmines and made supportive postings on Heather's website.

Paul allegedly told the newspaper editors: "Heather is a really decent person. All she does is good things. I see the other side to her that people don't see. The truth is Heather never seeks publicity for all the work she does with her landmine charity … She actually bothers to get off her backside and do things to help people. She can help young girls who have lost a leg get their confidence back. I can't do that and there are very few people on this Earth who can."

On 5 February 2005, Paul posted on Heather's website an 800-word open letter which branded Heather's media critics "malevolent and ridiculous." The letter listed and refuted media accusations of Heather's undue influence over Paul, including claims that Heather forced Paul to dye his hair, wear 'younger' clothes and attend parties and had been behind the 2002 *Back in the U.S.* reversal in Beatles' songwriting credits.

In addition, Paul agreed to spend more time in the US where Heather's media and campaigning activities were increasing. In June-July, she appeared in two episodes of the NBC soap opera *Days of our Lives*, as a counsellor to a soldier who had lost a limb to a landmine.

The US branch of Paul's MPL Communications had long operated from a former Manhattan townhouse at 41 West 54th Street. This was situated between Fifth Avenue and Sixth Avenue, near the offices of Eastman and Eastman. Paul decided now to convert the upper floors into a penthouse where he, Heather and Bea could stay.

Heather welcomed this, but asked Paul to allocate one of the other rooms in the building as an office where she could do charity business while Bea was sleeping. According to later (leaked) divorce papers (as cited by Sounes), Paul declined to go this far but did provide Heather with an office a 20-minute walk away.

Paul's 6 February Super Bowl XXXIX show went ahead. The 12-minute set comprised three Beatles songs *Drive My Car*, *Get Back* and *Hey Jude* and Wings' *Live and Let Die*, which was accompanied by a spectacular firework display.

Artists did not receive a fee for Super Bowl performances, but Paul's record sales received an estimated boost of $3.5 million from playing before Super Bowl XXXIX's crowd of 78,125 and 145 million US television viewers, with millions more watching in over 200 countries worldwide. Paul used the show to announce his autumn US tour.

Finalising *Chaos and Creation in the Backyard*

Paul worked with Nigel Godrich at Ocean Way, in January 2005, and at AIR Studios, London, in April 2005, adding the final overdubs and mixes to the tracks recorded in 2003-04.

During these sessions, Paul completed *How Kind of You, Friends to Go, I've Got Only Two Hands* and *Summer of '59*.

Twin Freaks

Personnel: Paul McCartney and Roy Kerr.

Producer: Roy Kerr, a.k.a. Freelance Hellraiser

Recording: 2004 at Hog Hill Mill Studio, engineered by Clive Goddard

Release date: 13 June 2005

Highest chart placings: UK: -; US: - [did not chart].

Length: 53:45 minutes

Tracks: 1. *Really Love You* 5:42; 2. *Long Haired Lady (Reprise)* 4:50; 3. *Rinse the Raindrops* 3:14; 4. *Darkroom* 2:30; 5. *Live and Let Die* 3:26; 6 *Temporary Secretary* 4:12; 7. *What's That You're Doing* 4:57; 8. *Oh Woman, Oh Why* 4:19; 9. *Mumbo* 5:24; 10. *Lalula* 4:25; 11. *Coming Up* 4:42; and 12. *Maybe I'm Amazed* 6:12.

Paul enjoyed dancing and dance music. During the 1990s, he included dance remixes as B-sides and extra tracks on his singles and maxi-singles.

In 1991-92, he commissioned DJ Steve Anderson to create *Deliverance (the Steve Anderson mixes),* sourced from the multi-tracks of *Off the Ground.* This resulted in an electronic house rave dance track in the style of the Italian house-music band Black Box whose *Ride on Time* had topped the UK singles charts in 1989.

Released anonymously in 1992 on a 12-inch promotional disc sent to UK club DJs, *Deliverance* reached number 9 in the national DMC (Dance Mix

Club) dance chart amid rumours that it was the work of a Brixton based house band or had come from Manchester's The Hacienda music venue. In 1993, *Deliverance* was released officially as a 12-inch single with *Hope of Deliverance* and on the *C'mon People* EP.

In 2003, the English DJ and electronic music producer Matt Edwards (1975-), a.k.a. Radio Slave, created a 7:25 minute dance mix of *Temporary Secretary*. Released to radio stations across Europe in December 2003 as a promotional 12-inch single, limited to 500 numbered copies, it became another club hit.

For the pre-shows to his 2004 concerts, Paul decided he would like a DJ to play remixes of his solo tracks. MPL invited interested DJs to send in mixtapes. The applicants included Roy Kerr, a.k.a. Freelance Hellraiser, who sent in a 5-minute mix.

Kerr described it as a "cut-n-past job" but it attracted Paul's attention. A fortnight later, MPL invited Kerr to meet Paul at their London office. As an icebreaker, Paul joshed with the laid-back Essex-born Kerr: "You don't look much like a Hellraiser." Kerr replied: "I'm not, the name's a bit of a joke."

Paul was aware, from 2001-03 UK music press articles, of Roy Kerr's pioneering work at the forefront of bootleg mash-up: a UK music scene in which vocals and instrumentation were spliced together from different songs to create a new song.

In October 2001, Roy Kerr's (The Freelance Hellraiser) *A Stroke of Genie-Us,* became a huge dancefloor hit and a highly influential track. It seamlessly merged vocals by Christina Aguilera (1980-), from her hit *Genie in a Bottle*, with guitar riffs by US indie-rockers The Strokes, from their 2001 single *Hard to Explain*.

Despite a cease-and-desist order issued by Aguilera's record label RCA, which halted physical sales, *A Stroke of Genie-Us* circulated virally through MP3 filesharing. So impressed was Aguilera that she engaged Roy Kerr to produce the *Freelance Hellraiser 'Thug Pop' Mix* of her 2003 single *Fighter*.

At their 2003 London meeting, Paul discussed with Roy his musical interests and how he came up with his mash-up ideas. Paul affirmed he liked the mix submitted and invited Roy to be DJ the pre-show for Paul's 2004 and 2005 tours in Europe and the US. Kerr accepted. The assignment involved Roy, dressed as a ringmaster, playing his McCartney mixes while Cirque du Soleil dancers performed on stage.

During these tours, Roy was treated as a band member, travelling in the private jets, tour bus and motorcades. Kerr recounted: "(Paul) was really fatherly and sweet to me … he called me 'Roy-boy.'"

At a vodka-heavy afterparty following the 20 June 2004 St. Petersburg concert, 20 June 2004, Paul made a special point of congratulating Roy. Getting Paul in a headlock, Roy responded: "This is amazing … we've got to make an album." The next morning, on the tour bus, Paul came over and said to Roy: "That's a brilliant idea, we'll do that."

Paul asked Roy to develop his pre-show mash-up set into a longer piece: *Twin Freaks*. In a later interview in 2022, Roy stated: "Paul gave me absolute free rein to do whatever I wanted. The only stipulations were no Beatles stuff, and I wasn't to play any original music over any of it."

Paul provided Roy with full use of Hog Hill Mill studio and access to the original multi-tracks of Wings, McCartney solo and The Fireman songs. Some of the original analogue tapes had to be baked so they could be digitised.

Roy noted: "I was a bit cheeky by including *Live and Let Die*, because Paul didn't own the multis to that (the Broccoli family do), but I just snipped the intro and looped it like an old Beatles loop, and he loved it."

The songs

Five of *Twin Freaks'* twelve tracks were based around McCartney songs from the early-1970s, four from the early-1980s, one from the 1990s and one from *Driving Rain* in 2001. *Lalula* drew on many songs.

In 2022, Roy recounted that, while his father was a Beatles fan: "I honestly didn't know much about Wings or Paul's solo work until I started DJing in the early-2000s … it was *McCartney II* (1980) that I'd discovered through DJing electroclash parties in the early-2000s, and it properly blew me away. Still does."

1. **Really Love You** originated in a Paul and Ringo jam for *Flaming Pie* (1997). The *Twin Freaks* mash-up mix has heightened energy, with Paul's raw, distorted vocals underpinned by a driving bass and electronic drumbeats, sampled from *What's That You're Doing* (1982).

2. **Long Haired Lady (Reprise)** was a laid-back stoner track from *Ram* (1971). On *Twin Freaks,* it is given a trance-beat introduction before looping into the refrain "love is long, yes, love is long." This mash-up, which includes a guitar riff from *Oo You* (1970), is a standout.

3. **Rinse the Raindrops**, a *Driving Rain* jam, is given a frantic, paranoid remix as well as spacy sounds.

4. **Darkroom,** from *McCartney II* (1980), is invigorated by electronic drum and dub mixes and bass from *Bogey Music* (1980).

5. **Live and Let Die** is radically reconstructed. The phrase "when you were young" is looped endlessly, while fragments of dialogue from the *Back in the U.S.* DVD and dub percussion add colour.

6 **Temporary Secretary,** an oddball *McCartney II* (1980) track, is reimagined with a repeated chorus and powerful drum and bass lines.

7. **What's That You're Doing**, a Paul and Stevie Wonder co-write from *Tug of War* (1982), is given a hard funk mix that emphasises Stevie Wonder's vocals and Paul's funky and propulsive bass.

8. **Oh Woman, Oh Why**, the B-side to Paul's first single *Another Day* (1971), is one of *Twin Freaks'* most complex mash-ups. It starts with an excerpt from the title song *Venus and Mars* (1975), followed by snippets of dialogue from *Back in the U.S.*, samples from *Oh Woman, Oh Why* (1971) and *Blue Sway* (1980), drums from *Loup* (1973) and the "we better get out of here" guitar riff from *Band on the Run* (1974). It was Roy Kerr's favourite track on *Twin Freaks*.

9. **Mumbo,** the opening jam track on *Wild Life* (1971), includes dub drums, transforming it into an extended, primitive dance groove.

10. **Lalula** mashes together fragments from ten tracks. They include *Old Siam Sir* (1979), *Momma Miss America* (1970), *Blue Sway,* and *Oh Woman,*

Oh Why. It is an example of how a skilled mash-up DJ can craft novel dance grooves from multiple sources.

11. **Coming Up,** from *McCartney II* (1980), is a track which John Lennon praised as "a good piece of work." On *Twin Freaks* it is mashed-up with bass and rhythms sampled from *Morse Goose and the Grey Goose* (1978). This adds power to the driving dance groove.

12. **Maybe I'm Amazed** starts conventionally on *Twin Freaks* before bass and drum echo and breathing is added from *Kreen-Akrore* (1970). After 2:45, the line "maybe I'm amazed at the way you" is repeated in a semi-instrumental dance-trance outro.

Release and reception

Twin Freaks was released, with little fanfare, on 13 June 2005, in Europe only, by Graze Records, as a double vinyl LP. It was available as a worldwide digital download but was not released on CD. From April 2012, it was made available on music streaming services.

The album's cover art and title came from a 1990 abstract painting by Paul, featuring two green and yellow faces with black masks and red lips. Roy Kerr selected the painting from the *Paul McCartney Paintings* (2000) book Paul had asked him to browse through for artwork ideas. Roy liked the painting's "vibe." The album is credited to Twin Freaks.

On 6 June, a 12-inch one-sided promotional single was issued, comprising *Really Love You* and *Lalula* and limited to 500 copies. A 12-inch promotional single of *Rinse the Raindrops/What's That You're Doing* was also released: restricted to several hundred copies.

An enjoyable album for fans of dance and trance music, *Twin Freaks* received a three-star rating from *Uncut* magazine, which praised its "audacious reworkings."

After *Twin Freaks*, Roy Kerr remained in high demand. In 2007, he formed a writing and production partnership Kid Gloves, with the DJ Anu Pillai, and in 2012 MyRiot with Tim Bran. In 2015, MyRiot produced and wrote songs for *Higher Than Here*, a UK top ten album by the English singer-songwriter James Morrison (1984-) and in 2018 for

Wax, a UK top twenty album by the Scottish singer-songwriter KT Tunstall (1975-).

Live 8

On 31 May 2005, Bob Geldof announced an anti-global poverty concert, *Live 8*, on 2 and 6 July 2005. It was timed to coincide with a Group of 8 (G8) meeting in Scotland of the leaders of Canada, France, Germany, Italy, Japan, Russia, the UK and the USA to discuss the Global Call to Action Against Poverty and the UK's Make Poverty History campaign.

Live 8 sought to levy moral pressure on the G8 to increase aid to poorer countries. This had some success when, on 7 July, G8 members pledged to double aid to poor nations to $50 million in 2010, with a half going to Africa.

Over 1,000 musicians participated in *Live 8*'s concerts in London, Paris, Berlin, Rome, Philadelphia, Moscow, the Eden Project (in Cornwall, England), Edinburgh, Barrie (in Ontario, Canada), Chiba (in Japan) and Johannesburg. *Live 8* was broadcast by 2,000 radio and 182 television networks to 3 billion viewers worldwide.

The highlight of *Live 8* was the re-uniting, after 24 years, of Pink Floyd for a one-off 18-minute set. Others appearing at *Live 8* included Kanye West (1977-), Madonna (1958-), R.E.M. and Stevie Wonder.

The 2 July concert in Hyde Park, London, before a crowd of 200,000, was opened by Paul. He played *Sgt. Pepper's Lonely Hearts Club Band* and was accompanied by U2 and their singer Bono (1960-). The song's lyric, "It was twenty years ago," was apposite as *Live 8* was held twenty years after *Live Aid*.

Paul returned hours later to close the concert. He performed *Get Back*, *Drive My Car*, with vocals by George Michael, *Helter Skelter* and a finale of *The Long and Winding Road* and *Hey Jude*, with all the artists on stage singing along.

Digital versions of *Sgt. Pepper's Lonely Hearts Club Band* and *The Long and Winding Road* were released online as singles. On 7 November, a four DVD set *Live 8* was released.

Chaos and Creation in the Backyard

Personnel: Paul McCartney (vocals, keyboards, bass guitar, acoustic and electric guitars, drums and percussion, flugelhorn, güiro, cello, vibrachimes, melodica, recorders, tubular bells, autoharp, harmonium, gong, toy glockenspiel, mood synthesizer); Millennia Ensemble (strings and brass arranged and conducted by Joby Talbot on tracks 1, 4, 6, 10, 12 and 13); Jason Falkner (guitars on tracks 4 and 8); James Gadson (drums on tracks 4 and 9); Joey Waronker (bongos, bass drum, shaker on track 8); Nigel Godrich (piano and acoustic guitar loops on track 2); Pedro Eustache (duduk on track 3); The Los Angeles Music Players (strings arranged by David Campbell on tracks 9 and 13); Abe Laboriel Jr. (tambourine and percussion on track 10); Rusty Anderson (acoustic guitar on track 10); and Brian Ray (acoustic guitar on track 10).

Producer: Nigel Godrich

Recording sessions: September 2003 (in RAK Studios, London), April, October and November 2004 and January 2005 (in Ocean Way Recording Studios, Los Angeles) and September 2004 and April 2005 (in AIR Studios, London)

Release date: 12 September 2005

Highest chart placings: UK: 10; US: 6.

Length: 43:38 minutes (46:53 including the hidden track 14)

Tracks: 1. *Fine Line* 3:06; 2. *How Kind of You* 4:48; 3. *Jenny Wren* 3:47; 4. *At the Mercy* 2:38; 5. *Friends to Go* 2:44; 6. *English Tea* 2:12; 7. *Too Much Rain* 3:25; 8. *A Certain Softness* 2:42; 9. *Riding to Vanity Fair* 5:07; 10. *Follow Me* 2:32; 11. *Promise to You Girl* 3:10; 12. *This Never Happened Before* 3:25; 13. *Anyway* 3:52; and 14. *I've Only Got Two Hands* (hidden track) 3:15.

Producer Nigel Godrich's set out "to make a great album that was true to Paul" and tried out differing recording approaches, sounds and instruments to see which worked best. Reflecting on the recording experience, he stated: "Paul was always very patient with me, I was making him do things that were uncomfortable for him, in ways where normally he wouldn't have to relinquish creative control."

Godrich entered the project with great respect for Paul as a musician and "came out with even more respect." But he was not intimidated working with an ex-Beatle. Indeed, one of his rules when working was: "'No Beatles stories,' because we had to keep our eye on what we're doing now."

In contrast to the affable George Martin, at times Godrich was blunt when rejecting melodies and lyrics he considered clichéd. This led to "a few shouty moments," most notably when the pair locked horns on the track *Riding to Vanity Fair.*

Paul agreed, stating: "There were some tense moments during the making of the album. Nigel wasn't sycophantic; he said from the off. 'I warn you. I know what I like'." But keen to make the best possible album, Paul accepted Godrich's approach.

The album's release was delayed until final writing sessions and overdubs in January and April 2005 satisfied both parties.

The songs

The album's thirteen main tracks range from 2:12 to 5:07 minutes and the total running time, at 43 minutes, is 24 minutes less than the bloated *Driving Rain.* Tight focus was a strength of this album.

Five additional tracks recorded during the *Chaos and Creation* sessions were released as singles' B-sides. A sixth, **She's So Beautiful**, a romantic ballad written for Bea and recorded in November 2004, found its way on to the album's Japanese edition.

1. **Fine Line** opens the album in an upbeat, poppy vein. Its line, "a long way between chaos and creation," provided part of the title for the album. Recorded in September 2004, *Fine Line* begins with what Paul termed a "chuggy" piano riff accompanying the phrase: "fine line between recklessness and courage." Midway through, the tempo downshifts on the words "come home brother." This leads into a punchy Beatle-ish string section, conducted and arranged by Joby Talbot in a

"tribute to George Martin." Paul described the song as a "philosophical one about knowing where you're going."

2. ***How Kind of You***, recorded in April 2005 – the last song Paul recorded during his sessions with Godrich - is a song of gratitude to Heather for "think(ing) of me when I was out of sorts." Paul also reflects on his last night with Linda and "how unafraid you were that long dark night."

Paul said the song was inspired by his interest in the way the English language is spoken and the quaint phrases used by "older posh English friends." Presented originally as a jangly guitar demo, Godrich created a sophisticated arrangement, setting Paul's fragile vocals above a sonic bed of piano and acoustic guitar loops.

3. ***Jenny Wren***, recorded in October 2004, is the 'daughter of *Blackbird*', Paul's 1968 Beatles US civil rights song. During a day off from recording, Paul took his guitar to a nature spot in a canyon near Los Angeles where he walked and relaxed and came up with the song's idea. Later that evening, he finished the song in the kitchen.

Godrich described *Jenny Wren* as: "a song that came out of the sky ... instant and visceral ... I'd been needling Paul about that kind of song."

Jenny Wren reprises the top line and bass line acoustic finger-picking style of *Blackbird*. It was based on Bach's Bourée in E minor for lute, which Paul and George had learned from a version by the American guitarist Chet Atkins (1924-2001). The song draws its name from England's smallest garden bird and one which Paul stated he felt always "privileged to see ... (as) they're very shy."

The song describes a girl from a poor, broken family who, after her heart was broken, lost her desire to sing and left home. It can be interpreted as an allegory on Heather's overcoming of life challenges.

In *The Lyrics* (2021), Paul stated that Jenny Wren was a 'brave girl' in *Our Mutual Friend* (1865), a Charles Dickens (1812-70) novel he had read many years before. In the novel, Jenny Wren was born with underdeveloped legs and a crooked spine but considered herself no different from other teenage girls. She compensated for her physical appearance by taking on a position of authority over every man she met, including her alcoholic father.

In Paul's telling of the story, Jenny Wren stops singing because she could see the world's foolish ways. In 2005 and 2021, Paul explained that underpinning the song was an environmental message: we are making a mess of the world, with, for example, "the ocean filling with plastic; it didn't get there by itself."

Godrich added a twist to the song by recruiting the Venezuelan multi-instrumentalist Pedro Eustache (1959-) to play the duduk, an Armenian woodwind instrument.

4. **At the Mercy** was written by Paul in Los Angeles in April 2004 during a weekend break between recording sessions. Doodling on his piano to the mantra of "at the mercy of a busy road," Paul hit upon some interesting sounding darker chords. The lyrics about dealing with the curve balls that life throws struck a chord with Heather, who had lost her left leg crossing a road.

The song has shifts in tempo and instrumentation and troubled lyrics. Paul plays piano, bass, cello and vibrachimes. Jason Falkner plays electric guitar, James Gadson drums and the Millennia Ensemble, violoncello, strings and brass. It was one of Godrich's favourite songs, containing "an intimacy vocally I was hoping to get."

5. **Friends to Go** was recorded in April 2005. Originally titled *Waiting on the Other Side*, Paul wrote the song in the style of George Harrison and plays all instruments, including drums, a flugelhorn and melodica. In explaining the song's lyrics, Paul stated that he imagined he was visiting a friend who lived on a housing estate and was watching and waiting outside for his friend's friends to leave.

6. **English Tea** is a pastiche song written by Paul after being asked in a café in Lisbon, when on tour in May 2004, what type of tea he would like. Recorded in November 2004 and April 2005, the song's melody, with a chromatic descending line, has echoes of George Harrison's *Piggies* (1968) but is played on piano in the genteel 1930s' style of Cole Porter (1899-1973). Strings and brass are played by the Millennia Ensemble and tubular bells and recorders by Paul.

Paul uses archetypal, upper middle class village England phases: "Very twee, very me … nanny bakes fairy cakes … miles of English garden stretching past the willow tree" and "peradventure" (perhaps), having come across the word in a Charles Dickens novel.

7. **Too Much Rain**, recorded in September 2004, is a stoical "get over it" song driven by a piano melody. Its inspiration was one of Paul's favourite songs, *Smile,* composed by the English comic actor Charlie Chaplin (1889-1977) for his 1936 film *Modern Times*. Chaplin's song had the line "smile even though your heart is aching," whereas *Too Much Rain* has "smile when your heart is filled with pain."

In interviews in 2005, Paul explained that *Too Much Rain* was about empathising with people feeling overwhelmed by problems that life may throw at them and saying: "I know what you're going through. I can relate to it." Specifically, Paul wrote this song with the life challenges Heather had overcome in mind.

8. **A Certain Softness**, recorded in April 2004, is a love song written by Paul during a boat cruise in Greece, which had been a surprise birthday gift. Paul termed the song "sexy, very romantic." It has a Latin vibe, with a mix of Brazilian bossa nova and Argentinian tango rhythms. Paul and Jason Falkner play classical guitars and Joey Waronker, who had played sessions with R.E.M and Beck, on bass drum and bongos.

9. **Riding to Vanity Fair** is an ominous, dreamlike song with a stop-start pace. The song has gorgeous instrumental touches on toy glockenspiel, electric guitar and bass played by Paul, drums by James Gadson, harp by the Los Angeles-based Stephanie Bennett and strings by The Los Angeles Music Players.

Paul presented the song as "an up-tempo thing" and Godrich told Paul that he didn't like it. During recording sessions in April 2004 and January 2005, the song was deconstructed and reconstructed. Its tempo was halved, making it "slow and moody," and the melody and words rewritten. Paul noted "it was a very interesting process … like working with a band member."

Paul stated *Riding to Vanity Fair* is about: "You're approaching someone for friendship, and they just don't want to know. They're just rejecting you … it's not about any particular person." But biographers have suggested the song was about Heather, noting that:

- In 2002, Heather had given an interview to the US celebrity fashion and pop culture magazine *Vanity Fair*.
- *Vanity Fair* (1848) was the title of a satirical novel by William Makepeace Thackeray (1811-63) featuring Becky Sharp, a poor, strong-willed young woman determined to advance in society.
- Vanity is a fictional town in *Pilgrim's Progress* (1678) by John Bunyan (1628-88) which held a Fair at which "all that is there sold, or that cometh thither, is vanity." Paul had read this book in his youth.

The song states: "I was open to friendship, but you didn't seem to have any to spare while you were riding to Vanity Fair."

Paul denied, in a July 2005 interview with Paul Du Noyer, that the song was about Heather. He stated that it was about another relationship and was a "therapeutic way of releasing myself."

Some have suggested that the subject of the song might have been Geoff Baker, whom Paul sacked as his publicist in September 2004. But the song's timeline and the facts about Baker and Paul's relationship make this unlikely.

Baker accepted his September 2004 dismissal, stating: "The pressure of 15 years of having been on call to the globe got to me and I cracked … It's been a blast and that's what it's meant to be. It's only rock 'n' roll." During his final year with Paul, Baker allegedly became dependent on alcohol and cocaine and was diagnosed as manic depressive.

After his September 2004 sacking, Geoff did not speak ill publicly about Paul. This was despite tough times, including prolonged periods unemployed, falling into debt and carrying out voluntary work, as a street cleaner, in his hometown of Lyme Regis, Dorset, in 2010.

Baker rejected an offer of £150,000 to write a 'warts and all' book about his time working with Paul. But he did write and publish, in 2010, a satirical novel *Rock Bottom*. It was a story of a self-absorbed fading rock star Ian Taylor, his demented, drug-addled PR Peter Forth and an extorting fan. Baker stated that Taylor was not based on Paul.

Riding to Vanity Fair is in some respects a bookend to *Riding into Jaipur*. Its dark mood and lyrics hint at storm clouds in Paul's marriage: "I bit my tongue … You put me down … but why pretend … I've heard enough of your familiar song."

Whatever the truth about its subject, it is a standout track.

10. ***Follow Me*** was the first track recorded for the album, in September 2003, and the only one to feature Paul's touring band: Abe on tambourine and percussion; and Brian and Rusty on acoustic guitar. Written in the key of C major, it is a positive feelgood song about the people in Paul's life who lifted his spirits.

11. ***Promise to You Girl***, recorded in November 2004, references the album's title in its nostalgic opening line: "looking though the backyard of my life, time to sweep the leaves away." The song's changes in pace and tone arise from it comprising fragments of two songs sewn together. It begins with a plaintiff refrain, before transitioning, via layered, harmony vocals, to a honky-tonk piano, with Paul vamping away. It features a McCartney guitar solo set against a backdrop of Wings-like harmonies. Paul described it as an optimistic song which began as a "Motown thing."

12. ***This Never Happened Before*** is a beautiful piano and strings-based love song composed in the style of Burt Bacharach (1928-2023) and the Frank Sinatra (1915-98) hit *It Was a Very Good Year* (1965). Paul recorded the song in September 2003 at the height of his romance with Heather and was one of the first songs he worked on with Godrich. It is underpinned by a melodic Höfner bass line and supported by strings by the Millennia Ensemble.

Paul stated that, while receiving a massage in the US, he played a pre-release version of the song and the massage therapist stated: "I love that song, it's magnificent." She told Paul she was getting married in a few weeks. Paul sent her a copy to play for her first wedding dance.

In 2006, the song featured in the romantic film, *The Lake House*, starring the American actor Sandra Bullock (1964-) and the Canadian actor Keanu Reeves (1964-).

13. **Anyway** is a song from November 2004 inspired by Paul waiting for hours for a call from Heather that never came. This explains the lyrics: "If you love me, won't you call me … I've been waiting, waiting too long." Paul described it as a Randy Newman-style song imbued with the vibe of the US deep south, "like Charleston or Savannah." Its opening piano riff is reminiscent of *People Get Ready* (1965) by Curtis Mayfield (1942-99). The song's anxious tone is heightened by the strings of the Millennia Ensemble.

14. **I've Only Got Two Hands** is a hidden instrumental track. It was formed out of improvised tracks Paul recorded during an hour in April 2005. There is an assortment of musical styles: rock jam; piano arpeggio; drum grooves; distorted electronica; and a car horn.

The album title and cover

The album takes its title comes from phrases in the songs *Promise to You Girl* and *Fine Line*. Initially, Paul had suggested *Backyard* for the title, but Godrich found this insufficiently intriguing. So, Paul added the "chaos and creation" phrase from *Fine Line*. Godrich texted Paul that this: "fits because that's sort of what this album has been about, chaos, creation and it's also home-made, it's a bit in your backyard."

The cover photo is of a youthful Paul sitting in the garden of the McCartney family's 20 Forthlin Road playing an acoustic guitar, with washing drying on the line. It was taken around 1962 by Mike McCartney. Titled, *Our Kid Through Mum's Net Curtains*, it was used also for the cover of the UK edition of Paul's 2021 book, *The Lyrics*.

Release, promotion and reception

On 29 August, *Fine Line* was released as a single backed with the unreleased *Comfort of Love* and *Growing Up Falling Down*. It reached number 17 in the UK and 31 in the US adult contemporary chart.

Comfort of Love, recorded in September 2003, is a pop song that features the use of metronome.

Growing Up Falling Down, recorded in April and October 2004, is an Asian-style track with Jason Falkner on guitar and Pedro Eustache on the didgeridoo, an Australian Aboriginal wind instrument.

On 21 November, *Jenny Wren* was released as the second single. It reached number 22 in the UK singles chart.

The 7-inch vinyl edition was backed by the unreleased **Summer of '59**, a skiffle-style song about girls in dancehalls in the late 1950s, recorded in April 2005.

The CD edition included the unreleased **I Want You to Fly**, a soft blues song recorded in April 2004, and **This Loving Game**, a ballad recorded in April 2004, with James Gadson on drums and lyrics about disappointment in a relationship, with the phrase: "somebody told me to walk away."

Ahead of the album's release on 12 September, Paul held interviews with music magazines including *Mojo* and *Music Week,* and the New Zealand DJ Zane Lowe (1973-) on the UK's Radio 1. He also appeared on the *AOL Music Sessions* in Miami on 15 September, performing six songs, including four from the new album.

On Thursday 28 July, Paul invited 50 friends and selected fans to Abbey Road Studio 2 for an intimate one-hour show, interspersed with anecdotes. This was broadcast on UK Radio 2 on 17 September, on UK television on 17 December 2005 and on PBS in the US on 27 February 2006.

During this show, Paul played four tracks from the album: *Friends To Go; How Kind of You; English Tea;* and *Jenny Wren*. He also performed the Beatles' *I've Got A Feeling, Blackbird* and *Lady Madonna* (a slowed down version); *Band on the Run,* accompanied by a harmonium drone and sounds produced by his finger circling glasses of water; Elvis Presley's 1956 hit *Heartbreak Hotel,* playing Bill Black's stand-up bass; *In Spite of All Danger*; and Eddie Cochran's (1938-60) 1957 single *Twenty Flight Rock,* which Paul termed the "audition piece" that got him into The Quarrymen.

On 15 November, Paul and his band played a 12-song set at the 5th AAM Benefit Gala at the Beverly Hilton Hotel, Los Angeles. It featured nine Beatles' songs, two rockabilly standards (*Whole Lotta Shakin' Going On* and *Midnight Special*), but only one song, *English Tea,* from the new album. The event raised $2 million for AAM.

Music critics reacted positively to *Chaos and Creation in the Backyard,* giving it typically 3-4 stars out of five. Some saw it as a late-career high. Critics liked its intimate, reflective lyrics and tone and the use of unusual instruments: the duduk; flugelhorn; autoharp; melodica; and Puerto Rican güiro.

In *The New York Times,* Jon Pareles (1953-) wrote: "Sir Paul chose a producer who favoured the experimental side: Nigel Godrich ... Sir Paul also lined up his best backup band since the Beatles: himself."

In *Music Week,* Paul Williams wrote: "McCartney has produced recordings that stand up with some of his best post-Beatles output."

A BBC review stated: "*Chaos and Creation in the Backyard* is a better album than anyone could reasonably expect from a 63-year-old who helped remould not just world popular music, but world popular culture."

Parlophone's managing director Miles Leonard (1967-) believed the freshness of the album made it attractive to younger listeners, stating: "There's the fanbase that will really enjoy the songs and melodies and craftmanship of the songs, but there's enough in this album to excite a younger audience."

With opening week sales of 91,545 in the US, the album debuted at number 6 in the Billboard 200: Paul's best performance since *Flaming Pie* in 1997. In the UK, the album outperformed *Driving Rain,* peaking at number 10 in its release week: *Life in Slow Motion* by David Gray was number 1 at this time. *Chaos and Creation in the Backyard* stayed three weeks in the UK's top 100.

The album went on to sell 1.3 million units worldwide and received four Grammy nominations for: album of the year; best pop vocal album; best male pop vocal performance (for *Fine Line*); and producer of the year (for Nigel Godrich). It lost out in the album of the year category to U2's *How to Dismantle an Atomic Bomb.*

Another US tour

Paul's autumn 2005 *'US' Tour* of North America referred to the collective we, rather than the USA. The tour began in Miami on 16 September 2005 and comprised 36 sold-out shows in 25 US cities plus one concert in Toronto, Canada. Once again, Paul and his band played to 14,000-17,000 seat venues.

During the tour, Paul made first-ever visits to Des Moines, Iowa, and Omaha, Nebraska. The tour ended on 30 November 2005 at the Staples Center in Los Angeles.

Seen by 568,000 and grossing $77 million, it was 2005's fourth-highest grossing tour, ranking behind The Eagles ($117 million from 59 shows), the Rolling Stones ($120 million from 43 shows), and U2 ($260 million from 90 shows).

At the 16 September opening show in Miami, Paul played 26 Beatles-era songs. These included the rarely played *I'll Get You, In Spite of All the Danger, Please Please Me, I've Got A Feeling, For No One, I Will, Till There Was You, Good Day Sunshine, Fixing a Hole, She Came in Through the Bathroom Window* and *Yellow Submarine*.

The eleven solo and Wings songs played included four from *Chaos and Creation in the Backyard: Fine Line; Jenny Wren; English Tea;* and *Follow Me*. No songs were played from *Driving Rain*.

After Miami, shows followed at Tampa (17 September), Atlanta (20 September), Philadelphia (22 and 23 September), Boston (26 and 27 September), New York City (30 September, and 1, 4 and 5 October), Washington D.C. (8 October), Toronto (10 October), Detroit (Auburn Hills 14 and 15 October), Chicago (18 and 19 October), Columbus (22 October), Milwaukee (23 October), St. Paul (26 October), Des Moines (27 October), Omaha (30 October), Denver (1 November), Seattle (3 November), Portland (4 November), San Jose (7 and 8 November), Anaheim (11 and 12 November), Sacramento (16 November), Houston (19 November), Dallas (20 November), Phoenix (Glendale 23 November), Nevada (Paradise 25 and 26 November) and Los Angeles (29 and 30 November).

Campaigns against the fur trade

In 2005, Heather became a patron of *Viva!* and became increasingly active supporting its campaigns promoting animal rights and veganism.

During 2005-06, Heather and Paul became immersed in the campaign against the fur trade and the fashion trade's use of animal furs.

In March 2005, Heather lobbied the European Parliament in Brussels for a ban on the fur trade between China and Europe. At the press conference, she emphasised her point by holding aloft a coat made from the fur of 42 Alsatian puppies.

Supported by PETA, Heather attended protests outside fashion firms in London, New York and Los Angeles. In September, during the New York demonstration outside the Sweetface fashion house, Heather was injured during a melee with security guards. Her prosthetic leg was twisted and knocked off, leaving her writhing in pain.

In November 2005, Paul and Heather were shocked by a video they received from PETA. Filmed covertly in a fur market in the Guangzhou region of southern China, it showed an Alsatian dog being skinned alive and dogs and cats being thrown from the top deck of a converted bus. Paul and Heather called publicly for a boycott of Chinese goods and of the 2008 Summer Olympics in Beijing.

During a 17 December 2005 a UK television interview by Michael Parkinson (1935-2023), Paul re-iterated this stance. Aked why he had not yet toured China, Paul stated it was because of China's inhumane killing and skinning of dogs and cats for the fur trade.

2006: Behold My Heart

Key events

8 February: Paul performs *Fine Line, Helter Skelter* and, with Chester Bennington of Linkin Park and rapper Jay-Z, *Yesterday* at the 48th annual Grammy Awards at the Staples Center in Los Angeles.

March and April: Recording sessions for *Memory Almost Full.*

13-17 March: Songs for Paul's classical oratorio *Ecce Cor Meum* are recorded at Abbey Road Studios.

29 April: Paul and Heather separate, announcing this formally on 18 May.

18 June: Paul's 64th birthday.

17 July: Paul petitions for divorce from Heather.

25 September: *Ecce Cor Meum* is released on EMI Classics.

26 September: Tony Bennett releases the album *Duets: An American Classic.* It includes a duet with Paul on *The Very Thought of You.*

24 October: The jazz artists George Benson and Al Jarreau release the album *Givin' It Up.* It includes a Sam Cooke track, *Bring It On Home To Me*, on which Paul provides vocals and Abe Laboriel Jr.'s father Abraham plays electric bass.

13 November: Paul's *The Space Within US* DVD is released. On the same day George Michael releases a 2-CD compilation album, *Twenty Five*, to celebrate the 25th year of its career. It includes a new version of *Heal the Pain* recorded with Paul.

20 November: *Love*, a soundtrack album of remixed and mash-up music from the Beatles, is released.

2006 was a challenging year for Paul personally. In January, he received notice from Rother District Council that The Cabin at Peasmarsh had been built without planning consent and must be pulled down as it harmed "the intrinsic quality and character of the High Weald Area of Outstanding Natural Beauty."

Paul appealed the ruling unsuccessfully. In August 2007, The Cabin was demolished. However, the lakeside wildlife-viewing pavilion was allowed to remain.

In early 2006, tensions in Paul and Heather's marriage reached breaking point, culminating in the couple's separation on 29 April. This was followed, from June, with UK tabloid newspapers publishing a series of hostile articles about Heather. On 17 July, Paul filed for divorce.

Paul did not tour in 2006 and played live just once: on 8 February at the Grammy Awards. But, in the spring he recorded further tracks for his 2007 album *Memory Almost Full* and on 25 September released *Ecce Cor Meum*, a choral classical album he had been working on since 1997. On 13 November, he released *The Space Within US,* a DVD of his autumn 2005 US tour.

There were four additional 2006 releases Paul had some involvement in:

- The 26 September Tony Bennett album *Duets: An American Classic.* This included Bennett-McCartney duet on the song *The Very Thought of You.*
- The 24 October the album *Givin' It Up* by jazz artists George Benson and Al Jarreau. Paul provided vocals on the Sam Cooke song *Bring It On Home to Me.*
- The 13 November George Michael compilation album *Twenty Five.* George and Paul duetted on the song *Heal the Pain.*
- The 20 November Beatles mash-up album *Love.*

Recording *Memory Almost Full*

Paul's only live performance in 2006 was on 8 February at the Grammy Awards at the Staples Center in Los Angeles. It was Paul's first-ever performance at the Grammys and, when opening his three-song set, he declared: "I have finally passed the audition."

Paul and his band performed *Fine Line* and a high-energy, barnstorming version of *Helter Skelter* to rapturous applause. Later, he came on stage midway through the performance by Chester Bennington (1976-2017) of Linkin Park and Jay-Z of their mash-up hip hop hit *Numb/Encore* after the song had segued into the Beatles *Yesterday*. Paul took over the lead vocals on *Yesterday* from Chester Bennington.

It was a performance that divided opinion. At the song's end, Jay-Z declared to the audience: "sounds so beautiful don't you agree?" The audience agreed. But, in 2021, *Far Out* magazine described this reworking of *Yesterday* as "excruciating and cheesy ... a painful, unaware cringe-fest." Whatever the verdict, Paul was gaining exposure to new audiences who had tuned in to the Grammys to see their favourite rap and nu metal artists.

Disappointingly, *Chaos and Creation in the Backyard* did not win any of the Grammy awards it was nominated for.

In March 2006, Paul entered Hog Hill Mill studio to record five tracks for his 2007 album *Memory Almost Full*: *Ever Present Past*; *Mr. Bellamy*; *Gratitude*; *Nod Your Head*; and *In Private*. Four of the tracks were set to tape during a six-hour creative burst.

Between April and June 2006, Paul recorded two further tracks: *See Your Sunshine*; and *Why So Blue?*

Paul and Heather separate

On 1 March 2006, Heather and Paul flew to Canada to protest the annual slaughter of 320,000 harp seal pups whose skins are used for fur in the fashion industry. Clad in bright orange thermal jumpsuits, the couple posed with a cuddly seal pup on an ice floe off Newfoundland and Labrador in the Atlantic Ocean.

Despite this public show of togetherness, Paul and Heather's incompatibility had reached breaking point.

On 3 April 2006, Heather underwent revision surgery on her left leg to reattach muscle tissue to the bone. Her spokesperson told the media that Heather had been experiencing discomfort in her leg in recent weeks. She said that Heather had been putting off having the operation as she would need six months to recover fully, including use of a wheelchair for two months. The spokesperson added that Paul had been "very supportive."

Following the operation, Heather recuperated at home while Paul had a brief holiday alone in France. During this break, Paul reflected on the couple's future. Paul admired Heather's campaigning spirit, but her intensity and assertiveness was becoming overbearing. Her free-speaking nature was on full display during a March 2006 interview with CNN during the seal cull protest. Heather admitted, in a 2015 interview: "I say what I think. If I think something is wrong, I'll say it. If I wasn't that type of person we'd still be married now."

During four days between 25-29 April 2006 the marriage reached a crisis point. Leaked extracts from later divorce documents revealed a series of rows. This culminated, on Saturday 29 April, in a realisation that the marriage had irretrievably broken down and the couple separated.

New living arrangements were agreed, with Heather selling her Thames Reach office property to Paul for £560,000 and Heather purchasing Pandora's Barn, a barn conversion near Peasmarsh, for £550,000.

On 18 May, a formal announcement of separation and joint statement was issued. It stated: "Having tried exceptionally hard to make our relationship work given the daily pressures surrounding us, it is with sadness that we have decided to go our separate ways…. Our parting is amicable and both of us still care about each other very much but have found it increasingly difficult to maintain a normal relationship with constant intrusion into our private lives, and we have actively tried to protect the privacy of our child."

On 18 June, Paul's held his 64th birthday barbecue celebration at Peasmarsh. Heather did not attend, but Bea did, along with Mike McCartney and Paul's children Heather, James, Mary, and Stella. As a gift, Paul's grandchildren recorded at Abbey Road a special version of *When I'm 64*.

The UK tabloids unload

Within weeks of the separation announcement, UK tabloid newspapers published headline-grabbing allegations about Heather's pre-1993 life.

The dam broke on 6 June 2006 when pictures of Heather posing naked in 1988 for a German sex-manual *Die Freuden der Liebe* (*The Joys of Love*) were made public. Heather stated the book was an educational "lovers' guide to caring relationships."

Sensationalist stories about Heather life in the late 1980s and early 1990s followed. They included allegations, in the *News of the World* on Sunday 11 June, by former escorts, that Heather had been a "party girl" with Arab princes and businesspeople in London and across Europe.

On 11 June, Heather's lawyers "strongly denied" the *News of the World's* allegations, stating: "These are not new stories and were refuted by her lawyers four years ago when first raised. The sources clearly are unreliable persons who have been paid for these stories. The timing of the article is clearly designed to cause maximum hurt to Heather, her husband and family at this sensitive time."

On 24 October, Heather's lawyers announced plans to sue the *Evening Standard*, *Daily Mail* and *The Sun* over "false, damaging and immensely upsetting statements" in stories about her divorce from Paul. The following day, *The Sun* responded with an article asking: "Come on Heather, what exactly did we get wrong? Is it that you're a [in boxes to tick if untrue] Hooker, Liar, Porn Star, Fantasist Trouble Maker, Shoplifter."

The timing was disastrous for sales of Heather's book, *Life Balance: The Essential Keys to a Lifetime of Well Being* (2006), written with Ben Noakes.

Concerned about the effect of these stories on Heather, who was said to be "in pieces," and Bea, Paul phoned Heather up to six times a day to provide emotional support. She assured Paul the allegations were untrue.

Paul termed the media attacks on Heather "a witch-hunt." On his website, he wrote: "It has been suggested that (Heather) married me for money and there is not an ounce of truth in this. She is a very generous woman who spends most of her time trying to help others in greater need than herself. I'm very sad to see that some insensitive people would choose a moment like this to spread these vicious rumours."

It was discovered later that *The Sun* and *News of the World*, part of Rupert Murdoch's News Group Newspapers (NGN), appeared to obtain some of their stories on Heather and Paul's relationship through illegally hacking Heather's voicemails. In July 2019, the High Court in London awarded Heather 'substantial' damages from NGN for this invasion of privacy.

The police also later reported in December 2011 that Paul's phone had been illegally hacked around the time of his divorce.

Paul files for divorce

During June 2006, Paul and Heather's lawyers tried to reach an amicable out-of-court divorce settlement.

Fiona Shackleton (1956-), styled by the media the 'steel magnolia' as she combined firmness and charm, represented Paul. She had acted for Prince Charles in his 1996 divorce from Princess Diana, who received a £17 million lump sum settlement plus £400,000 a year. Heather engaged Anthony Julius (1956-), a barrister from Mishcon de Reya who had represented Princess Diana in 1996.

Negotiations failed to reach a financial settlement acceptable to both parties and the divorce became acrimonious and contested.

On 9 July 2006, the *Sunday Mirror* published an article in which it published extracts allegedly from a 25 June private phone conversation between Paul and Stella. During the call Paul's daughter made unflattering comments about Heather. The newspaper alleged that Heather had bugged Paul's phone. This she denied. Given later court judgements against phone-hacking by the UK's tabloids, it is unclear who was responsible.

But this was a breaking point for Paul. He stopped wearing his wedding ring in public and, on 17 July, instructed his lawyers to file a Petition for Divorce on grounds of unreasonable behaviour by Heather.

In September, Paul told friends: "I don't know how to deal with it all. It's been the most terrible time for me and my family."

On 13 October, Heather's lawyers counter-filed for divorce on the grounds of unreasonable behaviour by Paul. In a Cross-Petition, details of which found their way to the press, Heather claimed that Paul had abused drugs and alcohol, been possessive and jealous, had, on occasions, been violent, had been unsympathetic to her disability and had not protected her from intrusive media attention and false press claims.

On 18 October, the *Daily Mail* published details of these leaked allegations, which were also reported on UK television news. Heather and her lawyers denied being involved in the leak.

On 18 October, Paul's lawyers vigorously rejected these allegations. And on 24 October they received public support from Geoff Baker, who told the *News of the World*: "To brand Paul a wife-beater is the most absurd claim anyone can make. I was with them for four years when she says a lot of this took place. On my son's life, I never saw him lay a finger on her (Heather) or throw abuse at her."

On 25 October, Paul's lawyers issued an Amended Petition setting out counter allegations against Heather of verbal abuse, extreme jealousy, false accusations of violence, leaking private phone calls and, throughout the marriage, a consistent inability to tell the truth.

Ecce Cor Meum

Personnel: The Academy of St. Martin in the Fields, conducted by Gavin Greenaway; London Voice, directed by Terry Edwards; Kate Royal (soprano); Colm Carey (organ); Mark Law (piccolo trumpet); Boys of Magdalen College Choir, Oxford; and Boys of King's College Choir, Cambridge.

Producer: John Fraser

Recording: 13-17 March 2006 (at EMI Studio, Abbey Road, London); organ recorded at the Tower of London.

Release date: 25 September 2006

Highest chart placings: UK Classical Charts: 2; US Classical Charts 2

Length: 56:50 minutes

Tracks: 1. *I. Spiritus* 12:00; 2. *II. Gratia* 10:50; 3. *Interlude (Lament)* 3:56; 4. *III. Musica* 15:14; and 5. *IV. Ecce Cor Meum* 14:50.

In spring 1997, Anthony Smith (1938-2021), president (1988-2005) of Magdalen College, Oxford University, invited Paul to write a choral work for the opening of a new auditorium. Smith envisioned "a choral piece which could be sung by young people the world over - something equivalent to Handel's *Messiah*."

Formerly a BBC television producer, Smith had worked with The Scaffold, the comedy, poetry and music band in which Paul's brother Mike performed between 1964-73.

Paul also knew the Magdalen College choir's director, Bill Ives (1948-). As a member of the King's Singers, Ives had been part of the Frog Chorus which sang on Paul's 1984 hit single *We All Stand Together.*

Paul and Linda visited the College and attended several of the choir's daily services. Excited that Smith "wanted something different …. (which) allows some latitude, it means I don't have to fit myself into any sort of box," Paul accepted the prestigious – although daunting and unpaid - commission.

Linda's death caused the project to be put on hold. A new Grove Auditorium opened in 1999 to a premiere of *Prometheus,* a film-poem by Tony Harrison (1937-). But Smith and the Oxford University Music Society encouraged Paul to persevere. In November 1998, Paul visited Magdalen College to attend an All Souls Day service reading of Linda's name in remembrance. He agreed to resume work on the commission.

In developing the new piece, Paul drew inspiration from a Latin inscription *Ecce Cor Meum* (Behold My Heart), he had noticed in May 2000 beneath a statue of the Crucifixion of Jesus while narrating a John Tavener concert in New York's Church of St. Ignatius Loyola. Recalling the Latin he had studied at school, Paul translated the inscription as: "Let me show you what's in my heart, the things that are important to me." *Ecce Cor Meum* would be Paul's spiritual confession.

During summer 2001, Paul composed the music on a synthesiser, assisted by David Matthews. He visited Magdalen College, Oxford, staying at the president's home and chatting with students in the college bar. Heather accompanied Paul on some of these visits.

In November 2001, the Magdalen College choir, conducted by Bill Ives, performed an early version of the work in the Magdalen College chapel and at the Sheldonian Theatre, Oxford.

Paul did not realise until this live performance that children were unable to deliver long sustained passages. He noticed that: "the solo treble couldn't come on for the second half – I think I'd used him up in the first half!" Paul told the audience this was still a work in progress.

Over the next four years, assisted by producer John Fraser, Paul reworked the piece, giving some of the previously choral sections to the orchestra. Paul stated, this meant: "the orchestra has plenty of nice passages to shine while the voices are resting."

John Fraser recorded *Ecce Cor Meum* between 13-17 March 2006 at Abbey Road studios. It was performed by the Academy of St. Martin-in-the-Fields (London), conducted by Gavin Greenaway (1964-), London Voices, the choirs of Magdalen College, Oxford, and King's College, Cambridge, and the English soprano Kate Royal (1979-). The organ was recorded at the Tower of London.

The songs

Ecce Cor Meum is an oratorio (a narrative musical work for orchestra and voices) made up of four movements and an interlude. Typically, a composer writes an oratorio by finding a text to set to music. But Paul, unaware of this, wrote the music first and then put his own prose to it. He stated: "it meant that it was a bit less conventional." He asked the Latin tutor at Magdalen College to translate his text into Latin and then selected the phrases he liked.

Ecce Cor Meum is infused by Paul's faith in a benevolent spirit and the importance of love. This faith came to Paul after surviving a road accident when a van transporting the Beatles skidded off the road in a blizzard and went down an embankment. Unable to get the van back on the road, the group asked each other: "What are we going to do?" One of them said: "Well something will happen." This became one of the guiding philosophies in Paul's life.

I. ***Spiritus*** **is** a plea for guidance on the powerful emotion of love. It begins with sopranos singing: "lead us to love ... teach us to find our love." A faster section follows, with menacing drums. The choir then sings: "take love away and we are lost." The movement concludes with the plea: "strengthen my love, keep my truth, make my soul blessed."

II. ***Gratia*** is a response to the first movement. It contains a lyrical McCartney melody and a soaring soprano by Kate Royal. With a nod to the Beatles, it includes the lines: "Life aboard this fast revolver still remains a magic mystery."

The ***Interlude (Lament)*** for solo oboe and wordless choral accompaniment is a tear-jerking pastoral section. Paul stated it was: "one of the things that got me working again (after Linda's death) because it was really a lament for her ... I vividly recall sitting ... at the computer, writing that piece and just weeping." The oboe is played by David Theodore, who had played earlier on Paul's *Beautiful Night* (1997).

III. ***Musica*** begins slowly, with the choir calling on music to: "lift us from sorrow, lead us to the light." The movement builds in tempo and intensity as basses introduce a new theme: "light our way ... lift up our hearts." This is followed by a hymn-like melody in which the choir sings "behold this heart of mine ... help to reveal my inner light."

IV. ***Ecce Cor Meum*** concludes with an attestation to the inner joy and revelation brought by music. It opens with the phrase "*Ecce cor meum ...* here in my music I show you my heart." The movement ends with: " although life sometimes is hard. we still pull through ... nothing else remains."

Release and reception

Ecce Cor Meum was released on CD in the UK and US on the EMI Classics label on 25 September 2006. It was not released on vinyl. The

CD reached number 2 in the classical music charts in both the UK and US and sold 60,000 units.

The work is accessible and melodic, with beautiful choral, string and brass passages that work well in a church setting. However, classical music critics provided mixed reviews:

- The *Daily Telegraph's* Geoffrey Norris (1947-) found its "musical substance ... not strong enough to support the piece's expanse."
- *Gramophone's* David Gutman termed it a "pseudo-classical ... creakily Victorian four-parter (with interlude), both short-winded and constipated, hopping disconcertingly from one episode to the next in shades of grey." He found the first movement "processional," the third a "sclerotic muddle" and the fourth "cramped albeit ... melodic ... in the vein of John Tavener." But he praised the second movement for: "it's pretty McCartneyesque melodic squibs ... this is the bit one would expect to be aired on Classic FM."
- The *Wall Street Journal's* Barrymore Laurence Scherer (1950-) was more positive. Noting the influences of Tavener, Gabriel Fauré (1845-1924) and Giovanni Gabrielli (1558-1613), he found: "the score's stylistic homogeneity shows an advance over the greater eclecticism of his previous concert works, and the engaging quality - the voice - is pure McCartney."

On 3 May 2007, listeners of Classic FM awarded *Ecce Cor Meum* the Classical Brit Award for the best classical album of the year at a ceremony in the Royal Albert Hall.

On 3 November 2006, *Ecce Cor Meum* received its UK premiere at the same venue. It was captured on a DVD released on 4 February 2008 and which includes a behind-the-scenes documentary on the making of the work.

Ecce Cor Meum was premiered in the US on 14 November 2006 at a sold-out Carnegie Hall in New York City: the concert was simulcast over public radio and webcast.

Between October 2007 and November 2008, *Ecce Cor Meum* was performed in church and concert halls in Canada, England, France,

Germany, Ireland, Latvia, New Zealand and the US. This included a 1 May 2008 concert in Liverpool Cathedral.

A guitar concerto

In early May 2006, shortly after his separation from Heather, Paul began work at Hog Hill Mill studio on a Spanish-style guitar concerto with Carlos Bonell (1949-), a renowned English classical guitarist of Spanish descent.

The working process involved Paul presenting passages he had composed on his guitar and, for strings and brass, on his computer. Bonell then transcribed this on musical staff paper and played the piece's more complex passages. The pair also improvised together.

According to Keith Smith, Paul's recording engineer and instrument technician since the 1980s, during the months following his separation, Paul worked at Hog Hill Mill most days on this and other projects.

On 4 May 2007, Bonell visited Hog Hill Mill to continue work on the concerto. According to Bonell, the piece had elements of baroque and Spanish music, but also passages that sounded like the Beatles. This recording session was featured in a June 2007 cover article in the *New Yorker* magazine.

Despite Bonell speaking favourably of the piece, on which he and Paul continued to work until 2009, the guitar concerto was never released. Two versions were recorded: one with classical acoustic guitar and another with electric guitar by Jeff Beck and orchestra.

The Space Within Us

On 13 November 2006, *The Space Within US* DVD was released. It reached number 3 in the US Music Videos Chart. A Blu-ray version, with 5.1 digital surround sound, was released on 18 November 2008. No separate CD or double-vinyl album was issued. It sold 225,000 units.

Mark Haefeli directed the DVD. Haefeli had been responsible also for *Back in the U.S.* and *Paul McCartney in Red Square*. The DVD shows Paul and his band performing 28 songs on 12 November 2005 at Anaheim, California. The setlist includes one deep cut from Paul's solo career, *Too*

Many People (1971), and four from the Beatles' era: *Till There Was You; I'll Get You; For No One;* and *I Will.*

The songs are interspersed with comments on Paul's influence by the 1993-2001 42nd US President Bill Clinton, Apple CEO Steve Jobs (1955-2011), film director Cameron Crowe, music producer Phil Ramone (1934-2013), jazz keyboardist Herbie Hancock (1940-) and rock guitarist-singer Lenny Kravitz (1964-). Academics also discuss how certain chord structures in Paul's music affect listeners emotionally.

There are crowd reaction shots of fans of all ages, including US actor Jack Nicholson (1937-), Foo Fighters' drummer Dave Grohl (1969-) and US record producer Rick Rubin (1963-). Paul is also filmed interacting backstage with fans and his team of roadies and stage staff.

The DVD's live tracks are: 1. *Magical Mystery Tour;* 2. *Flaming Pie;* 3. *Let Me Roll It;* 4. *Drive My Car;* 5. *Till There Was You;* 6. *I'll Get You;* 7. *Eleanor Rigby;* 8. *Maybe I'm Amazed;* 9. *Got To Get You Into My Life;* 10. *Fine Line;* 11. *I Will;* 12. *I'll Follow The Sun;* 13. *Good Day Sunshine;* 14. *For No One;* 15. *Hey Jude* (fragment); 16. *Fixing a Hole;* 17. *Penny Lane;* 18. *Too Many People;* 19. *She Came in Through the Bathroom Window;* 20. *Let It Be;* 21. *English Tea;* 22. *I've Got a Feeling;* 23. *Follow Me;* 24. *Jenny Wren;* 25. *Helter Skelter;* 26. *Yesterday;* 27. *Get Back;* and 28. *Please Please Me.* (The soundcheck songs are: *Whole Lotta Shakin' Goin' On; Friends to Go;* and *How Kind of You*).

The Anaheim concert had spectacular staging, with illuminated squares on the floor, Paul's piano on a rising section (leaving a hole into which Paul accidentally fell during one show) and a wall of video screens. In February 2006, Roy Bennett, the tour's set designer, won the touring industry's set designer of the year award.

The Space Within Us DVD/Blu-ray shows Paul and his battle-hardened band at the height of their powers. The sound is fuller than on *Back in the U.S.* and the vocal harmonies tighter. They deliver particularly powerful versions of *I've Got a Feeling, Too Many People, Helter Skelter* and *Get Back.*

A unique element of the filmed show was Paul performing *English Tea* to both the 17,000 audience in the Arrowhead Pond at Anaheim and, via satellite, to US and Russian astronauts aboard the International Space Station which was orbiting the earth 220 miles above.

The Beatles *Love* project

On 20 November 2006, the Beatles *Love* was released: a soundtrack album of the Cirque du Soleil's *The Beatles "Love"* show at the Mirage Hotel, in Las Vegas. The show combined stunning visuals, dancing and acrobatics with remixed and mashed-up Beatles music.

The project's genesis was a meeting in 2000 between George Harrison and the Cirque founder, Guy Laliberté (1959-). Both were fans of film, comedy, theatrics and Formula 1 motor racing. Guy visited Friar Park and George asked: "Do you think there's anything that you could do with the Beatles' music?" Guy proposed a Cirque du Soleil theatre-in-the-round, multi-sensory spectacle combining Beatles' music, acrobatics and theatre.

George and Guy convinced Paul, Ringo and Yoko Ono (representing the Lennon estate) to support the project. After George's death in November 2001, they agreed to take forward the work as a tribute.

Cirque du Soleil's initially envisaged having live musicians play the Beatles' music. But Apple Records insisted that only officially recorded music could be used.

In 2003, George Martin, assisted by his producer son Giles Martin and the Abbey Road remix engineer Paul Hicks, agreed to trawl through Beatles' master tapes to assemble a soundtrack.

Over two years, behind closed doors, the Martins and Hicks mashed together both released and unreleased Beatles recordings to create a 78-minute Beatles mix tape for the show. As Giles noted: "in true Beatles tradition, tracks were reversed, sped up and slowed down."

Love contains pieces from 130 commercially released and demo recordings of the Beatles. For example:

- Ringo's dynamic drums on *Tomorrow Never Knows* are mashed together with George Harrison's elegant vocals on *Within and Without You* to produce a new dance-floor friendly track.
- *Get Back* includes the opening chord from *A Hard Day's Night*, drum and guitar solos from *The End*, percussion from *Sgt. Pepper's Lonely Hearts Club Band* and a section from *A Day in the Life*.

- *Yesterday* includes guitar work from *Blackbird*.
- *While My Guitar Gently Weeps* uses an unreleased early Harrison vocal take, with a new string arrangement added by George Martin. Recorded at Abbey Road 37 years after the original song, it was George Martin's final Beatles string session.

Cirque du Soleil's theatrical director Dominic Champagne (1963-) secured approval from Yoko Ono, Olivia Harrison (representing the Harrison estate), Ringo and Paul on how each song would be theatrically presented. This is chronicled in *All Together Now: The Beatles Love Cirque du Soleil,* a documentary film released on DVD in 2008.

The Beatles Love Cirque du Soleil show opened at the Mirage on 30 June 2006. Paul, Ringo, Yoko, Olivia and George's son Dhani and John's first wife Cynthia (1939-2015) and oldest son Julian attended, sometimes singing along. The audience reception was ecstatic.

Nearly two decades later *The Beatles "Love"* was still being staged at the Mirage to packed houses.

The soundtrack album *Love* was released on 20 November 2006 as a 26-track CD, on two-disc vinyl and on DVD in 5.1 surround sound to an appreciative critical response.

The UK's *The Guardian* rock critic Alexis Petridis (1971-) gave *Love* a four stars (out of five) rating. He stated: "Overlaying sections of different Beatles songs to create new pieces of music is ... controversial but the results are largely fantastic."

Love reached number 3 in the UK, spending 15 weeks in the charts, and number 4 in the US Billboard 200. In February 2008, at the 50th Grammy Awards, it was awarded Best Compilation Soundtrack Album and Best Surround Sound Album.

2007: Moving Forward Reflectively

Key events

January-February: Recording for *Memory Almost Full* at Hog Hill Mill and RAK.

22 March: Paul joins Hear Music label.

2 May: *Ecce Cor Meum* wins best album at the Classical Brit Awards.

30 May: Paul's solo and Wings catalogue becomes available on *iTunes*.

4-5 June: *Memory Almost Full* album is released, followed by *Dance Tonight* as a single.

7 June: Paul performs at the Electric Ballroom, London.

13 June: Paul performs at the Highline Ballroom, New York; on **27 June** at Amoeba Music, Los Angeles; and on **5 July** at the *iTunes* Festival in London.

28 August: *Nod Your Head* is released as a single in the UK and US.

25 September: The various artists album *Goin' Home: A Tribute to Fats Domino* is released. It includes the track *I Want To Walk You Home*, with Paul on vocals.

Autumn: Paul begins a relationship with Nancy Shevell.

22 October: Paul performs in Paris at L'Olympia Bruno Coquatrix and on **25 October** at the Electric Proms at the Roundhouse, London.

5 November: *Ever Present Past* is released as a single in the UK.

12 November: *The McCartney Years* DVD box set is released.

11 December: *Memory Almost Full* receives three Grammy nominations.

December: Sessions begin for The Fireman album *Electric Arguments*.

Paul began 2007 with a holiday in Jamaica, followed by recording sessions, in the second half of January and first week of February, at Hog Hill Mill and RAK studio in London for *Memory Almost Full*.

Paul and Heather's divorce proceedings continued throughout 2007, becoming tetchy, with efforts at mediation failing and a court hearing being set for February 2008.

In August 2007, Paul began a relationship with Nancy Shevell (1959-), an American business executive.

Professionally, Paul changed music label and management team during 2007. He joined the Starbucks-owned Hear Music label who released, on 4 June, his new album *Memory Almost Full*.

Paul promoted the new album extensively though a series of filmed and recorded boutique shows at small venues between June and October. These included the Electric Ballroom, London (7 June), Amoeba Music, Los Angeles (27 June) and the Electric Proms in London (25 October).

On 25 September, *Goin' Home: A Tribute to Fats Domino,* a various artists' tribute album was released, featuring Paul singing the 1959 Fats Domino R&B song *I Want to Walk You Home*.

On 12 November, *The McCartney Years* DVD box set was released.

Difficult divorce proceedings

In 2007, Paul and Heather's divorce proceedings became increasingly fraught.

Between December 2006 and January 2007, Heather and Paul's lawyers failed to reach an out-of-court settlement. Heather sought £50 million of assets but Paul offered £20 million.

On 28 February 2007, Paul and Heather attended a week-long preliminary hearing at London's Royal Courts of Justice: Paul's first appearance there since the 31 December 1970 case to dissolve the Beatles' partnership agreement.

There then followed, in mid-June, a 3-day hearing in Sussex on shared custody and care arrangements for Bea. The court ruled that Bea would live with her mother but spend an equal amount of time with her father.

Paul provided Heather with £3 million to buy Pean's Wood, a seven-bedroomed secluded house, with a gym, staff cottage and stables set in 14 acres. Situated in Robertsbridge village, East Sussex, 13 miles from Peasmarsh, the house was near Bea's Preparatory School. Unlike Paul's children with Linda, Bea was to be educated at private schools.

In October 2007, Paul's lawyers tried to again settle the case at a mediation hearing. They offered Heather an undisclosed settlement on condition that both parties sign a confidentiality agreement to not speak publicly or write about their marriage. Heather and her lawyers rejected this. Consequently, a court hearing was set for February 2008.

Heather's PR adviser and lawyers counselled her to avoid television interviews ahead of the court hearing. But, on 30 October 2007, Heather appeared on the UK GMTV breakfast show. She denounced the media, stating: "I've had a worse press than a paedophile or murderer ... been called a whore and a liar ... and I've done nothing but charity for 20 years." She urged viewers to boycott tabloid newspapers and made controversial and misleading statements about Paul.

The following day, Heather's PR adviser, Phil Hall (1955-), a former editor of the *News of the World* before 2000, resigned. On 8 November, so did her lawyers, Mishcon de Reya.

A new manager and record label

The music industry faced new challenges in the 2000s from the rise of internet MP3 file-sharing and digital streaming: Apple launched the *iTunes* Store in 2003 and Spotify began in 2006. Between 1990 and 2000, annual CD album sales in the US increased fourfold to 950 million units. By 2010, MP3 downloads and digital streaming caused them to slump to 230 million. Traditional music distribution retailers struggled: Tower Records closed its last store in December 2006.

Paul stated in 2007, in a financial submission during his divorce proceedings: "I have created new work (since 2002) which, though critically acclaimed, has not been profitable." His music-related income came now overwhelmingly from touring and royalties from past songs.

Throughout his career from 1962, Paul had been signed to EMI: releasing his records in the UK on Parlophone and in the US on Capitol. By 2006, he had become dissatisfied with EMI's outdated marketing campaigns and disappointing sales. Paul noted that, like other traditional labels, EMI was "puzzled as to what's happening in its industry." David Kahne went further, likening the major labels to "the dinosaurs sitting around discussing the asteroid. They know it's going to hit. They don't know when and where it's coming from. But it's sort of hit already, with *iTunes*, and all of that."

With CD sales dwindling, EMI posted losses of £260 million in 2006-07. In September 2006, Apple Records issued a lawsuit for non-payment of Beatles' royalties. This was settled in June 2009 for £56 million.

In February 2007, Capitol Records merged with Virgin Records America to form Capitol Music Group, and Capitol's CEO Andrew Slater resigned. In August 2007, Terra Firma Capital Partners, a private equity firm, took over EMI. This prompted the departure of some artists, including Radiohead.

These developments persuaded Paul it was time to change management team and record label. He asked Stella, now head of her own successful fashion and perfume businesses, to probe her contacts for suggestions on a potential new manager. One of Stella's magazine editors, who had worked with the Icelandic art-rock singer Björk (1965-), recommended Scott Rodger, Björk's manager since 1995. As head of the Quest agency, Rodger also managed Arcade Fire, a critically acclaimed Canadian indie rock band.

Paul met Scott and they got on well. Scott agreed to serve as consultant for the rollout of Paul's new *Memory Almost Full* album. He was the first person external to MPL Communications that Paul had worked with and it was not long before Scott Rodger became Paul's new manager.

EMI offered Paul £24 million for a new four-album deal, but Paul rejected this. On 12 March 2007, he signed to Hear Music: a new label co-owned by Concord Music Group and Starbucks Entertainment, an arm of the Starbucks coffee chain.

Kahne had suggested Hear Music and Paul was impressed by the new label's enthusiasm and innovative ideas about ways to promote his work. Hear Music agreed to issue *Memory Almost Full* as the label's first release and to distribute it through both traditional music retail outlets and through Starbucks coffee shops worldwide.

In a November 2007 interview with the *Chicago Tribune,* Paul stated: "People had been telling me the last couple of years the way I was selling most of my records was in Best Buy and Wal-Mart … in supermarkets. So it was more logical to me to do it in Starbucks, because it has a musical connection."

Speaking via satellite at Starbucks' March 2007 annual meeting, Paul said: "It is a new world now and people are thinking of new ways to reach the people, and for me that has always been my aim."

Memory Almost Full

Personnel: Paul McCartney (vocals, keyboards, bass guitar, mandolin, guitars, mellotron, drums, percussion, vibraphone, flugelhorn, celeste, organ, tambourine, harpsichord, xylophone and autoharp); Abe Laboriel Jr. (drums, percussion and backing vocals on tracks 4, 5, 8, 9, 10 and 11); Rusty Anderson (guitars and backing vocals on tracks 4, 5, 8, 9, 10 and 11); Paul 'Wix' Wickens (keyboards and backing vocals on tracks 4, 5, 8, 9, 10 and 11); and Brian Ray (guitars and backing vocals on tracks 4, 5, 9, 10 and 11).

Producer: David Kahne (some engineering at Abbey Road was by Geoff Emerick and Paul Hicks).

Recording sessions: February 2004 (Abbey Road Studios, London), September 2003 and March to July 2006 (Hog Hill Mill studio) and January to February 2007 (Hog Hill Mill studio and RAK Studios, London)

Release date: 4 June 2007

Highest chart placings: UK: 5; US: 3.

Length: 41:59 minutes

Tracks: 1. *Dance Tonight* 2:54; 2. *Ever Present Past* 2:57; 3. *See Your Sunshine* 3:20; 4. *Only Mama Knows* 4:17; 5. *You Tell Me* 3:15; 6. *Mr. Bellamy* 3:39; 7. *Gratitude* 3:19; 8. *Vintage Clothes* 2:22; 9. *That Was Me* 2:38; 10. *Feet in the Clouds* 3:24; 11. *House of Wax* 4:59; 12. *The End of the End* 2:57; and 13. *Nod Your Head* 1:58.

Memory Almost Full had a long gestation period, with recording taking place in discrete sessions across 2003-04, 2006 and 2007.

In September 2003, Paul and his touring band recorded nine demos at Hog Hill Mill studio. Six progressed to full recording at Abbey Road in February 2004. Paul then filed these recordings away during 2004-05 while he completed *Chaos and Creation in the Backyard*.

In late 2005, with *Chaos* released and a Grammy nomination received, Paul stated: "I realised I had this album (*Memory*) to go back to and finish off. So I got it out to listen to it again, wondering if I would enjoy it, but actually I really loved it."

Between March and July 2006, Paul added instrumental overdubs at Hog Hill Mill studio and recorded six further tracks, playing all instruments. In January-February 2007, Paul recorded the track *222* at Hog Hill Mill and *Dance Tonight* at RAK Studios, London.

Additional mixing for the album was conducted at AIR Studios, London, Henson Studios, Los Angeles and David Kahne's SeeSquared studio in New York. Most mixing was done by Kahne at Hog Hill Mill. Mastering was by Bob Ludwig (1945-).

Paul explained his burst in creative activity in 2005-06 as an emotional outlet during a difficult period in his personal life: "Music is a great healer and it's a sort of therapy. Often if you are going through something difficult to get into your music is a great thing."

The songs

Memory Almost Full, with a running time of 42 minutes, was another focused album. Its deluxe edition includes three bonus tracks: *In Private* 2:08; *Why So Blue* 3:11; and *222* 3:38. Nine other songs were recorded but not included.

David Kahne described *Memory Almost Full* as: "Beatle-ish and classic McCartney-ish, but very contemporary. There's a timeless quality to it." For Paul, it was: "A very personal record and a lot of it is retrospective, drawing from memories ... from being a kid, from Liverpool and from summers gone. The album is evocative, emotional, rocking."

Tracks 1, 2, 3, 6, 7, 12 and 13 feature Paul on all instruments, while tracks 4, 5, 8, 9, 10 and 11 also feature members of his tour band.

1. **Dance Tonight**, recorded in January-February 2007, was the final song recorded for *Memory Almost Full*. Like the iconic riff by Peter Buck (1956-) on R.E.M.'s *Losing My Religion*, the song arose from Paul trying out a recently purchased mandolin. Ahead of a December 2006 meeting at the MPL office in Soho, Paul visited a favourite guitar shop and was shown a left-handed mandolin. He bought it and had to figure out how to play it, stating: "I found one chord, then another, then a real strange chord. I still don't know what it is, but it sounded great."

In his kitchen, Paul strummed a basic three-chord (F, C and B flat) pattern and began stomping. He recalled: "I start singing, 'Everybody gonna dance tonight.' Every time my little girl (Bea) would come running in and start dancing, so I fell in love with this song and with the mandolin. The song kind of wrote itself."

Kahne kept the instrumentation sparse to emphasise Paul's mandolin and his stomping on a piece of wood. An infectious, singalong song, with whistling, Paul later performed *Dance Tonight* in a duet with the Australian pop singer, Kylie Minogue (1968-), on 24 December for Jools Holland's 31 December 2007 New Year's Eve UK television show *Hootenanny*. *Dance Tonight* became a staple of Paul's live sets, with Abe supporting on whistling.

2. ***Ever Present Past***, recorded by Paul at Hog Hill Mill studio in March 2006, is a mid-tempo pop song that reflects on how past times have flown by so quickly. It builds to an infectious ear worm chorus about "the things I think I did when I was a kid." The song began life in September 2004 as a folk song called *Perfect Lover*. Paul and David Kahne developed a new arrangement with Beatles-sounding instrumentation, including a harpsichord and clavioline.

3. ***See Your Sunshine***, recorded by Paul at Hog Hill Mill between April-July 2006, is an upbeat R&B song inspired by Heather Mills. As Paul later stated: "It was written during a good time with Heather. I didn't want to deny those times." The lyrics read: "Step out in front of me baby … they want to see your sunshine."

Godrich rejected the song, but Kahne persevered, working with Paul to produce a slick, 80s-style song dominated by Paul's multi-tracked vocals and rumbling bass. Kahne stated that the track features "Paul playing counter-melody bass at his absolute best."

4. ***Only Mama Knows*** is a raucous rocker recorded live at Abbey Road by Paul and his band in February 2004, with overdubs added in January-February 2007. The instrumentation has echoes of Wings' *Jet* and rockers from *Off the Ground*. The song's lyrics are based on Paul imagining the predicament of a child abandoned by her mother "in the transit lounge of a dirty airport town."

In *The Lyrics* (2021), Paul explained that the inspiration came from a true story from his childhood of a friend who was adopted as a baby and brought up, with his brother, in an orphanage. Paul stated: "He would always wonder why his mother had left him … (but) sort of knew … she'd been knocked up by some guy … passing through."

5. ***You Tell Me*** was recorded by Paul and his backing band in February 2004, with Paul adding overdubs in March-April 2006. Paul wrote the song during a summer stay at his Pintail property on Long Island in the early 2000s after seeing a bright red cardinal coming out of a tree. This set his mind back to golden, but hazy, memories of past summers when the skies were blue, and it never rained.

With its acoustic guitar and continental-vibe, *You Tell Me* is reminiscent of *London Town* era Paul. Paul sings in a high key and his band members add soothing backing vocals and electric guitar breaks.

In *The Lyrics* (2021), Paul states that David Gilmour and Paul Weller sent Paul messages saying: "Wow I like that one." Kahne considered it: "maybe the saddest song Paul's ever written."

6. **Mr. Bellamy** was recorded at Hog Hill Mill in March 2006 during a day session that generated four tracks. It is a 10cc-style 'pop opera' song with interesting changes in tempo and story-based lyrics. The song's subject, the suicidal Mr Bellamy, is sitting on top of a building and the rescue team below are trying to talk him down.

While it has been pointed out that Mister Bellamy is an anagram of "Mills betray me," it is a stretch to believe the song is about Paul's relationship with Heather despite the line: "Nobody here to … interfere with my plans."

When asked in 2007, "Who is Mr. Bellamy?", Paul responded, "Well I never know who these people are. Who are Chuck and Dave from *When I'm 64*? Who is Eleanor Rigby? Who are Desmond and Molly from *Ob-La-Di, Ob-La-Da*? I don't know, I just make them up."

Paul had asked Radiohead's Thom Yorke (1968-) to collaborate on this track. But, while Yorke liked the song, he declined, stating: "The piano playing involved two hands doing things separately. I don't have that skill available. I said to (Paul), 'I strum piano, that's it.'"

With its adventurous instrumentation and the different voices adopted by Paul during the song, *Mr. Bellamy* is a standout track.

7. **Gratitude** was recorded by Paul in March 2006 at Hog Hill Mill. A piano-driven gospel-style song with raw vocals by Paul, it has been interpreted variously as a tribute to Linda or as a sarcastic take on Paul's crumbling relationship with Heather. But Paul stated: "I was just thinking of how much there is to be grateful for in life."

In his gritty, screaming Little Richard voice, Paul sings: "I'm so grateful for everything you've ever given me … I should stop loving you …but I don't want to lock my heart away."

8. ***Vintage Clothes*** was recorded in February 2004 with Abe, Rusty and Wix, with overdubs added by Paul in March-April 2006. It is a spritely and sophisticated pop song with frequent changes of tempo and Paul plays low distorted mellotron notes. It is the start of a four-song medley of nostalgic songs.

The song begins with "don't live in the past ... don't hold on to something that changes fast," but concludes, "what went out is coming back." Paul explained that the vintage clothes in the song are clothes he wore in the 1960s and had kept. For Paul, the message of the song is: "Wear the clothes from the past but move on mentally."

9. ***That Was Me***, also recorded in February 2004 by Paul and his band, segues in from *Vintage Clothes*. It is a rockabilly reflection by Paul on his past, covering: a seaside holiday; scout camp; school plays; walking in bluebell woods; and performing in the Cavern Club. Interest is maintained by octave shifts between verses.

10. ***Feet in the Clouds***, recorded in February 2004, is about Paul's schooldays. A complex pop track, *Feet in the Clouds* features well-arranged backing vocals and vocoder effects.

Paul stated: "I had a really motley group of teachers at the Liverpool Institute High School for Boys. Some of them were complete maniacs. School was very dark and gloomy ... it was an 1825 building. This seemed to affect the attitude of the teachers ... So the song is like a therapy session for me."

11. ***House of Wax*** was recorded in February 2004 with Paul's touring band. Paul added overdubs in March-April 2006. A moody, dramatic song, it begins with ominous-sounding keyboards and thunderous drums. Its surrealist lyrics conjure up visions of the 1953 gothic horror film, *House of Wax* starring Vincent Price (1911-93). Some have interpreted it as a critique of celebrity culture, with house of wax referring to Madame Tussauds or to a record plant.

In *The Lyrics* (2021), Paul stated that he decided to "resurrect that sixties thing" of reciting a poem over a backing track. He discussed this with Adrian Mitchell (1932-2008), a left-wing English poet with whom Paul had worked on his 2001 book *Blackbird Singing: Poems and Lyrics*.

The song begins dramatically with "lightning hits the house of wax" and "poets spill out on the street to set alight the incomplete remainders of the future." There is also the line "buried deep below a thousand layers lay the answer to it all."

In a December 2007 interview with US music writer Kevin O'Hare (1957-2012), Paul explained: "We've got this hugely complex life, multi-layered … in the background there is always this thing – what's it all about?"

Paul's impassioned vocals are enhanced by coruscating guitar solos in which Paul cuts loose in the untethered style of Neil Young. Kahne had been impressed by Paul's iconic guitar solo on the Beatles' *Taxman* and asked Paul to let rip during the sections in *House of Wax* where there were breaks. Kahne stated: "Paul said. 'Okay,' sat in the control room with his Casino (guitar) plugged into the vox and just whipped it up, and literally, a half hour later, the solos were done. I've never heard him play guitar like that. He just pushes the notes sharp perfectly at the right time."

House of Wax is a striking song that would surprise casual McCartney listeners. Paul enjoyed playing it live but did so mainly at smaller venues.

12. **The End of the End** was written by Paul in February 2004 at 7 Cavendish Avenue, his St John's Wood London home (since 1966), on the piano he had inherited from his jazz pianist father Jim. The piano had been bought pre-Beatles days by Jim from the North End Music Stores (NEMS) music shop in Liverpool owned by Harry Epstein (1904-67), the father of the Beatles' manager Brian Epstein.

Inspired by the Irish wake, *The End of the End* is a light-hearted and optimistic song about how Paul would like to be mourned on his death, ahead of commencing his journey to "a much better place." Paul anticipated that, at his funeral, "jokes (would) be told and stories of old … rolled out like carpets."

13. **Nod Your Head** was recorded by Paul at Hog Hill Mill in March 2006. It is a raw and short rocker improvised by Paul on piano with vocals added at the last minute. Although the weakest track on the album, its inclusion gives an energy uplift after *The End of the End*.

Bonus tracks

14. In Private is an instrumental recorded at Hog Hill Mill in March 2006. It begins with Paul tapping on his acoustic guitar before launching into riffs on acoustic and electric guitars, keyboards and harpsichord.

15. *Why So Blue* is a strong pop-ballad recorded by Paul at Hog Hill Mill between April-July 2006. It had its origins in a faster version recorded in October 2003 with his backing band. Surprisingly, it was not included on the main album. Dominated by piano and acoustic guitar, it is embellished with harpsichord and overdubbed strings.

16. *222* is an experimental, electronic-jazz track recorded by Paul at Hog Hill Mill between January-February 2007. Largely instrumental, the track is driven by a catchy bass riff over which Paul scats in falsetto, "look at her walking … taking my breath away." It features xylophone, clarinet and electronic keyboards.

The album's title and cover

The album takes its title from the 'memory almost full' warning on a mobile phone. Paul saw this as apposite, stating: "In modern life, our brains can get a bit overloaded." It is also a recognition of how the ageing process leads to reflection on the past.

Memory Almost Full is also an anagram of "for my soulmate LLM" (LLM being Linda Louise McCartney). Paul stated in *The Lyrics* (2021): "That wasn't at all deliberate, but I like the mystery of it."

Paul was keen for the design and packaging of the CD and album to create "a desirable object … something … I'd want to pick up from the shelf." He decided to use Humphrey Ocean's *Black Love Chair* etching for the cover image.

Release, promotion and reception

Memory Almost Full and related singles were released in a variety of formats between April and November 2007:

- On 20 April 2007, *Ever Present Past* was released to US radio.
- On 23 May, a music video of *Dance Tonight* was released on *YouTube,* receiving 1.6 million views. Directed by the French filmmaker Michel

Gondry (1963-), responsible for *Eternal Sunshine of the Spotless Mind* (2004), it is a surrealistic fantasy. A postal worker, played by English actor Mackenzie Crook (1971-), from the UK mockumentary *The Office*, delivers Paul a mandolin. On strumming it, dancing ghosts come to life, one of whom is actor Natalie Portman (1981-).

- On 4 June in the UK and 5 June in the US, the album was released on CD and digital download: Paul's first album to be digitally released. The release was accompanied by a worldwide listening party at over 10,000 Starbucks stores in 29 countries in which six million people heard the album. Starbucks' XM satellite radio also provided promotion and a limited-edition Paul McCartney Starbucks card was issued.
- On 18 June, Paul's 65th birthday, *Dance Tonight* was released as a digital download single.
- On 25 June, the album was released on vinyl.
- On 23 July, *Dance Tonight* was released as a CD single and 10-inch picture disc.
- On 28 August, *Nod Your Head* was released as a digital download single.
- On 5 November, *Ever Present Past* was released in the UK as a CD single and seven-inch vinyl single.
- On 6 November, a CD/DVD deluxe edition of the album was released. The DVD included five tracks performed live at the Electric Ballroom, London, on 7 June 2007: *Drive My Car; Dance Tonight; House of Wax; Nod Your Head;* and *Only Mama Knows.*

The album's PR and online/digital marketing campaign won industry awards in 2008. It was led by Stuart Bell, who served as Paul's press officer and publicist throughout the next decade.

Paul and his band promoted the album through a seven-show Secret Tour between 7 June and 25 October 1997. This involved filmed gigs at small venues, four of which were released later in various formats:

- Thursday 7 June at the Electric Ballroom, London. Before a 1,100-strong audience of fan club members and celebrities, Paul played twenty songs. Five were from *Memory Almost Full: Only Mama Knows; Dance Tonight; That Was Me; Nod Your Head;* and *House of Wax.* The celebrities attending included Mary, Stella, Olivia Harrison, David Gilmour, English model Kate Moss (1974-), English guitarist Jeff Beck, Irish actor Pierce Brosnan (1953-), Mackenzie Crook and English actor Emma Thompson (1959-). Five songs from the set were included on the 6 November 2006 deluxe edition DVD, including a blistering version of *House of Wax*.

- Friday 8 June on the *Later with Jools Holland* UK TV show (recorded on 5 June). Paul performed four songs, including two from *Memory Almost Full*.

- Wednesday 13 June at a 'secret gig' at the Highline Ballroom, New York. Paul performed 21 songs: five from *Memory Almost Full*. In the audience of 700 were US actor Whoopi Goldberg (1955-), US actor Elijah Wood (1981-) and guitarist 'Little Steven' Van Zandt (1950-).

- Wednesday 27 June at Amoeba Music store in Los Angeles. In a free gig announced 48 hours in advance, Paul and his band performed 21 songs: five from *Memory Almost Full*. In the audience of 900 were Ringo and his wife Barbara Bach, US guitarist Joe Walsh (1947-), English singer-songwriter Graham Nash (1942-), Olivia Harrison, Denny Seiwell, Laurence Juber, Jeff Lynne, the English 'swinging '60s' model Twiggy (1949-), American actress Rosanna Arquette (1959-), American actor Woody Harrelson (1961-) and Canadian singer-songwriter Alanis Morissette (1974-). Four of the live songs were released in November 2007 as a twelve-inch vinyl EP *Amoeba's Secret* and as B-sides to the *Ever Present Past* single. Two (*That Was Me* and *I Saw Her Standing There*) received Grammy nominations for best male pop and rock vocal performances. On 17 January 2010, *The Mail on Sunday* and the *Irish Sunday Mail* distributed free in the UK and Ireland a 12-track promotional CD, *Live in Los Angeles*. On 12 July 2019, the full performance was released on CD, vinyl and digital download as *Amoeba Gig*.

- Thursday 5 July at the first-ever *iTunes* Festival, at the Institute of Contemporary Arts, London. Before 350 fans, including James and Mary, Paul performed 25 songs: five from *Memory Almost Full*. On 21 August, a six-track digital EP *iTunes Festival: London* was released on *iTunes*. It included four live tracks from *Memory Almost Full*. The UK's Channel 4 used eleven songs from the show in a TV special that included an interview with Paul.

- Monday 22 October at L'Olympia Bruno Coquatrix, Paris: the French capital's most famous music hall (estd. 1888) where the Beatles played in 1964. Before an audience of 2,000, Paul performed 23 songs: four from *Memory Almost Full*. In November, France's Canal+ broadcast the show.

- Thursday 25 October at the Electric Proms, at the Roundhouse, Camden, north London. Paul performed 24 songs: four from *Memory Almost Full*. James, Mary and Stella were in the audience of 3,000. The gig was broadcast that evening on BBC Radio 2 and BBC 2 (television). On 3 December 2014, *iTunes* released 17 of these songs, but removed them in February 2015.

Memory Almost Full peaked at number 5 in the UK album charts in its week of release: *Good Girl Gone Bad* by Rihanna was number 1 at this date.

Memory Almost Full went on to stay six weeks in the UK's Top 100. It reached number 3 on the US Billboard 200 and was Paul's highest-charting album since *Flaming Pie* (1997).

Almost half of the first-week's sales came from Starbucks coffee shops and these sales were not counted by the Official UK Charts. The album's total global sales have been 1.2 million units.

On 18 May 2008, *The Mail on Sunday* newspaper gave away for free in the UK a slip-case version of the CD.

The single *Dance Tonight* (b/w *Nod Your Head [Sly David Short mix]*) reached number 26 in the UK and 69 in the US Billboard Hot 100.

Ever Present Past (b/w live at Amoeba versions of *House of Wax*, *Only Mama Knows, That Was Me* and *Dance Tonight*) reached number 85 in the UK and 110 in the US.

The album was nominated at the 50th Grammy Awards on 10 February 2008 for Best Pop Vocal Album, Best Male Pop Vocal Performance (for *Dance Tonight*) and Best Solo Rock Vocal Performance (for *Only Mama Knows*). It lost out in these categories to Amy Winehouse (1983-2011), Justin Timberlake (1981-) and Bruce Springsteen (1949-).

David Kahne considered *Memory Almost Full*: "an amazing album, as good as anything Paul's ever done." Music critics concurred.

Rolling Stone ranked it at number 22 on its list of the Top 50 albums of 2007. The magazine's reviewer Evan Serpick noted that Paul had told producer Kahne that he'd wanted *Memory Almost Full* to compare to everything he'd ever done. Kahne stated: "He was looking to make something great." Serpick stated: "While it's not quite *Sgt. Pepper*, it's pretty great. The album has a retrospective feel, with nods to McCartney's discography: *Nod Your Head* sounds like *Come Together* and *Only Mama Knows* feels like a more metal version of *Helter Skelter*. The second half includes a five-song medley that recalls side two of *Abbey Road*."

In the *New York Times*, Allan Kozinn (1954-) found the album had "a nostalgic quality" and, despite being recorded over a four-year period with a long hiatus, partly with a band and partly on his own: "has a consistent sound and feel ... (and) a simplicity that gives it a rougher, rockier, more homespun sound than most of his recent albums."

In *The Guardian*, Jude Rogers (1978-) gave a negative two-star review. She had expected a sorrowful. bitter post-divorce album: Paul's equivalent to *Blood on the Tracks* (1975) by Bob Dylan or *Across a Crowded Room* (1985) by English singer-songwriter Richard Thompson (1949-). But the album was upbeat, and she stated: "while (Paul's) voice remains remarkably unweathered, equally at home with a feral screech or a soft purr, his frequent, chirpy nods to his past sound lumpishly heavy."

Paul explained: "I still seem to come out positive and optimistic. I think that's my character."

In recent years, *Memory Almost Full* has gained further critical respect. In a review for the *Record Collector* (2023), the English music journalist and novelist David Quantick (1961-) called it: "McCartney's greatest solo album ... the songs, the lyrics, the overall coherence ... (make it) a classic McCartney album."

Memory Almost Full is stylistically diverse, with sophisticated pop, rock, baroque pop and electronic experimentation. It is Paul's standout album of the 2000s: one that can be ranked among his best, alongside *Ram, Band on the Run*, *Tug of War* and *Flaming Pie*.

Paul meets Nancy

In August 2007, Paul began a relationship with Nancy Shevell, an American who had separated from her husband after 23 years of marriage and who divorced in 2008.

Paul and Nancy's paths had crossed socially since the 1980s, as both had summer houses in the Hamptons, a seaside retreat on eastern Long Island for affluent New Yorkers. Nancy's $8 million property was more imposing than Paul's smaller Pintail haven in Amagansett.

Barbara Walters (1929-2022), the US news anchor and socialite, who was Nancy's second cousin and emotional confidante, brought the couple together. During Paul's August 2007 summer stay in East Hampton, Walters invited Paul to a dinner party that included Nancy.

Nancy Shevell came from a non-musical background and, like Linda, from a Jewish family. Brought up in Edison, New Jersey, her father Myron ran a haulage company with his brother Daniel. They lost control of the company in 1975 amid allegations of involvement with the Mafia. Daniel committed suicide but Myron rebounded by taking over New England Motor Freight (NEMF) and turning it into a successful, large trucking company.

An adventurous child, Nancy loved playing with toy trucks brought home by her father as presents. She studied transportation at Arizona State University, attending a generation after Linda, as the only woman in her class. Following university, Nancy joined NEMF and became its vice-president in 1986. She married Bruce Blakeman (1955-), an attorney and later Republican politician she had met when both studying at university. They had a son Arlen in 1991.

Nancy was successful in the male-dominated trucking industry, becoming a multi-millionaire. But she also had a social conscience, serving as an unpaid board member of New York's Metropolitan Transport Authority 2001-12. And, as a survivor of breast cancer, which claimed her mother Arlene's life in 1991, she set up a cancer resource centre in the

Hamptons. She was diagnosed with breast cancer a year after Linda, but with a type that responded to treatment.

Despite the 17-year age gap between Nancy and Paul, they were well matched. Neither liked ostentation and both were low-key, family orientated, enjoying privacy and the outdoor life.

During his August 2007 holiday in the Hamptons, Paul attended the 11 and 25 August $15,000 a ticket James Taylor and Tom Petty benefit concerts at the East Hampton Ross School.

On 3 September, the last night of his holiday, Paul attended a Long Island Labor Day party at the house of Jon Bon Jovi (1962-). An impromptu house band was formed, with Bon Jovi, Billy Joel, Roger Waters and Jimmy Buffett (1946-2023). Paul sang *Long Tall Sally*.

Paul and Nancy's relationship became public on 7 November 2007 when, walking beside the beach in the Hamptons, they stopped at a coffee shop and were seen in conversation and exchanging kisses.

In late November, feeling unwell, Paul visited a Harley Street cardiologist. Soon afterwards, he underwent a successful angioplasty operation, in which a fine tube was inserted via the groin and inflated like a balloon to open several blocked valves in his heart.

The McCartney Years box set

On 12 November 2007, *The McCartney Years* three-DVD box set was released. It comprised:

- 42 music videos from across Paul's solo career.
- Seven live tracks from *Rockshow* (1976).
- *Let It Be* from *Live Aid* (1985).
- Four tracks from *MTV Unplugged* (1991).
- Eleven tracks from Paul's June 2004 Glastonbury show.
- Three tracks from Super Bowl XXXIX (February 2005).

2008: The Fireman Returns

Key events

January to June: Recording sessions continue for *Electric Arguments*.

20 February: Paul receives Outstanding Contribution to Music at the Brit awards.

17 March: A court determines Paul and Heather's divorce settlement.

24 April to 19 July: Linda's photographs are exhibited at James Hyman Gallery, London.

18 May: *Memory Almost Full* is distributed free to readers of the *Mail on Sunday*.

19 May: Paul and Heather are formally divorced by decree absolute.

1 June: Paul performs at the Liverpool Sound concert at Anfield Stadium.

14 June: Paul performs in Kyiv, Ukraine.

19 June: At Hog Hill Mill studio, Paul records the Fats Domino song *I'm in Love Again*. Ringo Starr plays drums and Klaus Voormann bass. It appears on Klaus Voormann's album *A Sideman's Journey*, released in July 2009.

18 July: Paul performs at Shea Stadium in New York City.

20 July: Paul performs in Quebec, Canada, at the 400th Anniversary Concert.

August: Paul and Nancy take a road trip on Route 66.

25 September: Paul performs at the Friendship First Concert in Tel Aviv, Israel.

13 October: Nitin Sawhney's *London Undersound* album is released. It includes a collaboration with Paul on the track *My Soul*.

24 November: The Fireman album *Electric Arguments* is released.

In 2008 Paul's personal life moved on apace.

On 19 May, his divorce from Heather was formalised, after a court hearing on 11-18 February and a judgement on 17 March.

During the spring and early summer of 2008, Paul and Nancy holidayed in the Caribbean and Morocco. This was followed in August by a 2,000-mile road trip in a 1989 Ford Bronco along the old Route 66 across the US Midwest to Los Angeles. It was during this 'trip of a lifetime' that, as Paul told the UK's *Sunday Times* on 25 November, the couple fell in love.

Musically, 2008 was a busy year:

- Between June and September, Paul played high profile concerts in Liverpool (1 June), Kyiv, Ukraine (14 June), Quebec (20 July) and Tel Aviv, Israel (25 September).
- On 19 June, Paul recorded at Hog Hill Mill studio, the Fats Domino (1928-0017) song *I'm in Love Again,* with Ringo Starr on drums, for the Klaus Voormann album *A Sideman's Journey* (2009).
- Also in the summer, Paul recorded, with US country singer Dolly Parton (1946-) and English singer-songwriter Yusuf Islam/Cat Stevens the song *Boots and Sand* for Yusuf's album *Roadsinger,* released in May 2009.
- On 13 October, *My Soul,* a song Paul co-wrote and recorded in 2007, was released on Nitin Sawhney's album *London Undersound.*
- On 24 November, Paul released a new The Fireman album, *Electric Arguments*, recorded with Youth between January and June.

Paul's divorce settlement

Between 11-18 February 2008, Paul and Heather presented evidence at London's Royal Courts of Justice before Justice Hugh Bennett (1943-) who had the task of determining the financial terms of their divorce settlement.

Paul was represented by Fiona Shackleton from the London firm Payne Hicks Beach and the barrister Nicholas Mostyn QC (1957). Heather represented herself, with assistance from her sister Fiona, David Rosen, a solicitor-advocate and Michael Shilub (1955-), a Los Angeles attorney.

During the six-day hearing, Justice Bennett weighed the evidence provided by Heather and by Paul and their advisers.

In his summation, he described Heather as: "a strong willed and determined personality … (who) has shown great fortitude in the face of, and overcoming, her disability." But he concluded that: "much of her evidence, both written and oral, was not just inconsistent and inaccurate but also less than candid. Overall, she was a less than impressive witness."

In contrast, Justice Bennett assessed Paul's evidence to be balanced, He noted that Paul: "expressed himself moderately though at times with justifiable irritation, if not anger. He was consistent, accurate and honest."

The hearing sought to determine: i) Paul and Heather's individual wealth at the date of marriage; ii) How much this increased during the marriage; and iii) How much Heather, and Bea, needed financially going forward.

On wealth at the time of marriage, Justice Bennett found Heather's claim that she was independently wealthy when she met Paul to be "wholly exaggerated."

Heather asserted that Paul had £800 million in assets and wealth at the time of marriage. However, Ernst and Young, the accounting firm engaged by Paul, debunked this. They calculated Paul's wealth in 2002 at around £400 million, comprising:

- £240 million in business interests.
- £70 million in pension assets/investments.
- £34 million in property: in London, Icklesham, the Peasmarsh Estate (comprising farms and related houses bought in stages from 1973), Rye (in East Sussex), Essex, Somerset, Merseyside, Scotland, New York, Long Island and elsewhere in the US.
- £32 million in works of arts, horses and vehicles.
- £15 million cash in the bank.

Justice Bennett commented that, while Paul was extremely wealthy, he was a saver rather than spender: a mindset driven into Paul by his father Jim. Paul had no live-in staff or round-the-clock security, ate out infrequently, and spent his leisure time riding, cycling, dinghy sailing and doing yoga - not on superyachts, sports cars or conspicuous consumption.

As recounted in a May 2003 interview in *Mojo,* Paul often travelled in London by bus and Underground. In the evening, he might watch a DVD at home or film at the local cinema.

Between 2002-06, during the period Paul and Heather lived together, Ernst and Young calculated that Paul's wealth increased by £40 million through income earned from royalties, investments and touring.

Justice Bennett rejected Heather's claim that her contribution to Paul's career during this period had been "exceptional" and that Paul had restricted her career and charitable activities. Indeed, Justice Bennett stated that during the marriage Paul had been financially generous:

- He had paid all household bills.
- He had provided Heather an annual allowance of £360,000.
- He had gifted £264,000 of jewellery in 2005 and cash of £250,000 in December 2002 and £250,000 in December 2003 to enable Heather to buy, mortgage-free in May 2004, a £450,000 office property at Thames Reach, Hammersmith, London.
- He had lent Heather's sister Fiona and cousin Sonya £420,000 and £264,000 respectively to buy properties.

Following the couple's April 2006 separation, Justice Bennett observed that Heather's expenditure increased "reckless(ly)." Between October 2006 and December 2007, Heather reported personal spending of £2 million, but Justice Bennett considered that £1.25 million of this was overspending.

Heather claimed £125 million in assets in the divorce settlement. If granted, this would have been three times the UK's largest previous divorce payment of £48 million.

In his 17 March 2008 judgement, Justice Bennett awarded Heather £24.3 million in property and funds, plus, for Bea, school costs and £35,000 p.a. for a nanny.

In May 2008, Paul settled the balance remaining on property and funds through making a one-off payment of £16.5 million.

Under the settlement's terms, both parties agreed to maintain confidentiality over matters relating to the marriage and divorce.

Heather declared herself "very, very, very pleased" with the verdict. At the case's conclusion, she approached Paul's lawyer, Fiona Shackleton, and said "I'm not a loser." She then poured a jug of water over Shackleton.

A *decree nisi* was issued on 12 May 2008 and on 19 May a decree absolute. This ended the six-year marriage.

My Soul: Paul's reflections on Heather

On 20 February, two days after the court hearing, Paul and his band performed to 18,000 people at Earls Court, London, for the 28th Brit Awards: a UK annual music awards ceremony watched by six million on television. They played: *Dance Tonight; Live and Let Die; Hey Jude; Lady Madonna;* and *Get Back.* Kylie Minogue presented Paul with the Outstanding Contribution to Music award.

Post-divorce, Paul rarely spoke in public about Heather. Sharing joint custody over Bea, it was important to maintain cordial relations. But when asked in *Q* magazine if the marriage was the worst mistake of his life, Paul admitted it was: "a prime contender … but I tend to look on the positive side, which is that I got a beautiful daughter out of it."

In summer 2007, Paul co-wrote and recorded with Nitin Sawhney the revelatory song *My Soul,* for Sawhney's *London Undersound* album, which was released in October 2008.

My Soul is a hidden gem in Paul's catalogue. Singing with fragile, age-weathered vocals, Paul reflects on his relationship with Heather. He acknowledges that Heather rescued him from the dark days that followed Linda's death: "I was awakened by magic … I was alone in this world." He criticises the paparazzi, who hounded Heather throughout their relationship, for stealing people's souls. But Paul also sings: "I long to know all your secrets … (and) walk through your fire."

The song concludes: "My soul, your heart, two worlds apart."

Heather's new life

Following the court verdict, the *Daily Mirror* reported that Heather treated 25 friends and staff to a £250,000 week's break at Necker, a 740-acre luxury island in the Caribbean owned by Richard Branson.

Heather's party included her sister Fiona and brother Shane, Juliet Gellatley of *Viva!*, her PA, personal trainer, security guard, make-up artist, photographer, housekeeper, interior designer and Jamie Walker, who was overseeing £1 million renovations on her Robertsbridge home. Bea spent the week with Paul.

After the divorce, Heather lived at Robertsbridge, near Bea's school. Heather made public appearances during 2008-10 in the US and bought a New York flat. Bea was kept out of the public spotlight.

Heather continued to campaign for *Viva!*: donating to it the fee she received in 2010 for competing in *Dancing on Ice*, a British television series. But in February 2007, PETA cut its ties with Heather while keeping close ties with its long-standing patron, Paul, and his daughter Mary.

Heather's post-divorce career focused on health, nutrition and veganism. She studied nutrition at University College London and authored books on healthy living. She also competed as a Paralympic Alpine skier.

In 2007, Heather became owner of VBites, a vegan café in Hove. This spurred her to develop a successful, broader vegan foods business into which she invested part of her divorce settlement.

- In 2009, Heather purchased a vegan food company in Corby, rebranding it VBites Foods. It employed 100.
- She added a factory at Benton, Newcastle, employing over 40.
- In 2018, Heather bought a former Walkers Crisps factory, in Peterlee, County Durham, and converted it into one of the UK's largest vegan food factories, employing 300.

In December 2021, Heather married Mike Dickman, an English businessperson 17-years her junior.

Paul and Nancy holiday together

In March 2008, Paul and Nancy Shevell had a luxury break in Antigua, in the Caribbean. They stayed in a two-bedroom suite at the Jumby Bay resort on a 300-acre exclusive island, chilling out with walks, cycle rides and reading by the pool.

In the early summer, they spent a week in Morocco with Bea and Paul's brother Mike and his wife. Paul and Nancy had separate bedrooms as, in Paul's words, they were not yet "an item."

In August, Paul and Nancy took a road trip in a 1989 Ford Bronco. They drove west along the old Route 66, via Chicago through the US Midwest states and St. Louis, Missouri, more than 2,000 miles to Los Angeles. On the way, they stopped at gas stations and ate at diners. During this 'dream of a lifetime' trip, Paul and Nancy fell in love.

On 25 November, in an interview with the *Sunday Times* newspaper, Paul, speaking about his new relationship, said: "I just like being in love."

In *The Lyrics* (2021), Paul later stated regarding Nancy: "She's multifaceted. She ran a trucking company … so (she's) … very blue-collaresque … superpractical … very interesting to talk to about things. She's a sweetie."

When asked about the stress of dating someone so famous, Nancy responded: "I'm a cancer survivor, I run a trucking company and I've got a 16-year-old to raise. That's stress."

Prestigious concerts

Between June and September 2008, Paul headlined four prestigious concerts attended by three-quarters of a million: Liverpool Sound (1 June); the Ukraine Independence Concert (14 June) in Kyiv; the Quebec 400th Anniversary (20 July); and the Friendship First Concert (25 September) in Tel Aviv. On 18 July, he made a guest appearance at the Last Play at Shea concert, in New York City.

The Liverpool Sound Concert: 1 June

The Liverpool Sound Concert celebrated Liverpool's year as the European Capital of Culture. It was held at Liverpool Football Club's Anfield Stadium, with capacity limited to 36,000.

Paul and Liverpool F.C. waived their fees but Liverpool City Council paid MPL its insurance, stage and lighting costs, and licence fees. Among the spectators at the concert were Olivia Harrison, Yoko Ono, George Martin, Peter Blake, Stella, James and Paul's brother Mike.

Paul arrived in Liverpool 48 hours ahead of the show and drove around the city with James, Bea and John Hammel, his executive personal assistant. Keen to show Bea his non-privileged roots, they visited the rent-free council-owned home in Speke where Paul had lived between 1947-55 until his family moved to 20 Forthlin Road, Allerton.

Ahead of the concert on Sunday 1 June, Stella held a lunchtime fundraising fashion show at LIPA, attended by Paul, James, Bea, Olivia and Yoko.

Paul took to the stage at Anfield following sets by the Kaiser Chiefs and The Zutons and wore a black, sixties-style Beatles-style suit. Paul and his band's 26-song set began with *Hippy Hippy Shake*, a 1959 hit for the US rock 'n' roll singer-songwriter Chan Romero (1941-), which became a Merseybeat staple in the early 1960s.

Midway through the show, Paul played, *In Liverpool*, an unreleased acoustic song written in 1991. As an encore, Paul became the first Beatle to play *A Day in The Life*. To Yoko's evident approval, the song segued into John's peace anthem, *Give Peace a Chance*. A Campaign for Nuclear Disarmament (CND) symbol was projected on the screen.

The setlist was: 1. *Hippy Hippy Shake*; 2. *Jet*; 3. *Drive My Car*; 4. *Flaming Pie*; 5. *Got to Get You Into My Life*; 6. *Let Me Roll It/Foxy Lady*; 7. *My Love*; 8. *C Moon*; 9. *The Long and Winding Road*; 10. *Dance Tonight*; 11. *Blackbird*; 12. *Calico Skies*; 13. *In Liverpool*; 14. *I'll Follow the Sun*; 15. *Eleanor Rigby*; 16. *Something*; 17. *Penny Lane*; 18, *Band on the Run*; 19. *Back in the U.S.S.R.*; 20 *Live and Let Die*; 21. *Let It Be*; 22. *Hey Jude*; and as encores, 23. *Yesterday*;

24. *A Day in the Life/Give Peace a Chance*; 25. *Lady Madonna*; and 26. *I Saw Her Standing There*.

Paul's friend Dave Grohl played guitar on *Band on Run* and drums on *Back in the U.S.S.R.* and *I Saw Her Standing There*.

Liverpool's newspapers gave Paul's performance a glowing review. The *Liverpool Echo* declared: "If Anfield had a roof, Macca would have blown it right off."

The concert was shown late in the evening on BBC Two but did not get an official CD or DVD release. A 4-CD and DVD bootleg, *The Complete Liverpool Sound Concert*, exists. It was compiled from audience and soundboard recordings.

The Ukraine Independence Concert: 14 June

Paul played this free concert at the invitation of the Victor Pinchuk Foundation, a non-partisan charitable foundation founded by the wealthy Ukrainian businessperson and philanthropist Victor Pinchuk (1960-) in 2006. The event aimed to unite the country and strengthen understanding within Ukrainian society.

The concert was held in Independence Square (the Maidan) in the country's capital, Kyiv. It came 17 years after Ukraine had gained independence from the Soviet Union (on 24 August 1991).

The show drew a record 350,000 crowd and was beamed live to giant screens for 195,000 to view in six other Ukrainian cities. Ten million watched the live broadcast in Ukraine on Novyi television. Four million Ukrainian hryvnias (US$0.9 million) were raised to buy modern cancer treatment equipment for children. To coincide with the concert, Paul exhibited forty of his paintings at the Pinchuk Art Centre in Kyiv.

After heavy rain, the skies cleared as Paul and his band took to the stage at 9:30 p.m. The two-and-a-half-hour 34-song set included 24 of the 26 songs played at the Liverpool Sound: those not played were *Hippy Hippy Shake* and *In Liverpool*. The ten additional songs played were: *Only Mama Knows; All My Loving; Let Em In; Mrs. Vandebilt; Good Day Sunshine; Birthday; I've Got A Feeling; Get Back; Sgt. Pepper's Lonely Hearts Club Band;* and *The End*.

Paul played *Mrs. Vandebilt* live for the first time. This was in response to a petition from Ukrainian fans: the song had been immensely popular on local radio in Ukraine in the 1970s.

The Kyiv concert was released on bootleg CD and DVD. In 2022, following Russia's invasion of Ukraine, Paul and MPL were petitioned to make an official release to benefit Ukrainian refugees.

Last Play at Shea: 18 July

Attended by 55,000 people and headlined by Billy Joel, this was the final concert held at Shea Stadium, New York, before its demolition.

Shea Stadium held strong memories for Paul. It was a sports stadium used for baseball (the New York Mets 1964-2008) and American football (the New York Jets 1964-83) and on 15 August 1965 held the world's first arena rock concert when the Beatles played there before a record 55,600 screaming fans. Although the Beatles' 1965 set lasted only 34 minutes, John Lennon stated in 1970 that it was a career high: "At Shea Stadium, I saw the top of the mountain."

On 18 July 2008, towards the end of Billy Joel's 25-song set, Paul took to the stage. He was driven there by Pete Flynn (1938-2017), the same groundskeeper who had driven the Beatles from the stage in 1965. With his Höfner bass strapped on, Paul played a rousing *I Saw Her Standing There* backed by Billy on keyboards. Paul then left the stage as Joel closed his set with *The Piano Man.* As the final encore, Paul returned and closed the concert with *Let It Be,* playing grand piano and trading vocals with Billy.

The Last Play at Shea is available on DVD on CD and DVD, released on 8 March 2011.

Live in Quebec: 20 July

The Quebec 400th Anniversary Concert was part of a $155 million investment by Canada's federal, provincial and municipal governments to celebrate the 400th anniversary of the founding of Quebec by the French explorer Samuel de Champlain (1567-1635) on 3 July 1608. The city was the birthplace of French America.

Paul's free concert, attended by 270,000, was held on the Plaines de Abraham (Plains of Abraham), an historic park area used for sports, festivals and concerts.

Paul's appearance was not without controversy, as the Plains of Abraham was the site of a 13 September 1750 battle which ended in the defeat of the French army by British forces. Speaking French, Paul told the crowd: "C'est ma premiere visite a Quebec, and it's a great place."

The 38-song set included the 34 songs played in Kyiv plus *Fine Line, Michelle, Too Many People* and *She Came In Through the Bathroom Window.*

In 2009 an unofficial *Paul McCartney - Live in Canada* DVD was released in Brazil. It is drawn from a Canadian television recording of the concert but does not have the set's final seven songs. The full concert is available on a 2 CD Brazilian 2016 unofficial release: *Paul McCartney - Live at Quebec City 2008.*

The Friendship First Concert in Tel Aviv: 25 September

Israel banned the Beatles from playing in 1965 because the government feared they would corrupt the country's youth. Forty-three years later, the centrist Kadima government of Ehud Olmert (1945-), prime minister 2006-09, declared the 1965 ban to have been a mistake and encouraged Paul to perform in the country.

Palestinian groups urged Paul not to go because of Israel's embargo on the Gaza Strip, a Palestinian coastal enclave. But Paul was keen to bring a message of peace and believed his concert would help bring people together through music.

Ahead of the show on Thursday 25 September, Paul and Nancy visited the holy city of Bethlehem, near Jerusalem, administered by the Palestinian Authority. They visited the Church of the Nativity and its Grotto, where Jesus was believed to have been born, and lit a candle for international peace. Paul then jammed with Palestinian children at The Edward Said National Conservatory of Music.

Paul met what he termed "some cool people from a group called *One Voice*" who promoted the training of youth leaders and a negotiated two-state resolution to the Israeli-Palestinian conflict. During the concert,

Paul and his band wore *One Voice* badges. In March 2009, Paul joined the International Board of Advisors to *One Voice:* an organisation made up 50:50 of Israeli and Palestinian members.

Paul's Tel Aviv visit was accompanied by an outbreak of what the Israeli press termed 'Macca-mania.' There were posters of Paul throughout the city and cafés, bars and radio stations played Beatles and McCartney solo music non-stop.

The 25 September show before a crowd of 50,000 in HaYarkon Park (Tel Aviv's equivalent of Central Park, New York, and Hyde Park, London) was a resounding success. Lasting more than two hours, the 31-song set omitted nine songs played in Quebec: *Got To Get You Into My Life*; *C Moon*; *Fine Line*; *Michelle*; *Good Day Sunshine*; *Too Many People*; *She Came In Through The Bathroom Window*; *Penny Lane* and *Birthday*. Two additional songs were played: *Hello Goodbye* and *Here There and Everywhere.*

Electric Arguments

Personnel: Paul McCartney (all instruments and vocals).

Producer: The Fireman (Paul McCartney and Youth)

Recording sessions: December 2007 to June 2008 (Hog Hill Mill studio)

Release date: 24 November 2008

Highest chart placings: UK: 79; US: 67.

Length: 63:05 minutes

Tracks: 1. *Nothing Too Much Just Out of Sight* 4:55; 2. *Two Magpies* 2:12; 3. *Sing the Changes* 3:44; 4. *Travelling Light* 5:06; 5. *Highway* 4:17; 6. *Light from Your Lighthouse* 2:31; 7. *Sun is Shining* 5:12; 8. *Dance 'Til We're High* 3:37; 9. *Lifelong Passion* 4:49; 10. *Is This Love?* 5:52; 11. *Lovers in a Dream* 5:22; 12. *Universal Here/Everlasting Now* 5:05; 13. *Don't Stop Running* 10.39 (the track ends at 5:59 and is followed by 1:53 of silence and then the hidden track *Road Trip*); and 14. *Sawain Ambient Acapella* 4:53 (a bonus track on *iTunes*).

Electric Arguments was recorded in short bursts in late 2007 and early 2008 and finalised in June 2008. This was at a time when Paul was on a break from touring and in the final stages of divorce proceedings.

As in 1998, which was another time of emotional turmoil and flux, Paul felt liberated recording under The Fireman alter ego. It enabled him to "goof around" musically in Hog Hill Mill studio. The accompanying video for the project shows Paul improvising on his diverse array of musical instruments – acoustic, electric and pedal steel guitars, bass, drums, washboard, tubular bells, xylophone, pump organ, synthesizer and cello – and experimenting with distortion and varied vocal tones. It was music therapy under the benevolent guidance of his Fireman partner, Youth.

Paul entered the studio without any song ideas or lyrics. Performing a Brian Eno conceptual role, Youth suggested grooves and textures to explore instrumentally. With basic tracks in place, Youth then asked Paul to add vocals. Lacking prepared lyrics, Paul flipped through books of Beat poetry he had at hand and, in the "first thought, best thought" cut-up technique of William Burroughs (1914-97), sang those word combinations that caught his attention.

Paul told *Rolling Stone* magazine that recording *Electric Arguments* was: "like writing on the spot, which … lent an electricity to the whole sound ... like throwing paint at the wall, and then you just stand back and take a look at it and see if some of it looks good."

The album's thirteen main tracks were recorded on thirteen non-consecutive days spread over six months. They were buffed and polished with overdubs and remixing in June 2008.

The songs

Electric Arguments differs from the first two The Fireman projects. In November 2008, Paul told the *Daily Telegraph*: "There's no songs on the first two The Fireman albums; it's just trance stuff, and basically each track is one chord. On this record, I started saying maybe we should go for another chord somewhere and, whoah, it just exploded. Some of the songs even have four chords!"

Electric Arguments' first nine tracks have vocals, lyrics, guitars and conventional structures. The closing four tracks are ambient and experimental.

1. ***Nothing Too Much Just Out of Sight*** opens the album in a raucous Chicago blues rock and Led Zeppelin fashion. Paul adopts his *Kansas City* and *Helter Skelter* Little Richard scream. The song has fuzzed bass, drums, electric and slide guitar and distorted harmonica.

The song's inspiration came from a phrase, "nothing too much, just outta sight,' which Paul remembered from the 1960s. It had been coined by Jimmy Scott Emuakpor (1922-1986), a tall happy-go lucky Nigerian who had come to England in 1948 as a stowaway on a cargo ship and became a conga drum player on the London music club scene. In 1964, Jimmy played with the jazz musician Georgie Fame (1943-) and the Blue Flames and in 1965 with Stevie Wonder during his UK tour. Paul met Jimmy in the mid-1960s at the Bag O'Nails and other London clubs.

The phrase "ob-la-di, ob-la-da, life goes on, bra," used in the 1968 Beatles song on which Jimmy played congas during the demo, was a catchphrase Jimmy used when interacting with audiences. He sought a writer's credit from the Beatles. This was refused but Paul sent Jimmy a cheque to help him out of financial difficulties. Jimmy went on to play in the ska band Bad Manners but died in 1986 just a day after being strip-searched at Heathrow Airport on his return from a New York gig.

The indignant rhythm and lyrics of *Nothing Too Much,* with lines about unrequited love and betrayal, has led some critics to interpret the song as being influenced by Paul's divorce proceedings.

2. ***Two Magpies*** is another bird-themed Macca song based around finger-picked acoustic guitar lines. During his youth, Paul had been a birdwatcher in the countryside outside Liverpool armed with his *Observer's Book of Birds.* Paul said later that he was attracted to writing songs about birds – *Blackbird, Single Pigeon, Bluebird, On the Wings of a Nightingale, Jenny Wren* and *Long Tailed Winter Bird* - as "they are symbolic of freedom, of flying away."

A single magpie is a sign of bad luck, but two are bringers of joy. On his Peasmarsh Estate, Paul saw many magpies and said: "I don't shoot or catch them like a lot of people. They're not supposed to be good for other songbirds and a lot of keen gardeners don't like them, but I do. I've got lots. To me, it's double joy or triple joy. I'm very inspired on a spring morning if I see a crowd of eight."

Two Magpies begins with crackly low-fi acoustic guitar, captured on a voice recorder. This broadens out into an engaging studio recording of Paul finger-picking a simple melody and singing softly about seeing two magpies: "a girl and a boy, one for sorrow two for joy." The song ends with the sound of Bea giggling and calling for Paul's attention.

3. **Sing the Changes** is an exultant, high tempo (120 bpm) modern-sounding guitar-driven pop song with a catchy singalong chorus. In 2009, Paul stated this was the song he most enjoyed performing live. Between 2009-12, it featured in many concert sets. It was also the only The Fireman track that Paul included on his *Pure McCartney* (2016) compilation.

Paul plays mandolin, electric and acoustic, guitars, keyboards bass and percussion. The euphoric lyrics are snippets of unconnected phrases: "every ladder leads to heaven … feel the sense of childlike wonder … sing your praises as you're sleeping." The overall feel is one of liberation and new beginnings.

4. **Travelling Light** is a pastoral electronic-folk track with a floating melody played on piano, mellotron, guitar and flute. In a low, half-spoken voice, Paul sings: "I ride on the white wind … I follow the bluebird … I glide on the green leaf." At 3:40 the song increases tempo leading into a coda with the lyrics: "I'll be travelling tonight … across the sea, where she waits."

Travelling Light was the first song written for the album. Its inspiration came from Paul listening to sea shanties on a 2007 CD *What The Folk* released by Youth's folk label Butterfly.

5. **Highway** is a simple rocker with a catchy chorus of "highway (do ya, do ya, do ya)". There is prominent harmonica and layered guitars. Paul and his band played *Highway* regularly during their 2009-10 tours.

6. ***Light from Your Lighthouse*** is a medium-paced gospel-blues song from the 1920s. The most famous version was by Blind Willie Johnson (1897-1945) in 1929. The lyrics allude to 5:16 of the Gospel of Matthew. Paul sings in a gravelly tone reminiscent of Johnson and plays mandolin and guitar in a campfire manner.

7. ***Sun is Shining*** is a rolling pop-infused, uplifting track. It starts with gently strummed acoustic guitar and the sounds of chirping birds before a melodic bass is added. At 1:02, as the song's subject awakes, Paul begins singing the verse. This is followed at 1:53 with an infectious chorus: "the sun is shining down, the air is buzzing."

This song reflects growing optimism as Paul's relationship with Nancy develops. It is The Fireman's *Good Day Sunshine*.

8. ***Dance 'Til We're High*** is an uplifting number in the euphoric style of Roy Orbison (1936-88) and Phil Spector, with the verse building to a dramatic crescendo. The double-tracked vocals are layered with reverb. Chimes of tubular bells give the song a seasonal flavour.

9. ***Lifelong Passion*** is a swirling romantic song built around Indian rhythms on the harmonium, synthesizer and percussion and echoed vocals. The lyrics, "give me love, love, love … sail away" may reference George Harrison, whose *Inner Light* (1968) and *Within You Without You* (1967) imbue the song's Indian sounds. The song marks a change in the album's tone towards more ambient, spacy tracks.

Lifelong Passion was first released in June 2008 as an exclusive download for those who made donations to the AAM charity.

10. ***Is This Love?*** is a dreamy ambient track. It starts with flutes and builds in vibraphone and percussion. The simple lyrics have a mantra-like quality. They declare: "Love, flow like water through my face."

11. ***Lovers in a Dream*** is the album's most avant-garde track. It begins with unusual sounds on violoncello followed by spacy electronic distorted effects with an insistent electronic beat. The lyrics comprise eight repeated words: "lovers in a dream, warmer than the sun."

12. ***Universal Here/Everlasting Now*** is a progressive instrumental track. It starts with tinkling, classical piano accompanied by barking dogs.

Electronic keyboards are then added, along with incoherent words and the sound of birds singing. At 1:55, an insistent electronic drumbeat joins the mix, followed by distorted vocals. The song closes with classical piano. It is a track which would have fitted on *Rushes*.

13. **Don't Stop Running** has an attractive guitar and harpsichord riff on which are layered flute, keyboards and synthesizer. Paul's plaintive vocals sing lyrics drawn from phrases in a poetry book he had at hand: "silent lovers, angels smiling, don't stop running." *Road Trip*, which appears after a two-minute break, is replete with spacy synthesizer sounds.

14. **Sawain Ambient Acapella** (*iTunes* bonus track) is an alternative mix of *Lifelong Passion*.

The album's title

The album takes its title from a phrase in the 1973 poem *Kansas City to St. Louis*, by Allen Ginsberg (1926-97), about a road trip in a Volkswagen Beetle while listening to the Beatles' *Michelle* and radio talk shows. The poem has the line: "I roll on/ the ground/ the music soars above / the ground electric arguments / ray over / The ground dotted with signs for Dave's Eat Eat." Paul felt this: "seemed to fit the spirit of the album."

A leading Beat poet in the 1960s' counterculture, Ginsberg became friends with Paul in 1965. In 1996, Paul played a Clash-style guitar riff to Ginsberg's recitation of his anti-war and anti-right-wing poem *The Ballad of the Skeletons* set to music by the Patti Smith Group guitarist Lenny Kaye (1946-) and American composer Philip Glass (1937-).

Release, promotion and reception

Electric Arguments was released in the UK on 24 November 2008 by the independent label One Little Indian and in the US by ATO. The CD was packaged in a digipak, with a 48-page booklet of photographs of Paul and Youth during an abstract art painting session. Two of the pieces created were used for the CD cover and inside cover art.

Electric Arguments was the first The Fireman album to have the names of Paul and Youth on the cover. The CD's red slipcase stated in bold white letters: "Paul is The Fireman."

Electric Arguments was Paul's first album to be released in a super-deluxe format. This took the form of a 2 LP, 2 CD, 2 DVD package which included a digital download, accompanying booklet and two art prints. This was all housed in a metal box inside a brown paper sack.

CD 2 of the super-deluxe package comprises seven ambient and dub instrumental alternative mixes:

1. **Solstice Ambient Acapella** (15:11): a meditative ambient remix of *Is This Love?* with extended flute and Celtic vibes.

2. **Travelling Light Instrumental** (8:16): a remix of *Travelling Light*, with drums adding greater urgency.

3. **Wickerman Ambient Dub** (12:41): an alternative extended instrumental mix of *Don't Stop Running*.

4. **Morning Mist Instrumental Dub** (5:40): a guitar and mandolin dominated instrumental mix of *Sing the Changes*.

5. **Equinox Instrumental** (8:22): an instrumental mix of *Sun is Shining*.

6. **Sawain Ambient Acapella** (4:53): the *iTunes* bonus track.

7. **Sawain Instrumental Dub** (4:51): an alternative mix of *Lifelong Passion*.

DVD 1 in the super-deluxe edition contains high-definition audio recordings, music videos of *Sing the Changes* and *Dance 'Til We're High* and a 12:41 *In the Studio* documentary. DVD 2 comprises multi-track session files.

The super-deluxe edition was produced in an extremely limited quantity and was only available from McCartney's website, from July 2009. It was a trial run for Paul's release, from 2010 onwards, of deluxe Archive Collection editions of his solo albums.

On 24 November 2008, Paul publicised *Electric Arguments* with a press conference at the Fire Station restaurant in Waterloo, London, and an interview on UK's Radio 4

Sing the Changes was released as a single but did not chart.

Electric Arguments reached number 79 in the UK but stayed only one week in the Top 100. It was the first The Fireman album to make the US Billboard 200, reaching number 67. It also topped the US Billboard Independent Charts. Worldwide, it sold 140,000 units.

Critically, the album was well-received.

- *Rolling Stone's* Will Hermes (1960-) gave it four stars, acclaiming it as Paul's: "headiest music in years … it's freak folk by a forefather."
- The *Daily Telegraph* stated: "Embracing raw blues, delicate folk, gospel, country and dubby psychedelia, it's like a solo *White Album* and confirms the ex-Beatles' resurgence."
- In *Pop Matters*, Ron Hart gave it a 7/10 rating and enthused: "Over the last ten years, McCartney has released perhaps his strongest continuous string of albums since the early '70s … and while 2005's *Chaos and Creation* and 2007's *Memory Almost Full* … (are) much stronger releases … *Electric Arguments* is the most diversified work McCartney has put his voice to since *McCartney II* (1980) … and harbour(s) its own unique charm that will certainly appeal to long-time fans."
- *Uncut's* Peter Paphides (1969-) was less effusive, giving it only two stars, He stated: "The best thing about *Electric Arguments* is that it sounds like the work of someone who doesn't give a stuff what people are going to think. About time too." In 2022 *Uncut* (2022) raised its rating to four stars, stating: "*Electric Arguments* feels both unpredictable and adventurous: a quite exceptional record."

In 2015, Paul du Noyer concurred, describing *Electric Arguments* as: "possibly the finest record that a lot of his audience have never heard."

2009: A Coachella Conquest

Key events

8 February: Paul performs at the 51st Grammy Awards, in Los Angeles.

4 April: Paul performs at Radio City Music Hall, New York, at the *Change Begins Within* David Lynch Foundation Benefit Concert.

17 April: Paul performs at the Coachella Music Festival, at Indio, California.

June-July: Paul records *(I Want To) Come Home* for the film *Everybody's Fine*. It is released as a single in the US on 8 December.

7 July: Klaus Voormann's album, *A Sideman's Journey*, is released with Paul appearing on the track *I'm in Love Again*.

11 July to 19 August: Paul and his band performs 10 shows in seven cities in the US and Canada during the *Summer Live '09* tour.

20 July: Paul appears, with Dolly Parton, on *Boots and Sand*, a single issued by Yusuf Islam (formerly Cat Stevens). The song was recorded in 2008.

9 September: Remastered CDs of the Beatles' albums are released, as well as *The Beatles: Rock Band,* a music video game for a new generation of Beatles fans.

14 October: The American Society of Composers Authors and Publishers (ASCAP) names Paul Songwriter of the Year.

26 October: Paul makes his Broadway debut, performing *On a Slow Boat to China*, at the Minskoff Theatre in a concert celebrating songwriter Frank Loesser.

17 November: The *Good Evening New York City* live CD/DVD is released.

2-22 December: Paul performs eight shows in Europe.

In 2009, Paul's relationship with Nancy became closer and his environmental and vegetarian campaigning increased, with the launch in June of a Meat Free Monday campaign, supported by a dedicated song.

Paul and his band were highly active touring in 2009. During the spring, there were performances at the Grammy Awards (8 February), the Change Begins Within Foundation concert (4 April) and the Coachella Music Festival (17 April).

Between 11 July and 19 August, this was followed with a *Summer Live '09* tour of North America. The year ended, with a December *Good Evening Europe* tour.

Paul's July shows at the new Citi Field Stadium in New York were recorded and filmed for release, on 17 November, as the *Good Evening New York City* CD and DVD.

On 9 September, remastered versions of the Beatles' albums were released on CD, accompanied by the release of *The Beatles: Rock Band* music video game. These attracted a new generation of fans, boosting Paul's profile.

Besides *Meat Free Monday*, the only new song released and recorded by Paul in 2009 was *(I Want To) Come Home*. Written for the film *Everybody's Fine*, it was released as a single on 8 December. Nevertheless, on 14 October 2009, the American Society of Composers Authors and Publishers (ASCAP) named Paul Songwriter of the Year.

The sun is shining

In 2005-07, Paul seemed troubled and wary in interviews as his marriage crumbled. By 2009, Paul was in a happy new relationship with Nancy and appeared re-energised.

Paul and Nancy celebrated the 2009 New Year in Mexico before returning to New York.

Paul's adult children approved of Nancy. She was elegant, empathetic and egoless. In March, Stella and Nancy were photographed embracing at a New York gala.

James had struggled with the loss of Linda. In 2013 interviews with the *Daily Mail* and the *Irish Mirror*, James admitted that, after Linda died, he "went off the rails a little bit … (and) had my slightly dark period." He got "heavily into Nirvana" and dark gothic bands. He did not get on with Paul's new wife Heather and spoke infrequently with Paul.

Living in Brighton, waiting on tables, James fell back on alcohol and drugs and spent a period in a drug dependency rehabilitation centre in Arizona. But Paul's November 2007 health scare and James' witnessing an ethereal vision at night on the family farm in Sussex led to his reconnecting strongly with his father from 2008.

James bonded also with Nancy. In 2013, he described her as "beautiful and wonderful … my new mother … she's very genuine."

James resumed his musical career in 2009, playing low key gigs under the pseudonym Light. In 2010, he released a four-track EP, *Available Light*, produced by Paul and David Kahne and which included a cover of Neil Young's *Old Man*. In August 2011, a further EP *Close at Hand* followed and in May 2013 a promising debut album *Me*, with Paul playing instruments on many tracks.

Springtime shows

On 14 January, Paul promoted *Electric Arguments* during an appearance on the Sirius XFM radio show of Howard Stern (1954-). Paul also appeared on the Barbara Walters hosted ABC chat show, *The View*.

On 8 February, Paul and Nancy attended the 51st Annual Grammy Awards at the Staples Center, Los Angeles. Paul's song *That Was Me* had been nominated for best male pop vocal but lost to *Say* by John Mayer (1977-). Paul, Brian and Rusty performed *I Saw Her Standing There* to the 20,000 live audience and millions watching on television. Dave Grohl played drums since Abe was touring Japan with Eric Clapton.

During this February 2009 visit to Los Angeles, Paul spent time with Ringo Starr, who was recording his 2010 album *Y Not* at his home studio. Paul played bass on *Peace Dream*, a song which referenced John Lennon, and duetted on *Walk With You,* with Paul echoing Ringo's vocal lines one beat behind.

Change Begins Within: 4 April

Since 1968, Paul had practised transcendental meditation (TM). He incorporated it into his fitness/health regime, along with yoga, to bring inner peace and enhanced clarity of thought.

The Beatles had been introduced to TM by George Harrison's first wife, the English model Pattie Boyd (1944-). She persuaded the Beatles to attend an August 1967 lecture in London by Maharishi ('great seer') Mahesh Yogi, an Indian guru and promoter of TM. Intrigued by the ebullient, giggling Maharishi, the Beatles agreed to attend a TM study camp in Bangor, north Wales, the Maharishi was holding in late August. However, this visit was interrupted by the shocking news on 27 August 1967 that the Beatles' manager Brian Epstein had committed suicide.

The Maharishi invited the Beatles to Rishikesh, in northern India, in February 1968 for TM training at his ashram (spiritual retreat). They accepted and were accompanied by others including the Scottish folk-singer Donovan (1946-), the Beach Boys' singer-songwriter Mike Love (1941-) and the American actor Mia Farrow (1945-).

The Beatles planned to stay three months, but Ringo and his wife Maureen Starkey (1946-94) left after 10 days. Paul and his fiancée, the English actor Jane Asher (1946-), stayed for five weeks, leaving in March because of business demands. George, John and their wives returned to the UK 16 days later. Despite their earlier than expected departures, the TM training had a lasting effect on George and Paul.

David Lynch (1946-), an American painter and surrealist film director noted for *Blue Velvet* (1986) and *Twin Peaks* (1990-91), championed TM's ability to lower aggression and change lives. In 2005, he set up the David Lynch Foundation to fund TM teaching in schools and help at-risk children, homeless groups, war veterans and refugees.

Lynch organised a 4 April 2009 *Change Begins Within* benefit concert with the goal of teaching TM to one million at-risk children. Paul agreed to headline the event, which featured performances also by Donovan, Ringo Starr and US singers and songwriters Eddie Vedder (1964-), Ben Harper (1969-) and Sheryl Crow.

Held at New York City's Radio City Music Hall, the concert drew an audience of 7,000. Paul performed *Drive My Car, Jet, Got to Get You Into My Life, Let It Be, Lady Madonna, Blackbird, Here Today, Band on the Run* and, for the first time since 2002, *Can't Buy Me Love*. Ringo joined Paul on *With a Little Help from My Friends*. All performers then came on stage for *Cosmically Conscious,* a song written by Paul in 1968 and released on *Off the Ground* (1993), and *I Saw Her Standing There*.

The event raised $3 million for the Foundation. In 2017, a concert DVD was released. It includes an interview of Paul by Lynch.

Coachella: 17 April

The Coachella Valley Music and Arts Festival had its origins in 1993, when the grunge band Pearl Jam took a stand against the high service charges applied to ticket purchases: an ongoing issue. They decided to boycott music venues linked to Ticketmaster and hold a concert for 25,000 fans at the Empire Polo Club in Indio, California, near Palm Springs in the Colorado Desert. This demonstration event showed the site was suitable for a large, multi-performer festival.

The first Coachella Festival was held in 1999 and from 2001 it became an annual event, lasting three days from 2007. With groups performing simultaneously on several stages, Coachella audiences were exposed to diverse musical genres, including indie rock and EDM. Art installations also became a feature of the festival.

With acts booked based on artistry and critical regard and audiences that crossed the generational divides, Coachella became California's Glastonbury and one of the most popular music festivals in the US. Paul became aware of Coachella through Nigel Godrich who extolled its beautiful location and enthusiastic audience.

Paul and his band headlined on Friday 17 April 2009 before an audience of 60,000. They came on stage at 10:25 p.m., following sets by the English singer-songwriter Morrissey (1959-), Scottish indie rock band Franz Ferdinand, Canadian singer-songwriter Leonard Cohen (1934-2016) and US blues-rockers The Black Keys.

Paul played a two-and-a-half hour 34-song set. It finished just before 1 a.m. and breached the festival's strict noise curfew by 54 minutes. The set was unusually varied. There were 13 solo-era songs including Paul's first ever performances of two The Fireman tracks, *Highway* and *Sing the Changes*. Paul played the Beatles *Paperback Writer* for the first time since 1993.

US newspapers raved about the performance. The *Los Angeles Times* wrote: "The verdict from his Coachella debut on Friday? Never underestimate the power of a Beatle … the night belonged to Paul."

The Joint: 19 April

Two nights after the Coachella triumph, Paul and his band played on 19 April before a 4,000-capacity audience at The Joint, in Paradise, Nevada, near Las Vegas. The Joint, at the Hard Rock Hotel & Casino, had just reopened after a $60 million makeover.

Tickets for the show ranged in price from $195 to $700 and sold out within seven seconds of their release on 14 February. The audience included Nancy, the tennis players Andre Agassi (1970-) and Steffi Graff (1969-), the US singer Donny Osmond (1957-) and Donald Trump (1946-), who later became the 45th US president.

Paul's 34-song set was virtually identical to Coachella, but with *Honey Hush* replaced by a cover of the Jan Garber (1894-1977) song *Baby Face* and *Birthday* replaced by *I Saw Her Standing There*.

(I Want to) Come Home

In June 2009, Paul returned to recording at Hog Hill Mill studio, followed with overdubs in AIR Studios, London, in July 2009. According to Luca Perasi (2013), Paul recorded twenty songs during these sessions, with Geoff Emerick engineering.

One of these songs *(I Want to) Come Home* was released in the US as a single on 8 December 2009 and on 1 March 2010 in the UK.

Paul wrote *(I Want to) Come Home* in spring 2009 for the closing credits of *Everybody's Fine*, a family relationship film by the English director Kirk Jones (1964-) and starring US acting legend Robert De Niro (1943-), US actor Drew Barrymore (1975-) and English actor Kate Beckinsale (1973-).

Before beginning writing, Paul saw an advanced screening of the film in a viewing theatre in London. Paul identified with the De Niro character: a widower who embarks on a road trip to try and reconnect with his adult children and reunite them for a family Christmas.

(I Want to) Come Home has a wistful piano melody, complemented by a string arrangement by Paul and the Italian composer Dario Marianelli (1963-). It received a Golden Globe nomination for best original song of 2009 but lost, on 17 January 2010, to *The Weary Kind*, a song written by Ryan Bingham (1981-) and T Bone Burnett (1948-) for the country music film *Crazy Heart* (2009).

In 2012 the Welsh singer Tom Jones covered *(I Want to) Come Home* on his album *Spirit in the Room*.

Meat Free Monday

In 2009 Paul also recorded and issued the song *Meat Free Monday*. It was part of a Meat Free Monday campaign launched in June 2009 by Paul and his daughters Mary and Stella, with support from musicians Sheryl Crow and Chris Martin (1977-) of Coldplay. The aim was to raise awareness of the impact of meat consumption on climate change.

The idea of Meat Free Monday began in the US in 2003. Paul was persuaded by a 2006 UN report, *Livestock's Long Shadow*. This demonstrated that livestock rearing was responsible for 19 per cent of the world's greenhouse gas emissions - more than transport (13 per cent) - and would increase greatly if action was not taken. Methane produced by cattle was 21 times more powerful than carbon dioxide.

The song *Meat Free Monday* is upbeat, featuring Paul on guitar, bass, piano, drums and vocals. One of Paul's stronger 'political songs,' it was released as a free download on his website. Its lyrics read: "Meat Free Monday ... it's happening all over the world ... too much livestock warming up the land ... think about the future ... if we don't do something we face calamity."

Paul, Mary and Stella continued to promote Meat Free Monday in the 2010s and 2020s. By 2019, over 3,000 UK schools had a Meat Free Monday and a fifth of UK households had reduced their meat intake.

Back touring North America

After limited activity in 2006-08, Paul and his band resumed touring, with a five-week 10-concert *Summer Live '09* tour between 11 July and 19 August. It took in six US cities and one Canadian city and was planned around gaps in Paul's schedule as a hands-on father to Bea.

The 10 shows attracted over 375,000 spectators and brought in $34 million in gross revenue: helping to repay the costs of his divorce settlement. Tickets typically sold out within minutes of going on sale.

Hard Rock Calling: 27 June

Ahead of the tour, Paul made an unexpected appearance on 27 June near the close of a Neil Young headline show at the *Hard Rock Calling* festival in London's Hyde Park, before 65,000 people.

A long-time admirer of Young, Paul watched Young's two-hour searing set from the side of the stage. As a final encore, Neil played a grunge feedback version of the Beatles' *A Day in the Life*. Half-way through, a beaming and slightly tipsy Paul came on stage. With his arm around Neil, they sang together the song's Macca-written bridge.

On 27 June 2010, Paul returned to *Hard Rock Calling* in Hyde Park to play a memorable 39-song curfew-busting Sunday night headline set.

Summer Live '09 tour

Paul's *Summer Live '09* tour began in Halifax, Nova Scotia, Canada, on Saturday 11 July, outdoors at the Halifax Common. An unconventional choice, Paul was persuaded to play at Halifax by Neil Young, who had been impressed by the appreciative and knowledgeable crowds he had drawn in this Atlantic Ocean port-city.

Paul's 160-minute 35-song set before a rapturous crowd of 50,000, many travelling long distances, included a rare live performance of *Mull of Kintyre*. Paul was joined onstage by the local 78th Highlanders Pipe Band.

The Halifax concert also featured Paul's first solo live performance of the Beatles' *Day Tripper*. The concert was broadcast on Canadian TV.

The *Summer Live '09* tour resumed a week later in New York City, with three inaugural shows, on Friday 17, Saturday 18 and Tuesday 21 July (this show added after the first two sold out within five minutes), at Citi Field Stadium: the new home of the New York Mets. Citi Field was located near the demolished Shea Stadium. These three sell-out nights were attended in total by 120,000.

It was vastly different from the Beatles' 15 August 1965 Shea Stadium arena-rock debut. In 1965, tiny speakers and a screaming crowd meant the Beatles could barely be heard. In 2009, the Citi Field Stadium had a powerful modern sound system and giant video screens.

Paul and his band were on scintillating form, leading some critics to hail the Citi Field shows: "the concert experience of a lifetime." For the 17 July opening night, Billy Joel joined Paul to sing *I Saw Her Standing There*. And, for the first time since 2002, Paul sang *I'm Down,* reprising his 15 August 1965 Shea Stadium performance.

Following a 10-day break, the *Summer Live '09* tour resumed with shows at the FedEx Field in Landover, Maryland, (Saturday 1 August: audience 50,000), Boston's Fenway Park baseball stadium (5 and 6 August: audience 35,000 each night), Atlanta's Piedmont Park (15 August: audience 36,000) and Tulsa's BOK Center (17 August: audience 16,000 in the only indoor venue on this tour).

The mini tour closed on 19 August before an audience of 36,000 in Arlington, Texas, at the Dallas Cowboys Stadium.

Good Evening New York City

A 2 CD and one DVD *Good Evening New York City* audio and film recording from the Citi Field shows was released in the US on 17 November 2009 and in the UK on 14 December 2009.

The DVD was shot in high definition using 15 cameras and incorporated digital footage from 75 handheld flip cameras handed out to fans to capture the atmosphere from the audience perspective. The audio was

mixed in stereo and 5.1 by Paul Hicks, who had engineered *Let It Be …
Naked* and the Beatles album remasters.

The deluxe edition has a second DVD. It includes footage of Paul's pre-
show performance of seven songs on 15 July 2009 for the *Late Show with
David Letterman*. Paul performed before a crowd of 4,000 from the
outdoor marquee of the Ed Sullivan Theater, returning to the site of the
Beatles' US television debut on 9 February 1964.

The 35 tracks on ***Good Evening New York City*** were representative of
the 2009 tour's setlist. They included 20 Lennon-McCartney Beatles'
songs, one George Harrison Beatles song, one Lennon song and 13
Macca solo songs, including two The Fireman songs.

The CD/DVD tracks are: 1. *Drive My Car*; 2. *Jet*; 3. *Only Mama Knows*; 4.
Flaming Pie; 5. *Got To Get You Into My Life*; 6. *Let Me Roll It* (with *Foxy
Lady* snippet); 7. *Highway*; 8. *The Long and Winding Road*; 9. *My Love*; 10.
Blackbird; 11. *Here Today*; 12. *Dance Tonight*; 13. *Calico Skies*; 14. *Mrs.
Vandebilt*; 15. *Eleanor Rigby*; 16. *Sing the Changes*; 17, *Band on the Run*; 18.
Back in the U.S.S.R.; 19. *I'm Down*; 20. *Something*; 21. *I've Got a Feeling*; 22.
Paperback Writer; 23. *A Day in the Life*; 24. *Give Peace a Chance*; 25. *Let It Be*;
26. *Live and Let Die*; 27. *Hey Jude*; 28. *Day Tripper*; 29. *Lady Madonna*; 30. *I
Saw Her Standing There* (with Billy Joel); 31. *Yesterday*; 32. *Helter Skelter*; 33.
Get Back; 34. *Sgt. Pepper's Lonely Hearts Club Band*; and 35. *The End*.

Good Evening New York City was released on Hear Music and reached
number 16 in the US Billboard 200 and number 28 in the UK album
charts. It sold 940,000 units worldwide.

At the 53rd Grammy Awards on 13 February 2011, Paul beat off
competition from Eric Clapton, John Mayer, Robert Plant and Neil
Young to win the Best Solo Rock Vocal Performance award for his live
performance of *Helter Skelter*.

Good Evening Europe

Paul closed 2009 with an eight-show three-week *Good Evening Europe* tour
of indoor arenas. This took in three German cities (Hamburg, Berlin and
Cologne, where there were two shows), Arnhem (in the Netherlands),

Paris, Dublin (Ireland) and the O2 Arena in London. Over 140,000 attended this leg of the tour, bringing in $18 million in gross revenue.

Paul also made three appearances before and during this tour:

- On 26 October, Paul made his Broadway debut, at New York's Minskoff Theatre, in the *Chance and Chemistry: A Centennial Celebration of Frank Loesser* benefit concert for the Actors Fund. Paul co-chaired the event: his MPL Communications owned the song catalogue of Frank Loesser (1910-69), which included the Broadway musical *Guys and Dolls*. Accompanied by a small orchestra, Paul performed *On a Slow Boat to China*: a song his father Jim used to play at home when Paul was a child.

- On 12 November, Paul performed in London at the *Children in Need Rocks the Royal Albert Hall* benefit concert. Organised by the English singer-songwriter Gary Barlow (1971-) of Take That, the show was attended by 6,000. A week later, on 19 November, the concert was broadcast to six million on the UK's BBC One ahead of a fundraising telethon. Paul performed three songs: *Back in the U.S.S.R.; Get Back;* and *Hey Jude* (with Take That).

- On Sunday 13 December, Paul and his band performed *Drive My Car* and *Live and Let Die* at The Fountain Studios, in Wembley, London, during the Season 6 final of *The X Factor* music talent show. A record 20 million people watched on UK television.

The *Good Evening Europe* tour was preceded by band rehearsals during November at Hog Hill Mill studio.

The mini-tour began on 2 December at the Color Line Arena, a handball and ice hockey indoor arena, in the German port-city of Hamburg. It marked another return by Paul to the city which had been the pre-fame training ground for the Beatles.

Paul had first arrived in Hamburg in August 1960 as a callow 18-year-old. Between then and their final Hamburg gig on New Year's Eve 1962, the Beatles became a tight battle-hardened group and discovered sex and amphetamines. A fortnight after they left Hamburg, the Beatles released *Please Please Me* in the UK and their meteoric ascent began.

On 2 December 2009, Paul and his band came on stage over an hour late and received slow handclaps and boos. Aware that Paul had been delayed arriving in Germany, the arena had deferred opening its doors. This had forced the 16,000 spectators to wait outside on a chilly night. The audience included Nancy, James and Paul's brother Mike.

Opening with *Magical Mystery Tour,* Paul and his band soon won over the crowd, delivering a 150-minute 35-song nostalgia-heavy set. During the performance of early Beatles-era songs, photographs from the Hamburg years and blown-up newspaper cuttings were projected on large screens behind and beside the stage.

The Hamburg setlist was identical to that played in the *Summer Live '09* tour, except for three changes: the debuting of *Ob-La-Di, Ob-La-Da*, with its Oktoberfest beat, and *(I Want to) Come Home* and Paul's first performance since 1993 of his Beatles' classic, *And I Love Her*.

Paul's next show was on the evening of 3 December at the O2 World ice hockey, handball and basketball arena in Berlin. But ahead of this, Paul flew to Brussels on that morning to address the European Parliament during an international conference on *Global Warming and Food Policy: Less Meat = Less Heat.*

Despite having had only four hours' sleep, Paul privately met the European Parliament's President, the Polish politician Jerzy Buzek (1940-), and briefly addressed the European Parliament about his Meat Free Monday initiative. He did so alongside the Indian environmentalist Dr Rajendra K. Pachauri (1940-2020), who chaired the Intergovernmental Panel on Climate Change (2002-15). Paul then flew to Berlin for a concert that was attended by 17,000.

After Berlin, Paul had a short break. The tour resumed on 9 December at the Gelredome football stadium in Arnhem, the Netherlands, before an audience of 27,000. This was followed, on 10 December, with a show before 16,000 at the Palais Omnisport in Paris-Bercy, where Paul played *Michelle.*

On 16-17 December, Paul and his band played two nights at the 16,000-seat Lanxess Arena in Köln (Cologne). There they moved into festive mood by playing, for the first time ever, his perennial Christmas hit, *Wonderful Christmastime,* first released in November 1979.

Wonderful Christmastime was played again before 14,500 at the O2 Arena in Dublin, Ireland, on 20 December and at the O2 Arena in London, on 22 December 2009.

In the audience at the Dublin concert was Henry McCullough, specially invited by Paul. Before playing *My Love,* Paul praised the original lead solo by Henry and encouraged the crowd to applaud Henry, who was sitting in the balcony.

The 17,700 tickets for the 22 December London O2 Arena concert sold out online within four seconds. In the audience were Nancy, Mary, Stella, Bea, Ringo and Barbara Starr, Madonna and Kate Moss. The 37-song three-hour set included, as an encore, a performance of *Mull of Kintyre* accompanied by the Scottish Highland Bagpipe Band. It received glowing reviews. The *Sun* gushed: "Macca's as fab as ever."

Postscript: 2010 and Beyond

Paul ended the 2000s on a commercial and critical high. He had an innovative new management and marketing team in place and his personal life was happy and back on track.

Continuing creativity and commercial success

Between 2010 and 2024 Paul released:

- *Ocean's Kingdom* (2011): a classical album commissioned by the New York City Ballet. It reached number 144 on the US Billboard 200, number 1 in the US classical chart and number 2 in the UK classical chart. Units sold worldwide: 40,000.

- *Kisses on the Bottom* (2012): a covers album including 12 popular and jazz standards from the great American songbook of the 1920s to early 1950s and two new Macca songs written in the same style. The first new song, **My Valentine**, is a love song written by Paul for Nancy when on holiday together in Morocco. It features Eric Clapton on guitar. The other new song, **Only Our Hearts**, features Stevie Wonder on harmonica. Accompanying Paul on piano on the album is Diana Krall (1964-), a Canadian jazz singer married to Elvis Costello. *Kisses on the Bottom* reached number 3 in the UK and 5 in the US. Units sold worldwide: 650,000.

- *New* (2013): a mainstream pop-rock album which reached number 3 in both the UK and US. Units sold worldwide: 670,000.

- *Pure McCartney* (2016): a personally curated career-spanning compilation of solo-era tracks, released in 2 CD, 4 LP and 4 CD formats. Units sold: 400,000.

- *Egypt Station* (2018): a mainstream pop-rock album which included the anti-climate change denialism song, *Despite Repeated Warnings*. *Egypt Station* reached number 3 in the UK and 1 in the US Billboard 200: Paul's first US number 1 since *Tug of War* in 1982. Units sold worldwide: 500,000.

- *McCartney III* (2020): a self-produced DIY album. It reached number 2 in the US and 1 in the UK: Paul's first UK number 1 since 1989.

- *McCartney III Imagined* (2021): remixes of *McCartney III* songs by younger generations of musicians. It reached number 13 in the UK and 19 in the US.

- *McCartney I II III* (2022): a box set of Paul's three eponymous albums from 1970, 1980 and 2020.

- *The 7" Singles Box* (2022): a box set of 80 seven-inch vinyl singles originally released between 1971-2022.

- *Band on the Run 50th Anniversary Edition* (2024): in 2 LP or 2 CD formats and which features on the second LP or CD "underdubbed" mixes of the album's songs before orchestral arrangements, horns and overdubs were added at AIR studios in London by Paul and Tony Visconti (1944-).

- *One Hand Clapping Live Studio Sessions* (2024): a 50th anniversary release, in 2LP or 2CD formats, of the August 1974 One Hand Clapping live sessions during which the newly assembled Wings band is captured performing 32 songs ahead of a prospective tour.

Paul's 2013 and 2018 mainstream pop-rock albums sought to appeal to younger music fans through using in vogue producers and collaborating with grunge, rap and hip-hop artists.

In 2012, Paul collaborated with Dave Grohl and former members of Nirvana to write and record the hard-rock jam, *Cut Me Some Slack*, for Grohl's documentary *Sound City*. *Cut Me Some Slack* received a Grammy in 2014 for Best Rock Song.

On *New* (2013), Paul worked with four English producers: Giles Martin; Ethan Johns (1969-), who had worked with the US alt-rock band Kings of Leon and was the son of Glyn Johns (1942-), the Beatles' recording engineer in 1969; Paul Epworth (1974-), producer of the best-selling album *21* (2011) by the English singer-songwriter Adele (1988-); and Mark Ronson (1975-), producer for English jazz/R&B singer Amy Winehouse. The album has a modern pop-rock energy.

In 2014, Paul wrote and performed *Hope for the Future* for the video game *Destiny*.

In 2014-15, Paul collaborated with US rapper Kanye West, co-writing the UK and US top 40 singles: *Only One; FourFiveSeconds;* and *All Day*.

FourFiveSeconds, a country-folk song about heartbreak and redemption, performed with the Barbadian singer Rihanna (1988-), reached number 3 in the UK, 4 in the US and topped the US R&B/Hip-Hop Songs chart.

On *Egypt Station* (2018), Paul worked with the US producers Greg Kurstin (1969-), who had worked with Adele, and Ryan Tedder (1979-), who had produced a US hit for US singer Beyoncé (1981-).

In 2017, Paul played on *Songbird in a Cage*, a song he had written in 2011. It was included by the French-British actor and dream pop singer Charlotte Gainbourg (1971-) on her critically acclaimed album *Rest* (2017).

McCartney III, written and recorded by Paul at Hog Hill Mill studio during the 2020 Covid-19 lockdown and released in December 2020, saw a return to the organic Paul of *McCartney*. The 8:25 minute *Deep Deep Feeling* was an experimental ambient track that could have appeared on *Rushes* or *Electric Arguments*.

Paul invited younger artists to reimagine *McCartney III* tracks by remixing and, in some cases, adding vocals and instruments. The result was *McCartney III Imagined,* released digitally in April 2021 and physically in July 2021.

The artists who contributed included Beck, the US hip-hop singer Dominic Fike (1995-), the US art rock singer-guitarist St. Vincent (1982-), the US indie folk singer-songwriter Phoebe Bridgers (1994-), the English singer-songwriter with Blur, Damon Albarn (1968-), and the English graffiti artist and musician with trip-hop pioneers Massive Attack Robert Del Naja (1965-).

A simple wedding

Paul and Nancy's romance flourished in 2010-11. They holidayed and appeared together at key events, including Stella's fashion shows. Nancy remained discrete, not seeking out media attention.

On 5 May 2011, Paul proposed to Nancy, presenting her a $650,000 1925 Cartier solitaire diamond engagement ring.

The couple married on 9 October 2011 at Old Marylebone Town Hall: the same London registry office where Paul had married Linda in 1969. It was a family affair: Stella designed Nancy's wedding dress; Mary took the photographs; Mike was best man; and Bea bridesmaid.

Paul held the £50,000 wedding reception at 7 Cavendish Avenue, under a flower-adorned marquee. The 100 guests included Ringo, Jools Holland, Bono and the Rolling Stone's Ronnie Wood (1947-). Paul played *My Valentine* for Nancy, *Let it Be* and the Nancy favourite *Let Me Roll It*. At 1:30 a.m. on 10 October, responding to a neighbour's complaint, police noise control officers visited and asked Paul to turn down the volume.

Later in the week, Paul and Linda flew to New York to celebrate their marriage with American friends and family. On 22 October, a wedding party was held at the Bowery Hotel in Manhattan, New York. Among the guests were Yoko Lennon and John and Yoko's son, Sean Lennon (1975-).

It was to be a happy and enduring marriage.

The archive collection, *The Lyrics* and awards

On 1 November 2010, *Band on the Run* was the first release in the Paul McCartney Archive Collection (PMAC). The package included a remastered version of the album along with B-sides, live recordings, alternative takes and videos.

The *Band on the Run* PMAC release consisted of a digitally remastered album and alternative 2 CD plus 1 DVD or 3 CD plus 1 DVD special and deluxe versions. It won a 2012 Grammy for Best Historical Album: Paul's 15th Grammy.

PMAC editions followed: on 13 June 2011 for *McCartney* and *McCartney II;* on 21 May 2012 for *Ram;* on 27 May 2013 for *Wings Over America;* on 23 September 2014 for *Venus and Mars* and *Wings at the Speed of Sound;* on 2 October 2015 for *Tug of War* and *Pipes of Peace;* on 24 March 2017 for *Flowers in the Dirt;* on 7 December 2018 for *Wild Life, Red Rose Speedway* and *Wings 1971-73* (previously unreleased); and on 31 July 2020 for *Flaming Pie.*

The *Wings Over America* PMAC won a 2014 Grammy for Best Boxed or Special Limited Edition Package.

Paul also released half-speed vinyl remasters of his early albums and one later album: *Flaming Pie* (on 31 July 2020); *McCartney* (26 September 2020); *Ram* (14 May 2021); *Wild Life* (4 February 2022); *Red Rose Speedway* (22 April 2023); and *Band on the Run* (2 February 2024).

Paul's releases from *New* onwards featured a proliferation of formats and purchase options:

- *Egypt Station* was released as a single CD on 7 September 2018, as a deluxe 3,000-copy Traveller's Edition on 10 May 2009 and as a 2CD Explorer's Edition on 17 May 2009.
- *McCartney III* was released between 2020-23 in a multitude of vinyl and CD configurations.

Instead of writing an autobiography, Paul published, in November 2021, a two-volume, *The Lyrics: 1956 to the Present*. This set out the stories behind 154 of Paul's Beatles and solo songs. It was the output of interviews between Paul and the Irish poet Paul Muldoon (1951-), some of which were released on a podcast series in 2024.

In 2023, a paperback version of *The Lyrics: 1956 to the Present* was issued. It includes Paul's commentaries on seven further songs.

In a *The New York Times* review, David Hajdu (1955-) wrote: "McCartney shows how deeply he is steeped in literary history and how much his output as a songwriter has in common with the works of the likes of Dickens and Shakespeare ... Paul really is a word man, the more literary and cerebral Beatle."

From 2010, Paul received continuing recognition from his peers:

- On 2 June 2010, the 44th US President Barack Obama (1961-) presented Paul with America's highest award for popular music: the Library of Congress Gershwin Prize for Popular Song. The earlier recipients had been Paul Simon, in May 2007, and Stevie Wonder, in February 2009. The event included a 90-minute concert in the White House East Room for Barack Obama and first lady Michelle Obama (1964-), with Beatles songs being performed by Paul, Stevie Wonder,

Elvis Costello, Dave Grohl, the US pop-rock band The Jonas Brothers and US guitarist-songwriter Jack White (1975-). Paul serenaded the first lady with a rendition of the Beatles' *Michelle*.

- On 9 February 2012, Paul was awarded a star on the Hollywood Walk of Fame.

- On 12 February 2012, Paul was feted as Person of the Year by MusiCares, the charity arm of the Recording Academy.

A never-ending tour?

With shared custody of Bea, Paul arranged his annual schedule accordingly. He told his agent: "These are the weeks I can work and these are the weeks I can't work, because I'll be getting up in the morning seeing my little one off to school and stuff."

Paul and his band returned to the road on Sunday 28 March 2010, at Phoenix, Arizona, for a 38-show *Up and Coming* tour across the US, UK and South America.

The tour was seen by 1.2 million and comprised 15 shows in the US (including two nights at the Hollywood Bowl where Paul had played with the Beatles in August 1965), seven in the UK (including the Isle of Wight Festival and *Hard Rock Calling*, in London), five in Brazil, three in Canada, two each in Argentina and Mexico and one each in Chile, Ireland, Peru and Puerto Rico.

On 10 June 2011, Paul and the band then embarked on a 37-date *On The Run* world tour between 15 July 2011 and 29 November 2012. This included:

- A 13 November 2011 concert at Abu Dhabi, capital of the United Arab Emirates, to coincide with the Formula 1 motor grand prix.
- A concert in Moscow on 14 December 2011.
- In the early hours of 28 July 2012, a performance of *The End* and *Hey Jude* to close the London Olympics' opening ceremony.

Further tours followed between 2013-19:

- The *Out There* tour between 4 May 2013 and 22 October 2015: involving 91 shows worldwide, watched by 3 million and grossing $500 million,

- The *One on One* tour between 13 April 2016 and 16 December 2017: comprising 78 shows worldwide, watched by 2.2 million and grossing $350 million,

- The *Secret Gigs* between 9 June and 26 July 2018: consisting of five shows in Liverpool, London and New York City.

- The *Freshen Up* tour between 17 September 2018 and 13 July 2019: involving 39 shows worldwide, watched by 900,000 and grossing $120 million.

As he moved into his seventies, Paul's schedule typically involved thirty shows a year. He kept his stamina through cycling, some gym work, yoga and TM. But it was the adrenaline rush from the audience's warm reaction and Paul's love of performing that supported his on-stage vigour.

Shows planned for 2020-21 were cancelled because of the Covid-19 pandemic, but on 28 April 2022 Paul and his band resumed touring.

Following the critically acclaimed Disney+ November 2021 *Get Back* docuseries by the New Zealand film director Peter Jackson (1961-), Paul named his 2022 tour *Got Back*. It included 15 US shows, seen by 425,000 and grossing $105 million.

The tour climaxed with a triumphal three-hour headline appearance by an 80-year-old Paul at Glastonbury Festival on Saturday 25 June 2022. He received an ecstatic reception from the 100,000 at Worthy Farm.

In a five-star review in the *Daily Telegraph*, Neil McCormick (1961-), raved: "They may have to rename it Maccabury. Sir Paul McCartney delivered one of the most thrilling, uplifting, banger-filled, star-studded sets this 50-plus-year-old festival had ever seen, including a duet [on *I've Got a Feeling* - from the *Get Back* docuseries] with John Lennon from beyond the grave, more pyrotechnics than a Hollywood disaster movie and a climactic guitar battle [on *The End*] with not one but two superstars of different American rock generations: Bruce Springsteen and Dave Grohl."

In late 2023, the 81-year-old Paul hit the road again, playing seven concerts in six cities in Australia between 18 October and 4 November

2023, two shows in Mexico City in mid-November and nine concerts in five cities in Brazil between 30 November and 16 December 2023.

More in the pipeline?

In 2021-23, Paul worked, with Giles Martin, on what was marketed as the "final Beatles song," *Now and Then*. Giles and Paul used the machine-assisted learning (MAL) audio restoration and separation technology that had been developed by Peter Jackson's team for the *Get Back* docuseries. Building upon a poor sound-quality John Lennon home demo from 1977, they constructed a sonically impressive single which topped the UK charts in November 2023.

During 2023, Paul recorded songs with the American producer Andrew Watt (1990-), who had worked with Eddie Vedder on *Earthling* (2021), Elton John on *The Lockdown Sessions* (2021), Iggy Pop (1947-) on *Every Loser* (2023) and the Rolling Stones on *Hackney Diamonds* (2023). On *Hackney Diamonds,* Paul made a guest appearance, with a pulsating bass solo on the high-energy track *Bite My Head Off.*

Paul also guested on piano, with Ringo Starr on drums, on a new version of *Let It Be*, on Dolly Parton's album *Rockstar* (2023). In August 2023, this track was released as a single.

Speaking with the Brazilian press in August 2023, Paul stated that "composing is my hobby." He confided that he had some new songs he would release in 2024 or beyond. The catalogue goes on.

Macca in the Long Noughties: A Playlist

Selecting chiefly from Paul's mainstream and The Fireman albums, below is a 76-minute playlist of Macca's 20 finest 1998-2009 tracks.

1. *Watercolour Guitars* (from *Rushes*)

2. *No Other Baby* (from *Run Devil Run*)

From *Driving Rain*

3. *Lonely Road*   4. *From a Lover to a Friend*

5. *Back in the Sunshine Again*   6. *Riding into Jaipur*

7. *Vanilla Sky* (from the film *Vanilla Sky*)

From *Chaos and Creation in the Backyard*

8. *Fine Line*   9. *Jenny Wren*

10. *This Never Happened Before*   11. *Riding to Vanity Fair*

From *Memory Almost Full*

12. *Dance Tonight*   13. *Ever Present Past*

14. *Mr Bellamy*   15. *House of Wax*   16. *222*

17. *My Soul* (from Nitin Sawhney's *London Undersound*)

From *Electric Arguments*

18. *Sing the Changes*   19. *Dance Till We're High*

20. *(I Want to) Come Home* (from the film *Everything's Fine*)

Secondary Sources: Books

Allan, A., *Paul McCartney After The Beatles: A Musical Appreciation* (Meadow Music Publishing, Manchester, 2019)

Benitez, V.P., *The Words and Music of Paul McCartney* (Praeger, Santa Barbara, California, 2010)

Bernstein, B., *Each One Believing: Paul McCartney On Stage, Off Stage and Backstage* (Chronicle Books, San Francisco, California, 2004)

Blaney, J., *Paul McCartney The Songs He Was Singing: Vol. 3 The Nineties* (Paper Jukebox, 2012)

Blaney, J., *Paul McCartney The Songs He Was Singing: Vol. 4 The Noughties* (Paper Jukebox, 2012)

Blaney, J., *Paul McCartney The Songs He Was Singing: Vol. 5 2010-2019 Noughties* (Paper Jukebox, 2023)

Bowen, M., *McCartney Solo: See You Next Time* (Mark Bowen, 2009)

Carlin, P.A., *Paul McCartney: A Life* (JR Books, London, 2009)

Chrisp, P., *Another Day – Paul McCartney: Life Beyond the Beatles* (Sona Books, Solihull, 2023)

Dirani, C., *Paul McCartney: Em Discos e Cançoes* (Sonora Editora, Rio de Janeiro, 2017)

Dowlding, W.J., *Beatlesongs* (Fireside, New York, 1989)

Doyle. T., *Man on the Run: Paul McCartney in the 1970s* (Ballantine Books, New York, 2013)

Driver, R., *That Was Me: Paul McCartney's Career and the Legacy of the Beatles* (Lexington Books, Lanham, Maryland, 2023)

Du Noyer, P., *Conversations with McCartney* (Hodder & Stoughton, London, 2015)

Evans, M., *Paul McCartney: The Stories Behind the Songs* (Welbeck, London, 2021)

Jones, L-A., *Fly Away Paul: How McCartney Survived The Beatles, Found his Wings and Became a Solo Superstar* (Coronet Books, London, 2023)

Kozinn, A. & Sinclair, A., *The McCartney Legacy: Volume 1 1969-73* (Deyst, New York, 2022)

Kozinn, A. & Sinclair, A., *The McCartney Legacy: Volume 2 1974-80* (Deyst, New York, 2024)

Maccazine: Paul McCartney Fan Club Magazine, *Chaos & US Tour 2005* (Vol. 33, Issue 3); *Timeline 2005* (Vol. 34, Issue 1); *Timeline 2006* (Vol. 35,

Issue 1); *DVD Special* (Vol. 35, Issue 2); *Memory Almost Full Special* (Vol. 35, Issue 3); *Timeline 2007* (Vol. 36, Issue 1); *Timeline 2008* (Vol. 37, Issue 1); *Fireman Special* (Vol. 37, Issue 2); *Paul is live in 2009 – Part 1 (USA & Canada)* (Vol. 37, Issue 3); *Timeline 2009* (Vol. 38, Issue 1); *Paul is live in 2009 – Part 2 (Europe)* (Vol. 38, Issue 2); *Paul McCartney Compositions 1956-2018* (Vol. 46, Issue 2); *Concert Tours 1972-2002* (Vol. 51, Issue 1); *Special Gigs 1973-2023* (Vol. 52, Issue 2)

McCartney, P., *Paintings* (Little, Brown and Company, Boston, 2000)

McCartney, P., *Blackbird Singing: Poems and Lyrics* (Faber & Faber, London, 2001)

McCartney, P., *Wingspan: Paul McCartney's Band on the Run* (Little, Brown, London, 2002)

McCartney, P., *Back in the World Tour 2003 Programme*

McCartney, P., Dunbar, G. & Ardagh, P., *High in the Clouds* (Faber and Faber, London, 2005)

McCartney, P., *The Lyrics* (Allen Lane, London, 2021)

McGee, G., *Band on the Run: A History of Paul McCartney and Wings* (Taylor Trade Publishing, New York, 2003)

Miles, B., *Paul McCartney: Many Years from Now* (Henry Holt and Company, New York, 1997)

Mills, H. & Cockerill, P., *Out on a Limb: The Autobiography of Heather Mills* (Warner Books, London, 1996)

Mills McCartney, H., *A Single Step* (Grand Central Publishers, New York, 2002)

Mills McCartney, H. & Noakes, B., *Life Balance: The Essential Keys to a Lifetime of Well Being* (Michael Joseph, London, 2006)

Norman, P., *Paul McCartney: The Biography* (Weidenfeld & Nicolson, London, 2016)

Perasi, L., *Paul McCartney: Recording Sessions (1969 – 2013)* (L.I.L.Y. Publishing, Milan, 2013)

Perasi, L., *Paul McCartney: Music is Idea: The Stories Behind the Songs (Vol. 1) 1970-89* (L.I.L.Y. Publishing, Milan, 2023)

Record Collector, Maybe I'm Amazed: Paul McCartney's Solo Years Explored (Diamond Publishing, London, 2023)

Sandford, C., *McCartney* (Arrow, London, 2007)

Simpson, N., *The Unsinkable Heather Mills* (Phoenix Books, Beverly Hills, California, 2007)

Sounes, H., *FAB: An Intimate Life of Paul McCartney* (Harper Collins, London, 2010)

Uncut, Paul McCartney: The Ultimate Music Guide (NME Networks, Crawley, 2022

Podcasts, Websites and YouTube channels

Beatley Tone's Beatles Channel
https://www.youtube.com/channel/UCDyGAalQqO1p8leVc7sBgQA
Fab 4 Free For All *https://www.fab4free4all.com/*
Mean Mr Mayo
https://www.youtube.com/channel/UC1HMIzOmmQ-TpQYFVuSC_bQ
The McCartney McAlphabet *https://mccartneyabc.podbean.com/*
Paul or Nothing https://feed.podbean.com/mccartneypod
McCartney A Life in Lyrics
https://www.pushkin.fm/podcasts/mccartney-a-life-in-lyrics
2Legs: A Paul McCartney Podcast https://2legspodcast.podbean.com
Talk More Talk: A Solo Beatles Videocast
https://talkmoretalk.podbean.com
Things We Said Today Beatles Radio Show
https://beatlesexaminer.podbean.com
www.beatlesbible.com
https://chartmasters.org/paul-mccartney-albums-and-songs-sales/
www.mccartneymaccazine.com
www.officialcharts.com
www.paulmccartney.com
http://themaccareport.com
www.the-paulmccartney-project.com
www.setlist.fm

Made in the USA
Las Vegas, NV
28 October 2024

10609102R00125